LIFE

LESSONS

For my children,
Julia, Karl, Sophie Rose and Zoë

LIFE
LESSONS

A TREASURY OF CONVERSATIONS ABOUT LIFE

RITA DE BRÚN

NEW ISLAND

LIFE LESSONS: A TREASURY OF CONVERSATIONS ABOUT LIFE

First published in 2014
by New Island Books
16 Priory Hall Office Park
Stillorgan
County Dublin
Republic of Ireland

www.newisland.ie

PAPERBACK ISBN: 978-1-84840-380-2
EPUB ISBN: 978-1-84840-381-9
MOBI ISBN: 978-1-84840-382-6
HARDBACK ISBN: 978-1-84840-404-5

British Library Cataloguing Data.
A CIP catalogue record for this book is available from the British Library.

Typeset by JVR Creative India
Cover design by Mariel Deegan
Printed by ScandBook AB, Sweden

Contents

'The real voyage of discovery consists not in seeking new landscapes, but in having new eyes.'

– Marcel Proust

Introduction

As individuals we are all unique, but we are also very much the same. Our life circumstances and paths differ wildly, but behind the superficiality of class, status and wealth, most of us at one time or another ponder the same questions: what matters most, who are we at our very core, and what has life taught us?

In this collection, which is composed of snippets of one-to-one conversations I had with twenty-one Irish women and men, the sameness and interconnectedness of us all becomes apparent, as does the inherent goodness, humbleness and spirituality that is central to the sheer extraordinariness of some of those we admire the most.

If there is a central theme running throughout the conversations in this collection it is the human capacity for strength and the determination to accomplish great things. Of course, what is great for one person can be meaningless for another, but sometimes that is the point.

For some, the power of passion manifests itself in securing corporate success. For others, it is a matter of following a spiritual path and being of service to the poor, the sick or the vulnerable. For yet others, it is about poetic expression, creating great art, serving one's country in diplomacy, administering justice, defending human rights, campaigning for the welfare of animals, fighting stigma, keeping the peace or introducing people to the love of their life. All of the contributors share determination and focus, and many have fought against prejudice of one form or another to be true to their own vision of who they are.

All of those whose words you read in these pages found within themselves the inner reserves to accomplish what it was they wanted, or felt driven, to achieve. In sharing so much about their personal journeys, their responses to the events that shaped them and what life taught them along the way, they inspire the rest of us to do the same.

To the contributors – all of whom generously shared so much of what is intrinsically personal – I am deeply grateful.

– Rita de Brún

Willie Daly

Third-generation traditional Irish matchmaker who has made more than 3,000 matches since he began matchmaking more than forty-seven years ago

A quiet American

One Sunday, an American man came into my house. He was 54 years of age. He had a palish complexion, and he wasn't very good-looking. He told me he was looking for a woman, and he wanted her slim. He then added: 'I'm in a strange situation – my wife is not dead.' I was just thinking that, given his request, this wasn't that handy at all, when he added that his wife had been in a coma for years and he didn't think she had long left. I admired his honesty and wished I could have helped him in some way, but I had to explain that most of the women on my files wouldn't want a man who was married.

Because our house was packed that morning, I was in conversation with several people at the same time. Just then, a man came into the house to buy a horse I had for sale. I guessed he wanted me to show him the horse, but as I was in conversation with the American, I gestured to the yard outside and said that if he wanted to go out and take a look, I'd follow him out when I could.

Out he went, only to put his head around the door two minutes later: 'Which one are you selling?' he called. 'Are we talking about the one with the bare legs or the one with the hairy legs?'

'Hairy legs' I shouted back, at which point the American leaned closer, and, wholly in earnest, said: 'I'd like you to know that I'd hate a girl with hairy legs.' Just then the chap in the yard shouted in: 'Can I ride her?' 'You can of course,' I replied. 'Ride her around the yard.'

At this point the pale American looked almost ashen. He had no idea that the other man and I were talking about horses. He seemed to think that our yard was filled with women who were looking for husbands and that I was in the habit of sending men out there to check them out.

Around that time I had been getting a lot of calls from an Irish woman and her daughter. They were constantly ringing to see if I knew of a rich man who might marry the daughter. In return, they wanted this man to buy a hotel, which was up for sale in their locality.

The duo were always together when they rang, and while they'd primarily be calling looking for a match for the daughter, every now and again the mother would pipe in to say that she wanted a man as well.

I was still explaining to the American that it was horses we had in the yard, not women, when the phone rang. It was the mother and her daughter, looking as always for a rich man to buy them the hotel of their dreams.

I thought for a minute and said: 'I've an American gentleman sitting here beside me. I will put him on the phone to you and you can tell him what you're looking for.' I then turned to the American and explained a little about the ladies on the phone. 'Is the daughter slim?' was his only reply. I said that I'd never met either of the women, then laughingly added: 'Judging by her voice, she's slim.' At that, he took the phone and I went out to the yard to sell the horse.

Sometime later the American met with the daughter, only to discover she was small and stout. Since he had a thing against fat, he had no interest in her, but he did fall in love with the mother, who was 47 (I met her sometime later and she was a lovely looking woman with green eyes – very Irish-looking) and he bought the hotel of her dreams.

The American's wife later died, but as he and the Irishwoman weren't getting on too well they didn't marry. After a period they fell out with each other, and he returned to America. In fairness to the woman, she and her daughter were entirely upfront about what they wanted. There was nothing underhand about them.

From long black dresses to hot pants

I remember being at a horse fair in 1957 or 1958. That was a strange time in Ireland in so far as women's fashion was evolving from long black dresses to hot pants.

I saw these two brothers – bold, skutty, small little lads – that I went to school with. They were dressed like Teddy boys, and they were with these two women who were wearing hot pants. Now these two women had big bulging legs, and every eye in the fair was on them. Just then a man I knew approached and said: 'By God. They're two fine women aren't they? And showing some leg.'

'As a man with seventeen kids, I'm sure you've seen a woman's legs before,' I replied. 'I have, but I never saw my wife naked' was his response. Now this was a man of 54 or 55 years of age. I knew his form, and I knew he was telling the truth.

Motivation for marriage

A man who lived with his father and mother in a small-sized house would be prudent enough to realise that if he were to get married when his mother was 47 or 48 – when she might be doing a great job around the house, cooking, washing and sewing – she and any young bride he might bring home might not get on well together.

Many found the motivation to find a wife after their mother's death, when the dishes would start piling up unwashed, the darning wouldn't be done and the shirts and socks would start to smell. In so far as housework was concerned, he'd be looking for a replacement for his mother. That still goes on, but less so than it did years ago.

The Irish

We Irish have always been a lovely, mild kind of nationality; a sweet, shy kind of people.

One hundred per cent Irish people are getting scarce. I feel that in seven years or so there won't be enough one hundred per cent Irish men to go around.

There isn't a nicer woman in the world than an Irish woman. If I were to marry one hundred times more I would choose an Irish woman every time. Irish women are happy, sweet and lovely to look at. They have a beautiful sincerity about them.

When American men think of Irish women they visualise these beautiful females, barefoot while walking through flower-filled fields, or down at a river, wringing sheets. They imagine them living in little thatched cottages with flowers in the window boxes and climbing roses covering the walls. They have these pictures in their minds. It's a wonderful dream.

Dowry

When a new bride came to live with her husband's family, she would usually bring money with her – typically somewhere between fifteen and forty pounds. Two pounds back then was something like 500 now. Women who had no money for a dowry sometimes brought livestock. Now while that was considered important from a food perspective, money was preferred.

The money the new bride brought into the house was divided between her husband's sisters, so that when they married they'd have dowries. This was the norm in Ireland in the thirties, forties, fifties, sixties ... even into the seventies.

The search for an heir

When men in their sixties, seventies and eighties contact me looking for a wife, I think it's marvellous that they're still thinking like that at their stage of life. Men in their eighties tend to be particularly intent when they get that into their mind, and I hugely admire them for that.

I recently made a match for an 82-year-old bachelor. That was a tough one, because he said from the outset that he wanted a woman who would bear him a son and heir. I arranged for him to meet with many girls. Some said they would marry him, then decided against it. After a time, one London-based girl of 34 said she would. She wanted to come back home to Ireland, and she felt that this was her chance.

The discussions went on for three weeks. Eventually it was decided on a Tuesday that the bachelor would meet his bride-to-be on the Friday. Delighted, he was full of questions about what it would be like to have a woman living in the house with him. Unfortunately, he never found out as he died on the Thursday.

Looking for husbands

My father was a matchmaker, as was his father before him. While his work took him all over the place, he was a quiet man who preferred to be at home. One day he travelled to Ennis to make a match, and when he didn't arrive home by nightfall we were very concerned for his safety. There were no streetlamps in the countryside back then, and the roads were so bad that there was a real fear that he might have fallen into a ditch or a bog hole as he travelled in total darkness. He eventually arrived, and when he did he explained that he had to walk home that night – a distance of twenty-three miles.

While he wasn't a drinker, his matchmaking often took him to pubs. I often saw him throw whiskey onto turf fires rather than risk offending the person who had given him a drink. When he was out he was always the centre of interest because he would know of five or six young women whose fathers or uncles were trying to find husbands for them. He was paid something small for his work. Often he was paid in turf.

One November night in a pub in Milltown Malbay after a bad day at the fair (cattle prices were down), my father was approached by a small, nicely dressed little man of about sixty-four years of age. He was wearing a hat.

The man was telling my father that he had five daughters when someone who knew him came up and said: 'Jesus, John, how are you going to find the money to wed five daughters with cattle prices the way they are?!'

When he heard that, the little man banged his hand hard on the counter and roared so the whole pub could hear: 'What are you saying? My daughters' faces are their fortunes. But let that stop no man. There's one thousand pounds going with every one of them!' At that everyone laughed; it was such a grand statement, but everyone knew he didn't have that sort of money.

Before the night was over, three or four farmers in their late sixties came up with a view to getting their sons married off to that man's daughters, who were indeed great beauties. They knew that while the girls, all of whom were in their late teens, wouldn't be bringing dowries of one thousand pounds, they'd be bringing whatever they could, and that would have to do.

The plucking of the gander

When I was about 9 years of age my father and I cycled twenty miles to a house for what was known as 'the plucking of the gander.' This was the name given to the final negotiations – as in what came with the girl and what she could expect in return.

When we arrived the house was filled with people – a match being made for the man of the house was something of an event. He was tall, thinnish and kind of good-looking. While he was 64 years of age, the bride-to-be was a very pretty blue-eyed 26-year-old; a real country girl, with a lovely head of dark curly hair and rosy red cheeks. She seemed very happy about the match. I remember hearing her laughing – a lovely trait in a woman.

She had two representatives who negotiated on her behalf: an aunt and a neighbour. While the negotiations were going on she stayed in the kitchen with a bunch of oldish women. They were pinching her arms, breasts and backside while whispering to her. She was laughing at their antics. I had no idea what was going on, but my father told me later that they were probably explaining to her what she could expect when she was married.

In the corner of the room there were three or four old women. One was sewing a false bottom on a pair of trousers. At that time there was a superstition that if a man wanted his marriage to be lucky he would have to wear his trousers back to front in bed every night for the first five nights of the marriage, so as to ensure that nothing would happen between the couple.

Men went along with this custom as they were afraid that if they dismissed superstitions, or *piseogs* as they were called, they'd attract bad luck. The reinforced trousers provided an extra barrier to ensure the man physically couldn't do anything even though he was wearing the garment back to front in bed.

Years later, when discussing that custom with my mother, she told me that it had been introduced by priests. The thinking behind it was that as it was common for men in their sixties to marry girls of 18 or 19, the avoidance of marital relations for the first few nights of the marriage might give the girl time to become accustomed to the company of her new husband. This helped because many a girl found herself married to an old man who had no real respect for her. Of those who did, few had any notion of what it meant to treat a woman well. The truth was that some of these men knew nothing of romance – all they would know was what animals do.

After the wedding

For many of those who got married in Ireland long ago, there was no such thing as a honeymoon. After the ceremony, and maybe a night away, the man would bring his new wife back to live in his family home. Apart from a kitchen, most houses had just two small rooms: one for the parents and the other for their children.

Because there was nowhere else for them, the new couple would sleep in the room with the groom's brothers and sisters. There could be fourteen or sixteen sharing that room, with the boys on one side and their sisters on the other. The couple had no privacy. But there was always a lot of codding and teasing by the groom's siblings, and that kept things light-hearted.

Sharing

Fear of sharing is something that has kept a lot of people from taking a partner.

A farm of land is no good for a man if he can't share it. What good is anything if you can't share it? What good is anything if you don't have someone to love, or if you don't have someone who will put their arms around you at night?

What women want

When I started, most of the women for whom I tried to find matches were aged between 18 and 35. Very few were older than 37. Quietly, they would be looking for someone who was handsome – someone with nice hair and teeth. But while they'd have that in their heads, they'd settle for less.

When discussing a match for a woman with her parents, it was often said of the man: 'He's secure. He has a nice farm of land. He has old money.' All the while the woman would be imagining a handsome chap.

Every now and again, film projectors were set up in the towns and local girls would get to see the faces of Rock Hudson and Doug McClure, the actor who played Trampas in *The Virginian*, flickering across the screen. So, from the age of 14 or 15, many would get it into their heads that they wanted to marry someone with an actor's good looks. It was hard for them when they finally saw the men they were to marry.

It was common to see young women with toothless old men for husbands, and to hear people ask one another: 'How could a lovely girl like that get into bed with a man like him?'

The answer was simple: these men provided their wives with a home. Most of the women would have grown up in very large families, quietly dreaming of a time when they might have their own little home. So those who were offered marriage to a man with a decent place tended to go along with that. Some were in a position where they could and did choose less attractive men with nicer homes over attractive men with little to offer. They then had to live with the consequences of that decision.

While the husbands may not always have had the love of their wives, the decent ones had their respect. For many, it was only with the arrival of children that love entered the home.

Women who weren't in love with their husbands often found happiness by refusing to dwell on their own needs, wants and desires. The words 'me' and 'I' were rarely spoken by them. There was no attitude of entitlement. Their thoughts were for their children.

Domestic violence

I think fear is often a cause of domestic violence. Sometimes, a man who fears that his wife may be attracted to another man will lash out on impulse in a bid to exert control, then regret it. Insecurity and jealousy would come into it, but most of it would be fear. Love brings fear. The two are closely connected.

Settling

Because life's too short to compromise on love, I don't think it's ever a good idea to settle. Even at my age, I still have the patience to wait until I find magical love. But unfortunately, great love is not for everyone and not everyone finds it.

Intuition

Women are wise and intuitive. They have a remarkable ability to assess a man in an instant. But long ago, many a woman felt she couldn't walk away from an offer of marriage to a man she felt wasn't nice, even though she would have wanted to.

What life has taught me

The big thing that life has taught me is to have a lot of respect for people. No matter what their situation in life, they are all equally important. The best traits are not always visible; the worth of a man and a woman cannot be gauged by their dress or appearance.

A family of matchmakers

I have six daughters and two sons. They have all contributed in different ways to the matchmaking tradition of our family – and many still do. We all feel that if we can bring a bit of love, joy and happiness into the life of someone who might be in their fifties, sixties or seventies that is marvellous. After all, it's perfectly natural for older people to want partners. Loneliness doesn't evaporate once we reach a certain age.

When I was 28 my father made my match. Marie was 21 when she visited our pony-trekking school with some friends. When it started to rain, they came into our family home for shelter. While she was there, Marie heard my father (who was bedridden at the time) call for me. As I was out around the farm at the time, she peeped into the room where he was, and gingerly approached to see if she could be of any help. He asked her to pick up his pipe, which had fallen to the floor, and when she did he asked whether she would marry me. 'I would,' she replied, and we were married within six months.

While we drifted apart in recent years, we still have a wonderful family together. Ours was the last match my father ever made.

Lisdoonvarna

It's a myth that most of the women looking for love at the Lisdoonvarna Matchmaking Festival are American. I'd say that at most, 7 per cent of them are from the US.

The women who come to Lisdoonvarna from America are not that young. Most have lovely heads of long, curly hair, so it's only when they turn and you see their faces that you realise that they are older than you might have thought they would be.

American women who come to Ireland looking for husbands tend to look good for their years. Very many come looking for a third or fourth husband. This shouldn't put Irish men off, but unfortunately it can.

Because these women are very often financially comfortable, what they're looking for is a man to have fun with; a man who will dance, sing and play a few tunes.

Some American women work hard on improving their older Irish partners. They see them as a project. If the men have bad hair or teeth, and they're out of shape, the women work hard to improve them. They never say at the outset that this is their plan, but many do it all the same.

Untidiness is a lovely quality in an Irish man, but once a woman overhauls a man like that, he loses that quality. Some women tend to take over the minds of the men they love to the extent that they don't allow them to be their own men any more.

Very often these ladies feed up their men, and before you know it the Irishman looks very like an American person. By the time her work is done, the new Irish husband often looks a bit like the previous American husband, and when that happens it's often time for the woman to embark on a new project. I say that in a light-hearted way, because I know from my experience of working with them that when an American woman loves, she loves completely.

Internet dating

Any system that helps people to find love is a good system, and while there's no doubt that many find love through internet dating, it's not for everybody. Even though the internet is driven by people, it operates via machine, and machines are cold. They're also a little far removed from the warmness and tenderness and softness that love and romance is all about.

When I meet people who are looking for a match, we sit and we talk. During the course of the conversation, we might shake hands, or give or receive a touch on the arm or a pat on the back. The touch of human flesh has to be better than the touch of a machine, which is devoid of any real feeling or emotion. That is just one of the reasons why there will always be a role for the traditional matchmaker.

Soulmates

I used to think that everyone was searching for a soulmate. Now I am not so sure. I'd say that while the vast majority are, a very small percentage are more interested in repeatedly experiencing the excitement of being with someone new. These people are attracted by new energy. Some may have met their soulmates and not recognised the fact because their affections wouldn't run that deep, and because they are always keen to move on to the next one.

What matters most

I think the most fantastic thing in the world is finding love. Not everyone has that experience, but all is not lost for them. There is an old expression: where there is no love, put love and you will find love.

It's important not to be afraid of love. When you see someone you like a lot, you should never be afraid to go up and say: 'I think you are gorgeous. I think I have fallen in love with you.' It's important to make some gesture. The worst thing that might happen is you might be ignored or told they are married, but the only true disaster would be to *return home without knowing what might have happened.*

Trust and monogamy

Women are born to be monogamous. Men are not. I think most men are better than they get credit for, especially young men. Older men, because they can't do much, are usually assumed to be loyal.

I think that men are very honest and that women are more honest again, but where there is very rich love, very good love, there can be fear. I think what women don't know they assume, and they are not always right in their assumptions.

I sincerely believe that if you totally trust someone they will never let you down. I don't think that men stray much. But I also think that to be trustworthy at all a man must be trusted. When men are not trusted, and they know they are not trusted, they are more likely to do what they are accused of.

What older men want

It is a myth that most old men looking for brides want young ones. There are some that go to some parts of Asia looking for very young women, but they would be in the minority. When I tell people that I would like to meet a woman who is in her seventies or eighties, the general response is, 'You must be joking.' And it's true. I am.

The appeal of the older woman

It is very common for young men to fall in love with women of a certain age. This is far more common than is known. I know of a 64-year-old woman who recently had two men chasing her. One was 24, the other 73. She asked my advice. I said to her: 'An old man is like an old car. You'll be all night trying to get the engine started.' When I saw her in town a few days later I asked for an update. 'I didn't disappoint either of them' was her reply.

One night when I was out in town with a group of people – one of whom was a woman of 62 years of age – we met a 30-year-old man I knew. She had a beautiful head of hair and very dark eyes. He was a clean, handsome, well-dressed, good-looking lad of about six foot two, with a lovely head of short, dark hair. When he saw her he immediately asked for an introduction, then he asked her to dance. After the first dance, they had another, and that time they danced very closely.

This man had come to me previously looking for help in finding a match. He spent over an hour telling me what he wanted in a woman – what he'd like, what he would not like. He had told me he wouldn't want a woman who was older than 34 because he wanted kids. And here he was, clearly deeply attracted to this woman of 62. If I had said to him the day he came in to see me: 'I have a grandmother of 62 on my files. I think she'd suit you,' he would have thought I was mad.

Fear

I grew up hearing a lot of stories about haunted houses and ghosts and fairies, so I was really afraid of those when I was a young fellow. I am not completely over that fear.

We didn't have electricity growing up, so when we needed to go to the toilet during the night we had to go out in the dark. I used to be terrified of the dark. Even now I prefer light.

Something strange

Thirty-seven years ago I saw something strange. It was 11.30 in the morning, and I was out digging potatoes. I heard a whirring sound, and when I looked up I saw a red car-shaped frame in the sky. I watched it flying in my direction. There appeared to be two people in it. I could just make out the contours of the vehicle, but not much more than that. It was two red rectangular frames: a smaller one, where the roof of a car might be, and a larger one representing the body of the car. I don't know what that was. I did think though that it was something other-worldly. I don't know where it came from. When I looked up it was simply there. I saw it coming towards me for about three seconds. Then it stopped, made a noise, turned and vanished.

Deepest source of comfort and solace

I have a modest farm in County Clare. To an outsider it's a grand farm, but to me it's a kind of heaven. There's pure quietness there, and fields rolling down to the Atlantic. A lot of my matchmaking thinking is done in those fields. As life progresses we all get many a shock along the way. The company of others is always a great comfort. I find that both personally and through my work. As a farmer, I also take great comfort from the earth.

Life

Life has been magical for me. There is nowhere in the world where I would like to live other than where I do. There is nothing that I want to do in my life that I have not done.

What I fear

I have a big fear of dying and of the unknown. I also have a fear of confined spaces.

I have said to my family several times: 'If ever I get into really bad health and there's no hope of improvement, drive me up to the top of a mountain on a bad night, let me out, then drive away.' To that they always say, 'Don't worry, we will,' but I know they would never do that.

We have a family grave in the local church, but I tell my daughters I don't want to be put in there when I'm dead because I would be confined by the church walls. They try to rationalise that it won't matter to me then, but the fear remains.

According to my religion, everyone rises up on the last day. I wouldn't have strong thoughts about that, apart from the question that if everyone rises up together, where would everyone fit?

I don't often go to church these days, but I pray all the same. I pray to the Blessed Virgin Mary. I don't think she has ever let me down. I hardly ever ask for anything for myself.

Something surprising about me

When I was in hospital four years ago, a ward nurse came over to me as I was being wheeled to theatre and asked my age. She said she had three different ages for me. I asked her to call out the ages she had, and when she did, I picked one and told her that was it. I picked because I don't know what age I am. There were ten in my class at school. None of us were sure of our ages. Family details were recorded at our christenings, but for some reason our birth dates weren't logged.

Many years ago I got a letter from an old classmate who had moved to England when we left school. None of us had heard from her since. She wrote to say she was getting married, and she wondered if I could get together with some of our old classmates, come up with an age for her and write her a letter saying that was the age we thought she was. She said it would be best if we could make her younger than we thought she might be, as she didn't want her husband to be to be put off by what she supposed her true age to be. I met with some of the class, and we decided she was probably about 27 or 28 at the time, but even so, we wrote her a letter saying we thought she was 25.

Decades passed before she contacted me again. This time she sent a lovely letter to me at Daly's, the family pub in Ennistymon. She said that as her husband had died, and her circumstances weren't good, she wondered if I could possibly write her a letter saying I thought a mistake had been made years earlier in estimating her age, and that she was in fact a few years older. She wanted the letter to reflect her true age so she could claim her entitlements. I regret to this day that I was so busy at the time; her letter went out of my head and I never replied.

Love

Love is there for every one of us. It's there if we want it. It won't knock us down on the side of the street to get to us. We have to make a little effort to find it. I am very thankful to all of those who entrusted me with the important task of finding a partner for them to love, and this is something I hope to continue to do for as long as I can.

For those who are searching for love, it might help to remember that there's no old shoe but there's a stocking to fit!

Colm O'Gorman

Campaigner, author, executive director at Amnesty International Ireland, and 'survivor' of clerical sexual abuse

Toughest obstacle I've faced

Overcoming shame. And it wasn't my own. The shame that I carried for so many years wasn't my own. And for me that's one of the terrible consequences in any particular scenario when a society refuses to name shameful things that have happened. What it does then instead is it leaves the victims of those terrible tragedies carrying the weight of society's shame and of the perpetrator's shame. And that's an awful burden for anybody to carry and it really paralyses people. It paralysed me for years. So, realising that the shame I carried wasn't my shame was incredibly liberating for me.

The most powerful negative force in the world

In my view it's fear. Because it's when people are responding to or reacting to fear rather than confronting it that they are more likely to do terrible things, and that's when evil thrives.

Cruelty and disregard for human dignity

Fear and absence of love, both for oneself and for the other, breed cruelty and disregard for human dignity. I think if one truly loves oneself with honesty, humility and courage – because it takes courage to love yourself – then you can't but love others.

If we can find the capacity to love ourselves, we find the powerful truth of how we love or how we're compelled then to love others. When I say 'compelled' I don't mean that that is something you necessarily work at; a lot of the time you have to remind yourself that you do.

Living on the streets

I spent some time living on the streets, and what that taught me was that I had to get off the streets as quickly as possible.

I remember working with a clinical supervisor who worked with homeless young men during the time when I was on the streets. He asked how it was that I never came across any of the services that were available to the homeless back then. He couldn't believe that I hadn't, nor could he understand how he had never come across me, even though he knew everyone of my age who was on the streets.

The reason he never came across me and that I was not known to those who provided services to the homeless was that I kept away from them. Keeping very separate was my way of trying to stay safe and secure, and of surviving the set of circumstances I was in.

Shame and fear played a role as well. I was terrified that if I was discovered I'd be sent home, and I couldn't go home. I couldn't go home where I'd have to face what I had become or where I was, and all of those things that I couldn't even begin to intellectualise. I just knew that I couldn't go home. I was terrified. Not because of how my father would react or because I was frightened of him or anything. It was because I was so ashamed, and so frightened of that shame, and of having to face him in that shame. It was a survival thing. 'Just keep going' was what I told myself to do.

For years afterwards I used to say that the one thing all of that had taught me was that nothing could defeat me, as I'd always be able to get up again. And I did learn that. That was one thing I learned. But that also was an awful delusion, as it wasn't until later on that I learned the most important thing, and that is that you don't always have to get up, as there are times when it's a damn good idea to stay down or just rest.

It wasn't a case of my having such incredible self-confidence that I could take anything on. It wasn't that I could take anything on; it was more that I could survive anything that was done to me. And in a funny way that was an acceptance of the fact that really awful things had been done to me.

I used to tell myself, 'It doesn't matter because I will survive this. It doesn't matter if you do this to me. I will survive it.' And that then meant that I didn't have to say 'no', or stand up, or stop, or protect, or push back. So, as important as learning that 'I can survive this' was, learning that 'well, I shouldn't have to' and 'I don't have to' and 'I don't have to tolerate certain things' proved to be much more so.

The 'survivor' tag

One of the things that became incredibly important to me in my work as a therapist was the reason why I hated and still don't have an awful lot of time for the 'survivor' tag. To me, it was laden with demands upon and expectations of people, and with the celebration of those who survive.

Well, what about those who didn't, or couldn't? Or those who could just about cope? Maybe we should celebrate coping as much as we should celebrate survival. For me, it's much more about the fact that we should acknowledge and celebrate and love the humanity of the individual, whether they've survived, coped or fallen. And who's to say that their decision or their outcome was right, or wrong, or better? It's just their decision or outcome. It's just wherever they've gotten to.

Being forever associated with clerical abuse

I had to do a thing recently where I had to do a Google search on myself. And I didn't realise at the time that Google now displays images or photographs in association with searches. And when I did the search, an image of Brendan Comiskey, Sean Fortune and a bunch of others came up.

My book *Beyond Belief* came out in 2009. Sometime later I made a *Would You Believe?* film. After that, I remember getting a call from a member of Sean Fortune's family. He was someone with whom I'd had some contact before. We had good conversations; real, human conversations, and I had a lot of regard for that family – the journey they've had to go on was awful, dreadful. This time when he rang he said to me, 'When will this be over? When will this stop? When are you going to stop talking about this?' And you know, I feel the same way about it myself very often.

If there is a value in talking about what happened, then I think it's important that I do so, or that we do. At least, certainly I feel that responsibility – and I'm not talking here about a burden. Although, to acknowledge it, at times it actually is a big burden, because sometimes I'd really rather not talk about it. But it is a huge part of my life experience and it is a big part of what I've done, and the work that I've done around it has been a big part of my life. At its most simple, I suppose I took on that work because I felt a duty or responsibility to do it, and that is not something for which you can just abdicate responsibility. Of course I can make that choice. I can choose not to, and now I very often will choose not to do an interview about it. But if I can see that it has real value, real integrity, real purpose, and that it's important, then I will.

Identity, marriage and our extraordinary capacity to be magnificent

I am not defined by what was done to me. What says much more about who we are as people is not what was done to us, but how we responded to and worked with that. Our responses say a lot about who we are.

Identity becomes fascinating. For me there's also the sexuality element of all of that, and there have been times when I've had a very strong personal sense of frustration with the focus on sexual orientation.

It's not the gender of the person you love that says anything about who you are; it's the quality of *how* you love. It's how you love, not who you love, that speaks of who you are. We should be able to celebrate love in whatever form it takes.

On the recent anniversary of marriage equality being introduced in New York, there was this great photo montage on Twitter. There were photos of great celebrations, of people being in love and getting married, of everything from young couples to those in their eighties and nineties.

Some couples had been together 40 or 50 years before finally being able to get married. There were a load of shots from City Hall in Manhattan.

That's where Paul and I went to get married in 2011, and what was lovely about the whole experience of getting married in New York was the celebration. There was just the two of us and two friends: a really good friend of mine and his wife. Because they live out there, they were with us on the day and they were witnesses and all that stuff.

City Hall in Manhattan is a civic office, but the buzz about the place is extraordinary. There are all of these couples there: young, old, gay and straight. They're all there, getting married. You queue up and you get a little ticket. Then you get your marriage licence. Then you go and you queue up again. What was gorgeous about it was just the simple celebration of it. It was all about couples getting married because they loved each other – that was what was being celebrated. For me, that's what I'm all about.

So, in relation to identity, we latch on to labels or differences, and sometimes I think that we do that so we can hold people up and say, 'Oh look! Isn't this person extraordinary?' And we're saying that because they've done these things they're exemplary in some way. Whereas actually, in my experience, I've seen people demonstrate the most extraordinary capacity and ability and integrity and compassion and courage, in really ordinary, simple ways.

I was really very lucky to work as a therapist for as long as I was able to before I came back to Ireland. When I returned I wasn't able to do much of that any more because of the public dimensions of what I was doing.

As a therapist, you sit in a consulting room with people and you see the capacity of women, men and children to achieve extraordinary things in the situations that they need to confront in their own lives, or in their capacity to find a way within themselves, back to love or to life, or to whatever.

We make the ordinary extraordinary rather than recognising that we have within us this extraordinary capacity to be magnificent, to live lives of extraordinary beauty and dignity and compassion and courage and meaning and value.

We are not taught, we are not nurtured in a way that says we should be extraordinary. Sometimes, in Ireland in particular, there's that very idea of 'Who do you think you are, getting ideas above yourself? Would you stop?'

It's as though, somehow, it's embarrassing to be extraordinary. And it's not. It's ordinary to be extraordinary. Life is extraordinary. It is an extraordinary miracle that we're having this conversation. The fact that we are sitting here having this conversation is extraordinary. This is miraculous.

I think that every human being has the capacity to be extraordinary, to be truly wonderful, so there is something remarkably ordinary about that. Yet we have diminished our capacity to recognise that and to be that in ourselves. Or we have had it diminished.

Parenting plays a role there, and I mean parenting in its broadest sense – parenting by society as much as by individual parents – who suppress that capacity in the next generation. In some ways I think that happens because our capacity to be remarkable and wonderful has been suppressed in us, and we don't want to see that.

So, there has been a brutalisation of that capacity to be brilliant, to be all that we might be. It has been brutalised, and that is a very significant wound, I think, for an awful lot of people; maybe on a global level too. And that wound is such that we keep repeating it because we don't want to deal with it. We keep down the child who looks up and who challenges, or asks a question.

'Who are you to ask a question?' we demand. Who is a child to ask a question?

Why the concept of brilliance offends so many

In Ireland, we very often tell children off for being bold. Look at the language. Look at the word 'bold'. If there was the use of a word I'd ban, it's the use of the word 'bold' in the Irish context. The one thing we should be telling our children to be is bold.

But we tell them not to be. The words 'bold' and 'brazen' both mean courageous. Yet children in Ireland are told off for being either. Don't be too much. Be invisible so that nobody else has to be upset by your brilliance. These are the messages that so many Irish children absorb at home.

And why would anyone else be upset by their brilliance? Well, because they are so wounded by their own inability or fear or anxiety about being equally brilliant. Or because they're so insecure around it that they have to beat that down in other people. And that's awful.

The fear of looking at the darkness that exists within our society, within our families, within ourselves – that fear is really based on the best of who we are. So often we are frightened of seeing it because we would be offended by it. Why would we be offended by it if we were okay with it? We would only be offended by it because we would abhor it, because we would reject it, because it would demand, immediately, that we change. And we are frightened of change. We are frightened of being something other than that which we have been conditioned to be, or told we must be. We are frightened of being beautiful. We are frightened of being courageous. We are frightened of saying the things that we feel at a very deep level, and so we don't for fear of what we think is the worst of ourselves, for fear of our darkness, of our cowardice, or of our hatefulness; for fear of that, we deny the best of ourselves.

If we look at that, we will reject it and make different choices. And that has been my experience, not just in my own life, but with all of the other people with whom I've worked in different ways over the years.

As we face the darkness of who we are, we make different choices. And it's only when we deny the darkness that it takes over and that it becomes rampant. Recognising that has, for me, been one of the really valuable life lessons.

Why knowing what must be done diminishes fear

Fear was not something I experienced in my journey to get to the truth. At times I did feel an anxiety or a concern or the bubbling up of fear, particularly when I decided to sue the pope. I remember that, having made that decision, all I could think of, initially, was your man hanging under Blackfriar's Bridge: God's Banker. And immediately I said to myself: oh for God's sake, don't even go to that place of ridiculousness, and all the rest of it.

But the one thing that always kept me focussed, and again this is going to sound very righteous, was that whenever you look baldly at whatever type of circumstance you're in, if you're as honest as you possibly can be, the way forward is usually pretty clear and pretty obvious. So, what led to my deciding to sue the pope was a chain of events that began with my going to the guards to name what had happened to me.

I thought that this one bad man had done something terrible, but then I realised he'd been doing this to lots of other people, and I was really angry about that. And I thought: right, we need to get to the heart of this. And I asked how this could have happened. Then I heard that the dioceses knew about it, and I got more and more angry, and then I heard that it had been notified to the Papal Nuncio. Every time I asked a set of questions, there was an answer that led to another question, so it was always about just trying to understand how this had happened.

I thought: this is not okay. We need first to understand what has happened, then we need to name the fact that it was not okay, and then we need to try and make sure that it never happens again.

It was both outrage and determination that drove the desire to learn, to understand what had happened and to make sure it never happened again. At the heart of that was the fact that what had happened was profoundly wrong, and that was something that really fuelled me. So, when you hit those places and you know what's right, the steps that you need to take are very clear and fear doesn't really come into it. If I can paraphrase Rosa Parks a bit: When one's mind is made up, that diminishes fear. Knowing what must be done diminishes fear. It conquers it. And she was right, it does.

Sources of solace

Moments of human connection were the greatest sources of solace to me during the time I spent on the streets. When I was 17 and homeless on the streets of Dublin, there were moments when I'd be walking down Westmoreland Street, just around the corner from where the Amnesty International Ireland building is now, and somebody would say 'hello' to me. It would always be quite a shock whenever somebody looked me in the eye and said, 'Howya!'

It was the fact that they acknowledged my existence, just that, and that they weren't looking for anything, that they weren't looking to get anything from me, or to exploit me in any way.

It was just the fact that there was a moment of human acknowledgment. On the streets, a simple 'hello' or some small act of kindness was enough to connect me with the idea that I was alive; that I was still connected with life in some form.

There were many other examples of that, even when I was much younger. I remember when I was about 8 or 9 years of age being sent to a children's hospital in Dublin for about three weeks. That hospital visit was linked to the sexual abuse I experienced and to my constant bed-wetting as a result. There was a nurse who worked at that hospital, and I still remember her name: it was Mary Walsh. And Mary was fabulous. I can still remember, clear as day, hearing her coming down the hallway. Then she'd come in, jump up onto the side of my bed and sit there talking to me and giggling away. She was just lovely. She was just one of those people, and I remember her.

Connectedness

If you sit with any other being, there is a connection of being alive, of being in a moment together. We are living in this physical realm. We're living in this place, and I don't purport to understand what there is beyond this, and I don't feel the need to. But we are sharing this experience, and if all that connects us is the fact that we share this experience, then that's a pretty profound connection.

Because we're sharing this physical plain, this reality, we've come from it and we're in it, and our experiences of it will have so many commonalities. We all know what it is to be frightened, to be joyful, to be happy, to be sad, to be loved and maybe even to be despised.

There are communications between us that are not intellectual but behavioural, that are sensory, that are chemical. We are all connected on so many levels, and because of that I believe there's an enormous connection between people. And I can't think of a set of experiences where I haven't known that.

Best thing that ever happened to me

Becoming a family, meeting our children, becoming a family together. That has just been extraordinary, miraculous and incredible. Because of this, I feel I have been blessed. I certainly feel blessed. I feel very, very lucky.

Jimmy Goulding

HIV activist, writer and co-founder of Positive Now

Prelude to a rollercoaster of hell

I was a bitter, angry child. I never felt I belonged.

As a schoolboy I was abused by a priest in school. He picked me because I was destructive and because I wasn't learning. No sooner did he begin to abuse me than others did as well. Because I was too young to be aware that what was happening was abuse, I didn't look to my family for protection. Instead, I abused myself.

By the age of 13, I was addicted to alcohol and drugs. By 14, I was working as a prostitute. None of this was part of a conscious effort on my part to self-destruct. To me, the way I lived was not only normal for someone growing up in tough conditions; it was necessary for survival.

At that time I was involved with some of the most notorious groups in Dublin. I hung out with bank-robbers and drug-pushers. As a drug-addicted, alcoholic prostitute who also happened to be gay at a time when homosexual acts were criminal in Ireland, I felt we belonged together.

It was easy for me to get my hands on drugs and drink at the time. My friends used to encourage me to drink to get out of my head. I drank myself into a coma all the time. I did that because I wanted to block things out. I often woke up with black eyes and stitches in my head.

I was the only one of the ten kids in our family who went off the rails. It's hard to know why I did. But I was wild and gay at a time when it wasn't okay to be gay, and the abuse filled me with unexplained anger.

My family taught me to be genuine and to be respectful of others. But I got lost along the way, and as the years went by this brought disagreement among us. For a long time they saw me as this cunt who alternated between getting locked up and going back on the streets. But when I was a young teen they tried really hard to help me, and the more they did, the more I pulled away. As a result, there was no safety net for me.

Around that time I began to develop a reputation for shoplifting, and I came to the attention of the Gardaí. It helped that I was still living at home, but things started going downhill very fast.

Looking back, I think it's fair to say that my rollercoaster of hell began in earnest when I was 14 years of age, and lasted for eighteen years.

Who helped

When I was in my early to mid teens (I can't remember precisely what age I was) I jumped into the River Liffey. Because of that I was brought to Jervis Street Hospital, where the attending doctor said: 'You're too young to be locked up, so I'm going to sign you into St Brendan's hospital, and it will be up to your family to sign you out.'

I was horrified. But when I arrived at Grangegorman, I got the impression that the doctors there wanted to help me. Even so, when they prescribed medication, I knew that pills were never going to make me feel any better.

Harrowing as it felt to be in a psychiatric facility, my experience could have been worse. When the doctors learned I was gay, they told my parents. I hadn't done that because I didn't want to worry them – given that if I was caught I'd have faced criminal charges. For my parents' sake I was upset about the revelation, but that was nothing compared to the way I felt when I learned that the doctors had asked my parents for permission to treat my 'problem' with electroconvulsive therapy.

In fairness, it was not unusual to use ECT on gay people back then, nor was it uncommon to view homosexuality as a condition that needed curing. Even so, I was a mess when I heard the proposed treatment plan, and relieved beyond belief when my family refused to give permission and the ECT suggestion was dropped.

While this was a tough time for me, it was no easier for my mother. She was distraught that I had been put into a place like that. But the deepest hurt she felt was not for herself; it was for me, and for the way I had become hugely destructive and out of control. In the midst of all that was going on I could see the strain my situation was putting on her, and I'd remind myself that, while supporting me, she had nine other children to take care of as well.

I was discharged from St Brendan's seventy-two hours after I arrived, but I found myself back there several more times in the years that followed. Each time I overdosed, in a desperate bid for sympathy, I landed back there.

Back then, that hospital was a sort of safe haven for drug-addicted sex workers, and when I found out that some availed of its services when they had too many criminal charges to cope with, I began to do that too. Whenever

I had an armful of charge sheets, I'd go in with the sole intention of getting a psychiatrist's note for the courts.

Baggot Street Hospital

While very many alcohol treatment centres shut their doors on me, that never happened at Baggot Street Hospital. The staff there took me in and built me up. They taught me about self-esteem and self-awareness, and they showed me how to work on myself. They helped me to understand for the first time the reason why I was angry as a kid. They helped me to see that I had been abused by a priest and by other individuals I trusted, and that because I was so young I didn't recognise their behaviour for what it was.

Time and time again in the years that followed, the Baggot Street team stuck by me. They played a central role in bringing about my healing.

The darkest time

The darkest time in my life, the worst time, was when I was aged between 14 and 32. During that period, every aspect of my life got to me. My response was: why me? Why me? I had no realisation that I was creating the difficulties in my own life. Nor did I know how to fix things for myself. There was no blackboard in the sky telling me where to go and what to do, so all I knew was that I did not want to live.

The temptation to relapse

Despite the fact that I have been dry for nineteen years, I always feel that I am just a thread away from the lifestyle I left behind me.

Every now and again I feel I'm going to relapse, but so far the awareness of the nightmare that would bring has saved me from going down. I very nearly did that when I was in Thailand last year. But while I was on the edge I got a terrifying sense of what it would feel like to be locked up, and how bad it would feel if I got into a fight that resulted in my murdering someone. That feeling was so intense that I wanted to cut the holiday short and return home.

As there was no logical basis for those terrifying thoughts, my feeling was that they were being sent by my mother, who had just died. I felt it was her way of trying to protect me; that she was showing me how bad things could get if I were to take a drink or overdose. I felt she was warning me that, if I were to take one step in that direction, all of those terrible things would in time become my reality.

Angels

My mother and I were very close; so much so that my head was wrecked when she died. She always tried to protect me, and I tried to do that for her in return.

In times of crisis I never pray. Instead, I hand things over to Archangel Michael. I feel a force when I do that. Because he is known as a protector, I put a card with his image into my mother's coffin.

After her funeral I did an angel card reading in the hope of finding solace. The hairs on my head stood on end when the first card I pulled depicted 'a message from a deceased loved one.' It read: 'I am happy and at peace ...You did all you could ... Please don't worry about me.' I knew then that my mother was with me, and that gave me strength.

Years ago, I met Doreen Virtue when she was doing a workshop in Dublin. I told her that a friend of mine once said that when he died he would flash the lights on and off in my house whenever he came to visit. That happened when he died. It still happens. Her response was: 'Acknowledge his presence and feel the love that is being sent.'

When I started to get into self-help and angel books my family didn't know what to make of me. Because it wasn't the working-class way, they told me I was off my head. My response was to ask which 'me' they preferred – the 'me' who was off his head on drink and drugs, or the 'me' who was off his head on self-help.

Turning point

I was diagnosed as being HIV positive in 1990. I was 28 years of age.

The last time I'd been tested (three months earlier) the results had come back negative. That result surprised my counsellor. It also surprised me. Because of the drugs I took, and the sex work I did, I was high risk.

When I welcomed the positive diagnosis, my friends asked: 'Jimmy, how can you accept this?' My response was: 'No matter how hard or how often I try, I can't seem to get sober. I need to escape from this horrible hell. I look forward to death.'

At the time, many of my friends were dying of HIV. Others were living in fear of contracting it. I was the only one of my group who had no fear of dying. To anyone who questioned that, I simply said, 'I want to die.'

So, I accepted the prognosis that, given my lifestyle, the likelihood was that I'd be dead within three years.

In 1995, I was hospitalised. I was extremely ill, and my weight had dropped to six stone. Some of the doctors suspected meningitis. Others suspected blood clots. When

I could no longer walk, they sent for my family. They told them I'd be dead in three months and that it wouldn't be HIV that would finish me; it would be my addictions.

That prognosis hit my family hard. Their response was to thank the doctors, approach my bedside and say, 'Jimmy, you're on your own.' Then they turned and walked out of the hospital. Just one family member waved goodbye.

As I did not know what had been said to them, I had no idea why they chose to abandon me that day. Nobody had told me what the prognosis was, but even so I expected that I would die soon.

Left with my thoughts, I remembered the countless times they had visited me in hospital and how they couldn't have been more supportive, despite the fact that for the past eighteen years I had brought them nothing but trouble: drug and alcohol addiction, prostitution, police, prison, psychiatric units and hospitals. I had seen from the look on their faces that they were all truly sick of me; that they couldn't take any more.

My ex-boyfriend (I call him that because, even though he was officially my boyfriend at that time, there was no real support from him) was also at a loss as to how to deal with my fast deteriorating health. I remember him saying: 'Look at you. Just look at the state of you.'

I knew I had only myself to blame when he and my family walked away, but even so I was furious that they had done it at a time when I felt so close to death.

I thought about that, then said to myself: 'Fuck you lot. I'm going to get out of this.' But then I remembered that it had been years since I'd managed to stay sober for longer than three days, and I realised that 'getting out of this' would be easier said than done. Even so, no sooner had I decided to get well to prove a point to them than I changed my mind and decided I'd do it for me.

My family walked away that day only because of the enormous hurt I had put them through. It was the only time in my life when they felt they had to abandon me, and I don't blame them at all. The truth is that they have been my greatest support, and their walking away on that day was the catalyst that made me determined to change, and the reason why I found the strength to survive. It was a terrible time, but it was my turning point.

Brick by brick

Despite my best intentions, there were setbacks. The first came almost immediately. My counsellor in St James's Hospital advised me that she could no longer help me, and while she didn't say it, I got the impression that she thought that because I was a drug-addicted, gay, sex worker, I was beyond her help. When I told some friends about this, word filtered back to my family. That was upsetting, as even though my family's turning their back on me was the kick in the ass I needed to turn my life around, I still felt abandoned by them.

Hope came again when the team at Baggot Street Hospital's Alcoholic Treatment Unit welcomed me back once more. This time they didn't confine their treatment programme to my addictions.

Their work wasn't easy. When with their help I managed to kick the drink and drugs, my head went down and I couldn't look anyone in the eye. I wondered then if I needed tablets to help me cope. That setback didn't deter them. They worked to rehabilitate me on every possible level, and with their help I began to heal.

The Phoenix Park

When I was a sex worker in the Phoenix Park, I felt it was the fault of humanity that I was there; that society had let me down.

I was lucky to survive the many years I worked there. In that business you don't know who you're going with or whose car you're getting into, so you take your life in your hands with every customer you see.

Punters weren't the only ones who caused us problems. Some of the Gardaí gave us a very hard time, and 'queer-bashers' (as they were called at that time) were a constant threat.

Rape is part and parcel of sex work, and I was raped in the Phoenix Park. The same thing happened in the city centre. A guy got me into the toilets in Trinity College then beat me up. He didn't pay, but at least I got away. At the time, when prostitutes reported rape to the Gardaí they were often given a lecture – something along the lines of: 'You shouldn't be out there mixing with people like that. How can you be surprised that this has happened when you are working outside the law?' That attitude is no longer the norm.

Because male prostitutes don't have pimps, their survival is a matter for themselves. Most of us thought that if we operated as a group we'd stay alive. That strategy didn't work for my group. One by one, they all died. I don't know why I wasn't one of them, but I had a reputation as a 'tough man', and that may have made the difference.

What went on when I worked in the park still goes on today. 5 p.m. marks the beginning of what sex workers refer to as Married Men's Hour. This was the time when many of them would come looking for sex with a man before going home to their wives. When the shops closed for the night the shopkeepers descended; they were predictable that way.

I'd say that approximately 70 per cent of the clients I had were hiding their true sexuality domestically, professionally and socially. Many of them called themselves bisexual because they had wives and kids at home. In my opinion they were gay.

Working in the Phoenix Park was a soul-destroying experience. I didn't see any good in any of the clients. To me they were predators, nothing more, and every time I came away from them I felt sick.

Most of the sex workers I knew did not value their lives, or themselves. I was no different. There were many nights when I'd lash back a cheap bottle of VP wine or half a bottle of vodka to stun myself, to get rid of my nerves for long enough to do the punter. Those I most loathed working with were the ones I had to kiss. I dreaded that so much that once the deed was done I would be violently ill.

Dipper

Because I often took punters' wallets, I was known as a 'dipper'. One night I took the wallet of a client who was an Irish politician. When my friends heard this, they told me that because he had terrorist connections I should make sure he got it back.

I replied that I had friends who were in drug gangs, but later decided to return the wallet to him. I thought that the best way to do this was to get a friend of mine to ring his office to say that his wallet had been found and the finder wanted to return it. His secretary earnestly enquired if this was the wallet he had lost a couple of weeks earlier.

My friend knew that the wallet we had was the one he had lost the night before, but discretion prevented her from saying that. Later, when she told me the gist of the conversation, I assumed I wasn't the first sex worker to have robbed him.

Two great Gardaí

There were two Gardaí who would often come and chat with me when they were on duty in the park. One day, one of them threw me a ten-pound note (that was worth a lot more then than it would be today) and said: 'Jimmy, get out of here. Go on. Go and get something to eat.'

The same two Gardaí were the first to notice when I quit the drink and drugs. They remarked that it was great to see me looking so well. As the months went by, they asked why I was still working there when I no longer needed the money to fund my addictions. Their comments got me thinking, and I went back to Baggot Street Hospital looking for help.

It was then that I learned that sex work was another addiction of mine, and that I'd have to work as hard to quit prostitution as I had done to give up drink and drugs. That made sense when it was explained, but the knowledge wasn't enough to pull me out of the Phoenix Park.

It's hard to break a habit of a lifetime, and working as a prostitute in the park was the only way of life I knew. I had a circle of friends there, and they looked up to me. I was known for violence, particularly when I used to drink and take drugs. The violence frightened me, and while I was afraid of the violence within myself, others were frightened of me. Because of that, what I said went. I have no doubt that my reputation for viciousness played a role in keeping me alive. It certainly kept very many dangerous guys away from me.

When newcomers arrived to work in the park, someone would take them aside and point me out. 'That's Jimmy,' they would say. 'Never get on the wrong side of him.' Those words were taken at face value. Instead of avoiding me, the newcomers used to latch on to me and look to me for protection.

Dying of fear

There was a lot of negativity around HIV in the eighties and nineties, and while the virus killed many, the fear of contracting it and dying from AIDS dragged many down and caused their deaths.

Back then, AIDS was commonly known as 'gay-related AIDS'. It was considered to be a punishment sent by God to wipe out the gay community. As if that wasn't bad enough, it was suggested that the whole lot of us (those who were HIV positive and those who had AIDS) should be sent to Spike Island. Rumour spread that it was brilliant on Spike, that it was really 'out there' and that we would love it.

On prosecuting clients not prostitutes

It's important that any future sex-work-related legislation that might be introduced does not serve to drive prostitution further underground than it already is.

When you work on the streets as a prostitute, you have the advantage of meeting your future clients before you go somewhere with them. When they are face-to-face with you, you get to smell their breath and pick up on their energy. In that way you can assess whether they're the sort who are likely to put your life in danger.

Those who work in brothels don't get that chance. Once the client walks through the door, it's too late for assessment.

Some think that since sex buyers prey on vulnerable people, sex buying should be a criminal offence and sex working should not. That wouldn't work. It would be akin to suggesting that it should be illegal to buy cigarettes in a shop, even though those cigarettes are legally available for sale there.

Whenever I speak at conferences in Ireland and overseas about the rights of sex workers, I make the point that the vast majority of women who do this work do so to get the money either to bang up their arms or to feed their kids. Either way, they need the money it brings.

Very many have great difficulty in getting a client, and they'll have even more difficulty if the married men and the judges who use them were more likely to be found out. These men don't want to put their home lives and livelihoods in jeopardy. If they felt there was even more chance than there already is of their being found out, prostitution would be driven off the streets and into darker places.

Stigma

Despite the fact that being diagnosed as being HIV positive is no longer considered to be a death sentence, the stigma around it is just as bad today as it was in the eighties and nineties.

A few years ago, I got a foot infection. When the chiropodist I attended learned I was HIV positive, he said he didn't treat people with HIV. The fact that this happened on 15 June 2006 – Irish AIDS Day – may have been lost on him, but it certainly wasn't lost on me. I said that I was really worried about having an infection, so he looked at my foot, gave me a note and sent me off with two bandages and instructions to put those on the wound and keep them on until I got treatment.

Because of my positive status, I felt it was vital that I received the antibiotics I needed, so I rang Dublin AIDS Alliance in a panic. Their response was: 'Jimmy, you're very upset. Calm down, then come in and talk with us.'

Because I felt I had been discriminated against, I took a case to the Equality Authority. The fact that this case dragged on for close to four years was appalling and extremely stressful for me. The stress was increased when on the morning of the hearing the other side tried to settle.

My legal team from the Equality Authority was very supportive, and reassured me that nobody would think less of me if I took the offer on the table. Even so, I would have thought less of myself. The pressure to accept last-minute offers of this kind means that important legal principles are never really established, and landmarks never set. What happened to me would happen again unless somebody saw it through.

Despite advice to the contrary, I decided to decline the offer. I knew that I was in the right, that I had been refused treatment because of my HIV status, and that this was my chance to take a stand against stigma and discrimination. I heard there had been other individuals who had gone to the Equality Authority then settled prior to their cases being heard so their HIV status would not go public. I couldn't do that. I had to stand up for what I believed in.

Three years and eight months after the incident occurred I attended the hearing, with my legal team's warning that the chiropodist could get off on a technicality ringing in my ears. That didn't happen. I won. It was landmark victory.

What it means to be a positive person

In 2012, 341 people were newly diagnosed as being HIV positive in Ireland, with the highest proportion of those being among the gay and bisexual communities. Very many men are HIV positive and don't know it. Fear prevents them from going for testing, and many only discover they have it when they go looking for treatment for STIs.

Many men who engage in bareback sex don't know that those who are HIV positive are at an increased risk of heart disease. They believe that because HIV can be treated, it's easy to live with. Nothing could be further from the truth.

To survive, you have to take meds for the rest of your life – meds that can have massive side effects. For many, survival includes living with lesions, increased risk of heart attack and regular bouts of diarrhoea.

Something that fills me with despair

Men who won't get tested for HIV, yet have bareback sex with those they meet on dating sites.

Yoga

A few years ago I had to quit doing yoga for two years for medical reasons. During that time I thought everything had gone from me; that I was going under. These days I do yoga five days per week. It keeps me focussed, but more than that it keeps me going.

What I want

I am in a nice place, but I want to climb more spiritual ladders. What I most want is to reach enlightenment. When

I think about that, I wonder what that feels like and whether I have reached it already.

Four passions

Justice, honesty, kindness and Benjy – my 16-year-old Glen of Imaal terrier.

The LGBT community

Even though I have been openly gay for years, I was never accepted by the LGBT community in Ireland. I think that was because of my sex work and my addictions.

As a community, the LGBT is not averse to ostracising its own. Many gay men and women who have tested positive have experienced a huge amount of prejudice from within that community.

The fact that the biggest rise in HIV in Ireland is among gay and bisexual men is not something that has been sufficiently addressed by the LGBT community. Because of that, the message about the risks associated with having unprotected sex is not getting through.

In the past two months I have spoken with two men who had unprotected sex with men they knew to be HIV positive. Their attitude was: 'Oh, it will be all right. We'll get PEP [post-exposure prophylaxis].' They didn't take these risks for love; they did it to please two guys they had been hoping to shag for over a year.

A lesson learned

For years I believed that everything that was wrong in my life was someone else's fault. Taking responsibility for my own behaviour was a big step forward. When I did that, everything balanced out.

Self-help

The work of Louise Hay and Susan Jeffers helped me to find direction. It became part of the climbing frame I used to pull myself out of the hole I was in.

MSM

The term 'MSM' (men who have sex with men) has become part of common parlance, but I think that those who define their sexuality in that way are essentially men who fuck other men, yet refuse to be categorised as gay.

If I could be somebody else for a day

God, I just want to be me. But that's probably because it took me so long to get to where I am.

If I absolutely had to be someone else I'd choose to be someone with enough power to get rid of war. Failing that, I'd be someone like Barack Obama, and I'd use my power to help those who have been left suffering and marginalised on the edges of society.

Spirituality

I was baptised Catholic but I am now a spiritualist. Recently, I had a chat with a couple of Mormons who came knocking at my front door. I said that in my opinion spirituality was at the core of many religions, so it didn't matter whether a person was Buddhist, Hindu or whatever, as all that counts is goodness, kindness, honesty and expecting nothing in return for helping others. The callers didn't know what to say in reply.

Reincarnation

I believe in reincarnation and that each lifetime is a test.

Karma

I believe in the law of karma. I have to, given my background. Twenty years ago if I saw a purse, a wallet or a phone on the ground, I'd pick it up and put it in my pocket. Now I'd know not to do that, because it doesn't belong to me and because someone else might need it more. I feel much safer nowadays, mainly because I no longer feel that my actions are going to come back and hit me in the face.

My idea of beauty

Being in a peaceful place within myself and feeling taller than the sun.

Pat Byrne

Former Garda Commissioner

Tribunals

Instead of confronting situations as they arise, it has become more convenient and/or expedient for governments and politicians, when dealing with politically sensitive issues, to dispatch them to tribunals, thereby rendering them safely off the agenda for years.

When investigating crimes, you either have evidence or you don't. As Commissioner I was sometimes asked: 'How did the tribunal gather so much more evidence than you and the Gardaí?' The reason is simple: it's easier for tribunals to get evidence.

When a tribunal calls you in, you must appear before it. When it demands the documentation you have in relation to a particular issue, you have no right to refuse to give that. Lastly, you have no right of silence in a tribunal.

Now compare that system with what happens when the Garda Síochána investigates. A Garda calls out to an individual's house and says: 'I want you to come into the office.' The individual may reply, 'I won't go in.' The Garda may then say: 'I will arrest you and bring you in.' To do that, the Garda must have reasonable suspicion. If they do, they must immediately provide a caution to the effect that the suspect doesn't have to say anything unless they wish to do so. Not only does the suspect have the option of remaining silent, they also have the right to refuse to produce documentation. When the investigation is complete, the Garda then sends the evidence to the DPP, who decides whether or not to prosecute.

It's clear when one compares the two systems why it's so much easier for tribunals to gather evidence than it is for the Gardaí. Perhaps because of that, there's a perception that tribunals are hugely worthwhile and effective – so much so that their findings can put people in prison.

That doesn't necessarily follow, as what is said at a tribunal cannot be used in a criminal trial. Someone could say: 'By the way, I decapitated seven people,' but without evidence of the wrongdoing the Gardaí could not use that admission to bring that individual to court. It may steer an investigator in a particular direction, but the investigation would have to start from scratch. Citizens are often very frustrated when they realise that a tribunal is not a criminal court.

There is a misguided public perception that it's primarily wrongdoers who are brought before tribunals. There's a risk that the integrity and credibility of innocent individuals could be called into question by members of the public for no reason other than the fact that those individuals were called to give evidence at a tribunal. Remarks such as: 'Did you hear your man was up before the tribunal?' can have negative consequences for those summoned before them. This can be damning in the extreme.

Because tribunals make their findings on a balance of probability, I believe that their conclusions are opinions. When I compare the tribunal system with the court system

– where guilt has to be proved beyond reasonable doubt – I conclude that it would be very easy to solve crimes if, in the criminal court system, we had to prove the guilt of the defendant only on the balance of probability. But would that be right? I don't believe so.

In my opinion, while tribunals have brought into the open many issues that would have otherwise remained hidden from public view, they remain a hugely unwieldy, lengthy, cumbersome, overly expensive and at times very unfair way of conducting independent investigations, and from them there is no court of appeal. For these reasons I favour the use of the Commissions of Investigation.

The wrongdoing of some Donegal-based Gardaí

While I was disappointed, I wasn't shocked at the findings of the Morris or any other tribunal, because I had been aware of the evidence as it was revealed on a day-to-day basis by witnesses. What annoyed me was the difficulty Assistant Commissioner Kevin Carty experienced in carrying out his investigations because of a refusal to cooperate by some of those involved. The findings of the Morris Tribunal seriously damaged the reputation of the Garda Síochána.

Judge Morris at one stage made a comment to the effect that if certain members of the Garda Síochána had cooperated with and been truthful to Assistant Commissioner Carty when he was carrying out his investigations, there would have been no need for a tribunal. I agree. I had appointed Assistant Commissioner Kevin Carty and his team to investigate the issues that arose in Donegal. He was an exceptionally competent investigator, and had worked on many difficult operations both national and international over the years.

The evidence that emerged at the Morris Tribunal highlighted the damage a small nucleus of people can cause to a large organisation like the Garda Síochána. It also showed that the system in place allowed those individuals to undermine the Assistant Commissioner's authority to investigate them.

The behaviour of the Gardaí concerned, and their refusal to cooperate with the Garda Síochána investigation, undermined public confidence in the force and was an embarrassment to the honourable members of the Garda attached to the Donegal division. While a minority may have believed that the activities investigated by the Morris Tribunal were typical of Garda behaviour nationwide, the vast majority would have known that this was not so. We had a force of 11,000 at the time, and the Donegal-based Gardaí who were implicated in the activities that were subsequently investigated by the Morris Tribunal represented only a tiny percentage of the divisional force.

When a system breaks down like this I ask the question: how is it that such wrongdoing could go on for a number of years without someone noticing and reporting it? It is true that the Donegal division, like other border divisions, was at the forefront of the battle with paramilitaries of different kinds for a number of decades, as well as confronting crime, so the supervisory focus on the activities of personnel may not have been what it should have been. It is the responsibility of local management in any Garda division and district to be aware of and deal with concerns that arise in their respective areas of competence. If they are unable to do so, they are obliged to bring such concerns to the notice of the respective branch of Garda headquarters.

The Morris Tribunal, like others, has given its findings, and while we may not agree with all of them, we have had to accept them, learn from them and move on.

Getting off on a technicality

There was a public outcry when it emerged that evidence to be used in a case against a (now former) judge was inadmissible in court because the search warrant used by the Gardaí to access that evidence had expired.

My understanding of the case was that, when the validity of the warrant was challenged, it was established for the first time in Irish law that a seven-day warrant expires at the same time on the seventh day as it came into force on the first. Because that had never before been confirmed, the Gardaí believed that the warrant they used on the seventh day of the seven-day warrant was valid.

There were also questions as to why the Gardaí waited until the seventh day to conduct their search. But there was nothing sinister about that – their investigations were ongoing right up to the time of the search. I presume they were monitoring developments and gathering evidence until the last moment so as to strengthen their case.

When I read the newspaper reports I thought that the public would think it was intentional; that for some reason the Gardaí were working to get this individual off. This perception could have damaged the reputation of the Gardaí, but it couldn't have been further from the truth. The conspiracy theorists came to the fore, but you can be assured that nobody was more disappointed than the investigating Garda members. I believe that people eventually realised that it was just the search warrant technicality that caused the problem.

Garda corruption

People get fed up when I say 'You will always get bad apples.' I say that a lot, because it's true – they exist in all organisations.

I remember an occasion when, during a serious crimes investigation, it was brought to my notice that undercover surveillance had discovered that one of our Gardaí was working for a criminal gang we were investigating. He was investigated, charged and convicted, and served time in prison. We did the same when we discovered that one of our members was working for the provisional IRA. I have always found that in investigating our own people there was an added persistence in gathering the evidence to put such a person before the courts. Not that we were always successful, of course.

We also had the Disciplinary Regulations route to follow as an alternative. Some argued that this created 'double jeopardy' for the member under suspicion, but I didn't think so. Court judgments supported the principle that that while disciplinary action could not be pursued with regard to the actual offence/crime that was dismissed in the criminal courts, that did not prevent the Garda Síochána from pursuing disciplinary action against the Garda member for the behaviour surrounding the crime.

While shock and outrage was the general response to the criminal actions of some of our members, my reaction was: 'Did we not always realise that some would betray us in this way?' It would have been naïve for us to assume that we had 11,000 perfect people in the force. One has to be realistic. If as few as one half of one per cent of the force were covertly doing wrong, that would be more than sufficient to create major difficulties for a police service.

Phone tapping

The Garda Síochána, as the national police service and the national security service, has a responsibility that in most other countries is carried out by two different agencies; in the UK there exist forty-three different police services and the Security Service (MI5). The Garda Síochána is responsible for all aspects of criminal investigations and intelligence gathering on issues of State security and this includes phone interception. Phone interception is carried out by warrant under Ministerial authority. It is also now under judicial oversight. It is, however, managed and controlled by Crime and Security Branch in Garda HQ. The Garda Síochána may legitimately monitor phones while investigating crime and while investigating issues that touch on State security. In my time, that type of activity was extremely well supervised. I have no doubt it's the same today.

In relation to the recording of phone conversations in Garda stations, it was always the practice that calls to Command and Control centres and Communication Rooms in rural divisions would be recorded as these centres were the recipients of emergency 999 calls on a twenty-four-hour basis. The reasoning for this is obvious. The recording or monitoring of other phone conversations to or from Garda stations was never intended, nor was it policy.

Whistle-blowing

Whistle-blowing can affect all organisations. Some whistle-blowers are genuine, some are not, and there can be reasons for the emergence of both. It is not unknown for those who make reports to do so for vexatious reasons, potentially resulting in innocent people being put under investigation. Some whistle-blowers may have ulterior motives, and can seriously damage a successful business or organisation. There are, however, perfectly genuine people who suspect that wrongdoing has not been addressed by an organisation. If concerns are not properly addressed, one cannot complain if the whistle-blower then takes it further. In my experience, most issues of complaint or criticism can be dealt with comprehensively within the structure of an organisation.

It's commonly believed that just as accountants shouldn't investigate accountants and doctors shouldn't investigate doctors, police shouldn't investigate police. The Garda Síochána has an excellent track record of dealing robustly with complaints against Gardaí, but in the interests of justice being seen to be done, I think it's always good when investigations are seen to be independent. Internal discipline must always be a matter for the Garda authorities. Garda oversight, however, is best served by a properly established external body. Recent events support this view.

Investigation into the death of Veronica Guerin

I don't think anyone believed John Gilligan when, on his release from prison in October 2013, he said he had nothing to do with the murder of crime reporter Veronica Guerin. From the earliest stages in July 1996, the Gardaí knew who was responsible for her murder. A very effective investigation team under the supervision of Assistant Commissioner Tony Hickey dealt with this brutal murder.

Gilligan had also said that he never assaulted Veronica when she called to speak with him at his home. That was not what she told me when we spoke straight after she met with him. In fact, Veronica related exactly how he had assaulted her.

As a consequence of her killing in Dublin, and that of detective Garda Jerry McCabe in Adare in June 1996, there was a view abroad – and at the highest levels of government – that the Garda Síochána would not be able to deal with gangland crime in Ireland. That perception was wrong. I was appointed Commissioner shortly after the killings of Jerry and Veronica, and I found that convincing people that we were more than able for the challenge was no easy task. Tactics and units that were deployed to counter paramilitary activity were now used to complement those dedicated to fighting organised crime. Gangs were broken from the inside. Former gang members turned, and went on to testify in court. A witness protection programme was established.

I look back on that as a very successful operation as a whole, and while I can't say that we were able to convict every one of the criminals involved in the killing of Veronica, I can say that, at that time, the thoroughness of our investigations smashed organised crime in Ireland.

John Gilligan was sentenced to twenty-eight years for trafficking cannabis in 2001. That was reduced to twenty years on appeal. As a consequence, the Criminal Assets Bureau (CAB) was established, headed by a Garda Detective Chief Superintendent reporting to me as Commissioner. The key objective of this multi-agency unit was to follow the money trail of those involved in organised crime. I think its success over the years speaks for itself.

A great disappointment

Who killed the missing women, and where are their bodies? These are questions I often ask myself, and I feel great disappointment that, having served seven years as Commissioner, we still don't have the answers.

I think it likely that the deaths of at least three of Ireland's missing women may have been at the hands of one single individual. Without a crime scene, though, there are no forensics, and so we have had very little to work on. To review all such cases I later set up Operation Trace to review and examine these and any similar incidents that came to our notice. Such a practise is ongoing. These cases are never closed, and any information, even if seemingly insignificant, is pursued. The mystery of the deaths of these women strikes me every now and again, and every time a body is found.

Capital punishment

I was part of the unit that arrested Noel and Marie Murray for the murder of Garda Reynolds in Raheny in the seventies, and I was in court when Judge Pringle of the Special Criminal Court sentenced them to death. Despite the sentence, few thought that the executions would take place, and indeed their sentences were commuted.

I am very much against capital punishment, and would never like to see it reintroduced in Ireland. Criminals only rarely consider the ultimate penalty for their crime prior to its commission; they are much more likely to consider how best to evade capture than anything else.

When one looks at the USA, the death sentence does not appear to deter people from committing murder. Yes, it's cheaper for the State to execute rather than keep someone in prison for years, but I think it is an atrocious and barbarous act to end the life of another, whatever the reason, justification or mandate. Do mandatory sentences deter criminals from carrying out a particular crime? I don't think so. Does the fact that murder in this country carries with it a mandatory sentence of life imprisonment deter people from committing murder? I don't think so. Getting caught remains a criminal's greatest fear.

Some say of evil individuals: 'That fellow should be shot – that's why we need the death penalty.' I know that may be a throwaway remark, but if it means that we should have the death penalty for certain horrific crimes, I personally disagree. When an individual is sentenced to death, somebody has the task of pressing the button, pulling the lever or otherwise taking some action to end that life, and that, too, is horrific. The film *The Green Mile* is worth watching when one suggests that reintroducing the death penalty is worthy of consideration. Although this might sound like a simplistic or emotive approach to the question of capital punishment, I would maintain that some points of view are much more easily held 'at a distance' than when confronted by the reality of what that point of view actually entails.

There is also, of course, the risk of a mistake being made. The criminal justice system, for all its safeguards and legal principles, is ultimately administered by fallible human beings who are capable of getting things wrong. In the case of the death penalty, any such mistake is irrevocable. One's view on capital punishment should not be formed on the basis of one's willingness to be the executioner; it should be based on one's willingness to be a wrongly accused defendant.

Prison

Prisons can at times be a breeding ground for criminals. Many come out of prison as a bigger danger to society than they were when they went in. There are of course others who benefit from a term of imprisonment, but career criminals can benefit in a very different way while incarcerated.

Some prisoners opt to socialise in circles where commitment to crime is fostered. One of the many who strengthened his criminal networks while in jail was John Gilligan. While in Portlaoise Prison he associated with individuals who, on their release, joined his criminal gang.

Those who are convicted of crime pay penalties. If they get sentenced to time in prison the penalty is being taken out of society and put away. I don't agree with those who resent prisoners being given access to televisions or other facilities. I don't care if they get to watch SKY Sports while they're inside. Their liberty has been taken away, and that is the point. Criminals go to prison *as* a punishment; they do not go *for* a punishment.

The importance of timely reporting

In relation to supervision, it is vital that problems that come to light are tackled immediately. This became apparent to me during the two and a half years I spent as Assistant Commissioner in charge of Personnel (HR).

When problems such as a dependency on alcohol, gambling, domestic issues or illness issues etc. come to the notice of supervisors, they should be dealt with immediately and not put on the long finger hoping that they go away. They do not. Often, particularly in large organisations, rather than confronting the problem a compassionate approach would have been taken. At times this worked, but more often than not it only exacerbated the problem. Once problems arise, deal with them immediately – don't let them fester! Misplaced kindness can cause greater problems, and can ultimately cost people their jobs.

Police Force

The Garda Síochána polices this State on behalf of and with the assistance of the community. The relationship between the Garda and the community is a unique one, and is often envied by other policing organisations. Policing is in no way a namby-pamby occupation. While police organisations were historically known as police 'forces', the consensus now is that they should be described as police 'services'. That is fine, but it doesn't mean that the use of force is now a thing of the past. Citizens expect their Garda members to enforce the law and to stand toe to toe with those who transgress and who challenge them while so engaged. The Garda member represents the citizen, and as such must treat people in a fair and reasonable manner, and sometimes has to be firm and forceful.

A police force is only as good as the people it has, and so it is essential that they are properly trained, properly resourced and properly paid. Our people are highly trained, however resourcing is vital in ensuring the efficiency and effectiveness of the organisation. It is vital that we pay our Gardaí properly. Many of the younger people, like others outside the Garda, are financially so hard-pressed, particularly by negative equity and mortgage repayments, that they see no light at the end of the tunnel. This is not a very reassuring or healthy situation. Worldwide experience, in terms of ensuring the integrity of police organisations, points to the necessity of ensuring that one's police force is adequately paid. One has to accept that, in the context of the dire financial situation in which this State has found itself in recent years, to resource the organisation to its former levels is not on the immediate horizon.

Arming a police force.

To arm the Garda Síochána in general would, in my view, be a retrograde step. We have armed detectives, and our armed Regional Support Units are well equipped to confront armed criminals when the need arises.

It is obvious that in the last thirty years street violence and the use of firearms and knives has markedly increased. Organised gangs have displayed an attitude of complete disregard for human life, and this has filtered down to some of those engaged in street violence. The experiences of Gardaí have confirmed, if it were not already obvious, that a confrontational and violent culture is an increasing problem. If society continues to become more violent, however, resulting in citizens and Gardaí being killed or injured, the question as to whether they should be armed will in my opinion need to be reviewed. Armed backup to uniformed officers responding to dangerous situations is a must, and if this is not maintained then society and the Gardaí in general will call for a new approach. At this time I don't believe the rank-and-file officers of the Garda would wish to be armed, although that may change.

Complaints

When we consider the number of complaints made to GSOC against Gardaí (over 2,000 in 2012), it's easy to assume that this is an accurate reflection of Garda wrongdoing. It isn't. One has to look beyond these figures. As a matter of practice, most professional/career criminals will, when caught, make a complaint against the arresting Garda. This is a common tactic to slow up the process of their being brought to justice. Because of this, the most active policemen and women – those who are at the coalface of policing – tend to have the most complaints made against them.

Blue flu

Despite the fact that 80 to 85 per cent of Gardaí rang in sick on 1 May 1998, in what was effectively a strike action, recorded crime that day was at an all-time low. That surprised us, and others. The day was an unusual one, and many, including lawbreakers, were waiting for something to happen. A major and tragic incident did in fact occur, in that one of those involved in a paramilitary armed robbery was shot dead in a confrontation with armed Gardaí. Crime in general, however, was way below normal levels.

In fairness, there was a level of policing that day comprising the specialist units, probationary Gardaí and those of ranks from Sergeant up.

Because I spent twenty years of my service at Garda, Sergeant and Inspector levels in the Garda Síochána, I fully understood the issues that led to the organisation of the day making a decision to do what they did. I also firmly believed there was no need for it at all. I earnestly requested the Garda Representative Association not to go ahead, but to no avail. In the end, the 'Blue Flu' day achieved nothing for the Gardaí. Instead, it became a catchphrase to criticise the force. It didn't bring the Gardaí closer to their goal. Everything they got, in terms of pay, they were going to get anyway.

That said, there is no other organisation in this country that is not allowed to strike. For that reason, I have always maintained that the fact that our police force cannot take industrial action should be acknowledged in some manner.

Walking out on a speech

I think it discourteous and disrespectful for anyone to stand up and walk out when an invited guest is speaking, and I would never approve of such behaviour. If individuals don't want to hear what is being said by a particular individual, they should stay outside. Alternatively, they could attend and show disapproval by abstaining from clapping when the speech has been made. Stony silence can have a great impact.

Zero tolerance

Zero tolerance was debated in Ireland at a time in the late 1990s when the Fianna Fáil Spokesperson on Justice suggested it as the way forward. While he was very keen on the idea, I was sceptical and said so.

While it worked to a degree in New York, it could never work here. Irish society is different to American society. Irish policing is different to American policing. In the US it's policing by the gun and the holster – it's a different confrontational mode. Taking beggars and vagrants off the streets in the way the New York police did when zero tolerance was introduced would never be the Irish way. It also, of course, requires major resourcing.

Zero tolerance is about enforcing every law. The Irish way, however, is the polar opposite of this. The first thing Irish people do when they get into trouble is to ask: 'Who do I know who might be able to get me out of this spot?' Public representatives are continually lobbied to intercede for people for all manner of things. That does not happen in New York.

There are people in this country who say they support the policy of zero tolerance, particularly if it is utilised to police people outside their social class, society, community or family. Once it touches someone close to them, however, they can have different views.

Policing in Ireland is very much about interacting with people and convincing them not to do things. That can entail the use of discretion. In my view, some level of tolerance is better than none. Without that we would pave the way for fear-based policing and jammed prisons. Let's have more law enforcement in Ireland, but let's say no to zero tolerance.

The cover-your-ass approach to policing

Fear of getting into trouble prevents many from taking action. This shouldn't be the way. What is central is whether a particular course of action is the right thing to do. If it is, then that's what should be done. We all have a duty and an obligation to do the right thing and to take responsibility for it.

Sometimes it can take an extraordinarily long time for decisions to be made. Risk-taking, while necessary at times, is often ignored in favour of a safer approach. This was something that I found very frustrating. Bureaucratic processes can go on and on. This is not only true of State organisations; in all walks of life there are those who won't get off their asses and act until everything has been thoroughly checked and double-checked, every potentially bad possibility mulled over, every previous bad result coming back to haunt them. This 'cover-your-ass' approach is detrimental to progress.

Crossing the line

It's commonly thought that kids who grow up in rough neighbourhoods and broken homes are more likely to turn to crime. I don't believe that at all. Such a background doesn't help of course, but a lot of other issues come into play to steer a person towards a criminal career.

In my opinion, socio-economic background is not what sets people on the wrong path. Greed, opportunity, economic necessity and a moral compass that's way off line are far more likely reasons. Another is evil. Some people are bad to the core, and smart and intelligent with it. Fortunately, people like that are few and far between, but they do exist.

As to whether you are doomed if you cross a line you've set between right and wrong, it depends on where the line is. Nobody can be right all of the time. While some say it's either black or white, when it comes to right and wrong I have found that life is made up mostly of grey.

When people are seen emerging from Garda vans in handcuffs, members of the public tend to assume they're bad people. Some are. Some aren't. Some are very unfortunate people.

Over the years I have known people who were convicted and sentenced for very serious crimes. Some of them, and I must say they were a small minority, were people who had reacted, spontaneously and violently as a result of having been taunted unmercifully, with tragic consequences.

Despite what they did, they were often likeable individuals who were deeply sorry for what had happened. Encountering people like that brought home to me the fact that, under certain circumstances, perfectly ordinary, previously peaceful types discover too late that, when goaded, they are capable of terrible acts of spontaneous violence, which they neither would nor could have anticipated.

When it comes to human nature, there really is no black and white. Nobody is all good. Nobody is all bad. That is something Gardaí understand better than most. Perfection is difficult to achieve.

Clerical abuse

The scandal of clerical abuse was appalling. One simply cannot ignore the strength, influence and power of the

Church in Ireland up to recent years. This affected the whole range of society from the top to the bottom. This created a climate in which denial and incredulity were the response to any allegation of abuse, misconduct or crime by any cleric. A number of allegations of clerical abuse emerged during my time as Commissioner, when I saw first-hand the very many barriers our investigators faced in getting to the truth. Instead of the Church taking responsibility and cooperating fully, priority was given to the protection of organisations. I accept that many large organisations act similarly when challenged, but that is indefensible when crimes against children are being investigated. When the extent of that stance emerged, it was discouraging for everyone. It took some time for a change of attitude to emerge. The persistence and the professionalism of the investigating Garda officers assisted in bringing about this change.

Biggest security threat to Ireland now

There is a chance that Sellafield may blow up and destroy us all, but I don't think that will happen!

What is happening in the Middle East at this time must be a cause of concern for those in Europe. How it develops and how it spreads will be monitored closely. The problems involved in these confrontations are not ones that will be quickly or easily rectified. The possible spread of international terrorism into Europe, with its impact on energy resources and on international markets, could become a challenge in the future, and is an issue for which we may have to be prepared. In so far as this becomes a problem for mainland Europe, we will have to play our part.

Closure of Garda stations

Over the years, it was necessary to reduce the opening hours of some stations, particularly those in what one could describe as remote, rural areas (I grew up in a few of them). Since the foundation of the State we had over 700 Garda stations, which had been handed over from RIC days – an impossible number to man on an ongoing basis. If we were starting out again we would never have that many. Some such stations were reduced to one hour for three days in the week. I didn't like closing them, but it had to be done for practical reasons. There was no point in having a Garda sitting there all day with little to do. At the time, some suggested that if lights were left on in unmanned barracks, local communities would feel safe. I don't believe in that philosophy.

The recent closure of a number of Garda stations at the same time created agitation, both for the Minister and for the Commissioner. The biggest obstacle that Garda management faced over the years in trying to bring some sensible balance to the number of stations required was local politicians. They didn't want a local station closed any more than they wanted a local bank or post office removed. As understandable as this is when considered from their point of view, it resulted in an archaic system of police station locations. Over the decades there should have been an ongoing programme with an agreement on the need for the reduction of the number of stations, along with community consultation on how this could best be achieved. Such an approach might have gained the understanding and sympathy of the local communities by better addressing their concerns.

White-collar crime

White-collar crime has long been perceived as less serious than other types of crime. One often hears something along the lines of: 'Ah, sure, there was no violence involved,' despite the fact that the crime may have destroyed the lives of and wiped out the savings of elderly and vulnerable people. We hear of this happening when rogue solicitors wrongfully take, and lose, client monies.

The prime reason why the problem of white-collar crime has not been adequately addressed in Ireland is because it is so rarely reported. Rather than involving Gardaí, there has been a tendency by employers to sack those responsible and keep quiet about what happened. Investigating such crimes is often very complex, and hugely time-consuming. The 'proof' needed in terms of evidence for the prosecution can be quite a complex matter.

If a working-class individual with a job in a shop were to put their hand in the till, the chances are that they would be arrested and charged. A middle-class individual who did the same thing in his family business would most likely walk free. The well-to-do tend to look on this sort of crime as harmlessly errant so far as family are concerned. A typical response would be to label the perpetrator a 'black sheep', then encourage them to start a new life elsewhere.

As to why anyone carries out white-collar crime, usually it's because the opportunity presents itself, they get greedy, and in the end feel they will get away with it. We are dealing with greed and corruption and very serious criminal behaviour. Because of relatively recent events and third-party consequences, it now appears that such crimes are being reported more often, and investigated by the appropriate authorities.

Climbing the career ladder

My grandfather was a member of the Garda Síochána, as was my father and his two brothers. Even so, my father never encouraged me to join the Gardaí. That isn't to say that he discouraged me – he didn't. He just wanted me to do whatever I liked.

I was never a man with a vision of getting to the top of my career. I was thirteen years a Garda, seven years a Sergeant and three years an Inspector, so most of my service was at the bottom end of the organisation. I progressed fairly quickly thereafter. But I was lucky in that opportunities came my way, and that played a part in my being the youngest Garda Commissioner to come through the ranks.

I began as a uniform Garda, then in 1972 I went into the Special Detective Unit (SDU). At this time the whole focus of the Irish government was on security and policing – so much so that in the 1970s and 1980s one million pounds per day was being spent in Ireland on policing and security to counter the activities of paramilitary organisations.

I was committed to and successful at my work, and I think that was recognised. I was never a nine-to-five man. I worked hard, and went for promotion at every opportunity. Admittedly, it took me twelve years to do the Sergeants' exam. But when confronting paramilitary organisations, sitting exams was low on my priority list. That's not to say I was not ambitious. I was, in so far as I was ambitious if an opportunity arose. When I saw those around me getting promoted, I decided to do my exams so I'd be eligible for promotion. My approach was: I'll put myself forward and see how it goes. Other than that, I kept my mind on my work.

My attitude was always: do your darned best to do your job and don't be annoyed if somebody disagrees with you.

If you try to please everybody, you're not doing your job. I also believe that when you are wrong you should say you are wrong. That can be hard to do, but if you know you're wrong and can't bring yourself to admit that today, perhaps you will be able to do that tomorrow.

As a kid

I had a great childhood. I was a bit wild. But while I might have done stupid things, I didn't do bad things.

As a kid I attended four different national schools. Because of that I had to learn quickly how to integrate with others. As the new guy coming into a school time and time again, I could easily have been hammered had I not learned to survive. Back then, it wasn't only the other kids who would be doing the hammering; it was the teachers. That is the way it was back then; corporal punishment was the 'in' thing.

My father was a superintendent in Cork City when he retired, but in his Sergeant days we lived in Dunmanway. It was a different world. At that time, if our family didn't go to Mass together, or if my father attended out of uniform, there would be comments and criticism.

The local doctor, the parish priest and the Garda Sergeant were the influential people. Back then, while the law may not always have been applied 'by the book' throughout the country, justice was applied nevertheless. Very often it was applied by way of summary jurisdiction – as in the resolution of conflict on the street. Issues were dealt with and sorted out, often with no charge or conviction being made. While the end result was often akin to someone being tried and convicted, this was done informally, outside of the traditional channels. It was not unusual for members of local communities to approach the local Sergeant and say: 'Bring Johnny down to the cell for a couple of hours. That will sort him out.' That's how problems were handled at the time.

I asked my father a few years ago what would have happened when he was a Sergeant had he arrested a parish priest on foot of a complaint. 'I'd have been in trouble' was his response. Some might think that to be a strange reaction, but he was right. They were different times; times when the Irish government thought nothing of consulting the Archbishop of Dublin before passing legislation.

My father's job caused us to move around a lot. Besides Dunmanway, we also lived in Knocknagree, Eyeries on the Beara peninsula, Rathcoole and Bandon, all in Cork. In Rathcoole in the mid-1950s there were five houses, a Garda station (with one sergeant and one Garda) with no electricity and no running water, and a railway station with a little side shunting-track on it. When the driver would be shunting a couple of wagons he would bring me onto the engine. I'd be black with soot when I went home to my mother, telling her that I wanted to be a train driver when I grew up. I loved the steam engines. I wasn't interested in diesel, but I changed loyalty as the years went on.

What life has taught me

Life has taught me to be understanding of situations, to avoid jumping to conclusions and to refrain from pillorying individuals because of something someone may have said about them. It also taught me the importance of always asking for the view of 'the other side'.

While my initial instincts are inclined to be fairly accurate, life has taught me to refrain from reacting in haste. In my time as Commissioner, while deciding how to respond to a particular incident or event, I made a habit of putting the matter aside for a short while before taking action. At that level, reactions can have consequences, so it's important to be careful with them. There were times when I was asked to comment about incidents or events when I said nothing, because I knew that at the time that the only answer I could have given would have been used against the organisation. In those instances the best course of action for me was to say nothing for a little while and see how things developed.

There have been occasions when I was tempted to react in written form to some issue on a file or communication on my desk while thinking 'I'll show him.' But instead of succumbing to the temptation, I took time to reflect. That done, I'd often shelve my initial reaction and adopt a different stance. It's a good idea if you're tempted to write something to take someone to task to actually write it – don't post it, just put it in the drawer and look at it the following morning. More often than not you will then shred it.

Who I am at the core of me

I could say that I am a humble human being, but most others might disagree. At the core of me I am a very ordinary person, someone who loves people and who loves communicating with others.

I fear no one – apart from my wife when she is annoyed with me. In truth, though, I never fear anyone or anything. It's an emotion that never enters my mind.

I am a people person, and someone who is relaxed in demeanour. I am also a great believer in sincerity, so much so that I dislike insincere people; hypocritical people. Hypocrisy and dishonesty are traits that put me off.

I enjoy life. I have something great to look forward to every day. Maybe it's because I am a realist that I tend not to worry about things. Sometimes I worry about my family, but when I catch myself doing that, I say: 'Why am I worrying?' and I stop.

The extent of my struggles can be summed up as follows: every evening at around 6.00 p.m. I ask myself, will I have a glass of wine or will I not have a glass of wine? I ponder that for a moment and then I have one.

I love my lifestyle. Yesterday morning I fed six horses for my daughter and her friends. I do that most mornings. I don't have to prepare the feed; it's all left ready for me.

I am big into fixing things. Whenever something needs to be fixed at home or in my kids' homes, I am the man for the job. I absolutely love working with my hands. While I tackle most tasks, I stay away from plumbing.

I think I'm a good judge of character. My wife wouldn't always agree. Seriously though, I think I can accurately assess most people quickly and I'm fairly clued in to body language. Of course that doesn't mean I'm always right. My instinct has let me down once or twice.

I'm a Catholic, but not a good practising Catholic. When I think of what's happening around the world in the name of religion, I think how much better it would be if people could be allowed to get on with their lives. In my personal life I'm a 'live and let live' kind of person.

The goodness in people astonishes me, particularly the goodness in young people. Most are a damn sight more aware of and conscious of what is the right thing to do than we were at their age. When I think of what I was like when I was young, and when I compare that to how my kids are, I can only conclude that they are better people.

What matters most to me is my golf handicap, which is thirteen at the moment. I am kidding of course. Nothing matters more than family to me.

I have always believed that, no matter where you are in an organisation or what position you hold in society, it's important to know the names of the 'little people'. In my experience, while the 'big people' will let you know who they are, the little ones tend not to. That's why, for me, it has always been important to make sure I know their names. The person who is coming in with a cup of coffee for me, the person who is brushing the yard above in the depot, the guy who is on the gate: these are the people I want to know. I see myself as that sort of person. It's in me to be like that. It's who I am. That probably comes from my rearing. It also comes from moving around so much in my job.

I was never a goody-goody, so I would always be cautious of throwing stones at others. I am extremely thick-skinned. I learned to be that way; to take the rough with the smooth.

I also take risks. I remember Veronica Guerin remarking to me about one particular operation: 'Byrne, you'll never get Commissioner if this gets into print ...'.

'Print it,' was my response. 'Print it, because it's the truth.'

She said, 'Think of the risk you're taking.'

My response was: 'I'm paid to take calculated risks, Veronica.'

John Carmody

Founder of Animal Rights Action Network (ARAN)

A turning point

My turning point came when I was 14 years of age. It happened when a newspaper published a graphic shot of a seal-hunt in Canada on its cover. I was horrified by what it showed: baby seals had been skinned, their agony etched on the bloodstained ice that stretched the breadth of the photograph.

I have always had a strong sense of injustice. At 12 or 13 I became a supporter of Greenpeace, and while I was concerned about the environment, it didn't touch me as deeply as the hurting of animals.

I felt profound sorrow for the 3-week-old seals and for the terrible wrong that had been done to them. In response I wrote a letter to the Canadian Embassy in Dublin, asking that they try to stop that from happening again.

I also wrote to PETA (People for the Ethical Treatment of Animals). In reply they sent me an information pack, which opened me up to a world of animals being skinned for fur, or chained and caged in circuses until they reach the point where they are going absolutely insane from confinement and from the behind-the-scenes suffering they're forced to endure.

It also opened me up to what happens to animals in the name of medical research. I was repulsed by what I learned, and that revulsion was the catalyst that led to my later becoming an animal rights activist. I played my part by taking part in demonstrations, becoming a vegetarian, founding ARAN (the Animal Rights Action Network) and becoming PETA's organiser in Ireland.

Medical research

For the most part, countries are increasingly unwilling to tolerate cruelty to animals for the purposes of entertainment. The use of animals in circuses, for example, is something that is widely condemned, and most people would agree that no animal in this day and age deserves to spend its life in chains, generally in cramped and confined quarters, forced to perform repetitive acts in front of bright lights and screaming people. Many countries around the world have passed legislation to ban this kind of needless cruelty.

When it comes to the emotive issue of medical research, though, most people seem to want to draw a moral distinction and support it. Of course we all, and I include myself in this, want to see progress in medical research, and many important advances have been achieved. It is worth considering, however, that despite the large numbers of animals that have suffered and died for this reason, not to mention the vast amounts of public funding this research attracts, we still do not have the cures we need for many diseases. Is it not possible that a different form of research might have been more successful? It alarms me that the many undercover investigations conducted by animal welfare charities into the use of animals in research tend to reveal not only very significant levels of cruelty, but also somewhat shabby research methods. In some cases, investigations have even revealed data falsification and illegal practices.

If research using animals is, quite apart from the suffering involved, expensive, unreliable and unnecessary, surely we can find a better way to do things?

Something I avoid

I wasn't always a vegetarian. I ate my way through the animal kingdom before deciding I could no longer do that. This is something I say at every opportunity as I feel it helps the ARAN cause to show that those who work for animals are no different from anyone else; we're just people who make choices that reflect our respect for other creatures.

I avoid taking the high moral ground while trying to bring about change. It's not for me or for anybody else to look down on others because they may not live as we think they should. When we point the finger at or judge others, they either become defensive or they switch off. Either way, we lose their support.

Like most people, I wasn't always a super animal lover, but just as I made changes in the way I live when I became aware of what was happening to them, I hope that others will too when they learn the truth. We have a long way to go as a society in many different ways, but through my work with ARAN I have seen massive changes in public perception over time. At a point when enough people are unwilling to 'look the other way', change follows. Anything that anyone can do to make a difference, even a small difference, matters.

ARAN

In the early days of ARAN we did a lot of running around and a lot of screaming and shouting. We thought that would change the world. We know different now.

We used to turn up at petrol stations that were linked to animal testing and shout: 'Shame on you!' But while ARAN was more 'in your face' than it is today, I never did anything extreme or illegal. Looking back, I have no regrets about my earlier methods of campaigning as they shaped the way I work today. Now our focus is on getting the public onto our side.

My calling in life

I feel that working for the protection of animals has been my calling in life. Very many have become kinder to animals because of me and because of ARAN's work. When I look back over my life I want to be able to say to myself that in my lifetime I wasn't one to turn my head away; I was able to overcome the feeling that I couldn't make a difference. My work has stirred me to strive hard to make this world a better place. I know first-hand that individuals can and do make a difference.

What fills me with anger

Injustice.

Getting the basics right

When ARAN broke a story about cruelty to cats, I was asked why I was so upset about the fate of one unfortunate creature. My response was: if we can't get the basics right; if we can't learn the importance of respecting animals first, we have no hope of respecting one another. Until we manage to do that, there will always be war, there will always be hate, and blood will always be shed.

I very much believe that acts of cruelty to animals are not mere indications of a minor personality flaw; they are often symptomatic of a deep mental disturbance. Research in psychology and criminology has shown that people who commit acts of cruelty to animals rarely stop there. 'Murderers very often start out by killing and torturing animals as kids,' said the influential FBI profiler Robert K. Ressler. It is not the case that most people who hurt animals will go on to kill people, but there is no clearer warning of a disturbed personality than the willingness to hurt something that cannot defend itself. Abusers target the powerless; that is why, so often, an animal will be the first target of abuse, but will not always be the last.

Hope

Most parents do not have the awareness to educate their kids about the importance of respecting all living creatures, both animal and human. But some do, and that gives me hope. A lot of work is needed in terms of educational programmes, and these are the things on which ARAN tends to focus with our grassroots outreach programmes, awareness-raising and advertising campaigns.

Societies are becoming increasingly aware of animal rights. The Chinese are moving away from using animals for cosmetic testing. There is cause for hope, so much so that I believe that two generations from now we won't have animals in circuses or fur farms, and it will become the norm to treat animals with the respect they deserve.

The havoc we wreak

The devastation caused in the Philippines by Typhoon Haiyan highlighted how vulnerable we are when nature shows her might.

When we are struck hard in this way, we tend to ask: is there a God? We do this when, really, we should be looking at ourselves in the first instance. We should take responsibility for the fact that we're the ones who have screwed this planet over and that it's because of us that there is so much climate change.

We have done untold damage to the natural environment, yet we have the cheek to move into the habitats of animals and screw them around for no reason other than the fact that they are living as nature intended. There have been badger and deer culls in Ireland, but no good has come from them. They do not properly address any problems of overpopulation, certainly not in the long term, and there is almost always a more humane option available. Recently in Northern Ireland the TB problem was addressed without the use of a cull. Instead, alternatives including biohazards were used to prevent the spread of TB to bovines.

When a cull is called for by the government, the hunting organisations are the first to say 'We'll help out.' Many culled deer have ended up in restaurants in Dublin.

The desensitised

I have encountered some who have become so desensitised to the animals that are their victims that they snigger and laugh when they see them gasping on their own blood before they die. I try hard not to judge these people, because if I do, I absorb hatred into myself. Instead, I hope that someday they will see that what they are doing is wrong, because until that happens many more animals will suffer. I don't focus my energy on individuals like that. I focus on the people on the streets: those whose minds and lives may be changed by the images that depict what happens in slaughterhouses.

Militants

While there has been an extreme, militant side to the animal rights movement, I have never agreed with the killing or hurting of anyone. That said, I understand that those who engage in extreme action on behalf of animals do so because they have become so deeply frustrated by the wrong that is being inflicted on these creatures that they feel they have to take drastic action on their behalf.

Some do that by releasing animals from cages; we at ARAN do not. If we were to spend our time jumping in and out of laboratories, fur farms, circuses, zoos, factory farms and slaughterhouses, we would achieve very little in the long term and would have a public relations nightmare on our hands. The industries that we wanted to expose for wrongdoing would end up looking like the good guys and activists would end up looking like the bad.

My position, and the ARAN position, is that the only true way to bring about change is through showing the public what is happening to animals in those terrible places, and lobbying for change.

Politicians

In Ireland there is much support for and apathy towards the raising of birds and animals for slaughter and the cultures of hunting, culling and baiting. The support comes from both rural and urban communities. Unfortunately, support also comes from politicians. I live in hope that those concerned will educate themselves fully on animal rights issues and that that will lead to positive change.

ARAN is not about shutting down anything. We don't want to put people out of jobs. But we do want everyone to behave with decency and respect towards animals. We believe that the people who are involved through their work in inflicting suffering on animals could, with education, grasp the simple concept of treating them with kindness. I sincerely believe that if we were all kinder to animals there would be less violence on the streets; there would be less hatred. In my opinion, all of these things are connected.

Whilst I believe that significant social change is needed, I do not see people losing their jobs as a result of people opting for a healthier, more humane diet. On the contrary, I see the potential for further and different forms of investment. We are already seeing huge change in terms of high street restaurants offering vegetarian options on their menus. As more and more people demand more vegetarian options, we are likely to see even the bigger restaurant chains following suit. It is already beginning: in India you can go into a vegetarian-only McDonald's!

Educating the children

I think everyone who hears ARAN's message does something to be kinder to animals. That's why the earlier kids become aware of the importance of treating animals with kindness, the better. The messages we relay in schools are age-focussed. We talk with young children about the importance of respecting animals, and we make the point that even though they look different, they are very like us in many ways.

We point out that because animals don't speak our language, many sadly believe that they can't talk. We explain that they can and they do – in their own way – even though we don't always understand them. Then we try to relay the fact that because animals can experience pain, suffering and loneliness, just as we do, they have to be protected and minded.

What I want

I would like people to become more aware. Our single biggest problem as a society is that we are so switched off in so many ways. Because of that, it is our goal at ARAN, and it is my personal goal, to try to flick that switch back on.

When we are unaware, when we have our blinkers on, there is so much we don't see. But everyone needs to see what is happening to animals. Everyone has a moral duty to find out.

I want people to research what happens to the animals they eat and whose skins they wear on their backs. I want them to think twice about their entertainment choices. If they're off to the US and they plan to see an orca show, they should consider that the chances are that the poor creature being forced to swim around and perform in what is essentially a human bathtub was once ripped violently from its home and family. They should imagine what it might feel like for that orca to be in the same living hell over thirty years later. When they've done that, they might think again about the part they're playing in the suffering of that captive creature.

We have to see things for what they really are. We have to open the shutters and become aware that for every instance of cruelty there is a better and kinder option.

What matters most

What matters most to me is that we all become as kind as we can possibly be.

A vegetarian planet

Whether or not a person eats meat depends on the type of individual they are and on their level of awareness. When the vast majority of people become aware of what happens to animals behind the scenes, they make life changes. They absolutely do.

Perhaps we will one day become a vegetarian planet. The environment will play a role. Nature is going to push and viciously attack. We are going to see more hurricanes, tornadoes and other shows of nature's might. We have unleashed murder on this planet and on those who are most vulnerable; both human and animal.

We will look back in horror at the role we played in bringing about such destruction, and when we do we will realise that we failed to grasp something as simple as the importance of being kind to a dog, a cat, a cow, a pig, an elephant, a tiger or whatever. That realisation will bring change. There will be increased cognisance of the inherent suffering and cruelty that has been inflicted on creatures, and that awareness will change the way we live.

As a matter of fact, I would have no problem with tribal communities continuing to do what they have done for centuries. But the situation in the modern world is different.

Today we have taken the industrialised use and abuse of animals, sadly, to a whole new level.

There is no doubt about it: the earth cannot sustain modern-day factory farming methods forever. We are seeing the effects of climate change like never before, and today we know that one of the biggest causes of climate change is animal farming. If change is to come, it is unlikely to come from politicians; it will be increasing problems caused by climate change and global warming that will get us there.

What the world needs now

Increased awareness. Anyone who cares should be kinder to animals and to other humans. Everyone should redouble their efforts to be kinder in general. When we see injustice we should speak out or intervene if possible.

Caring is important, but to make a difference to the suffering of others, caring isn't enough. There has to come a turning point; a time when you will make changes to the way you live so as to right in some way the wrong that you have become aware of.

To highlight the horrors that animals are suffering, some lobby for change by writing emails or good old fashioned letters to TDs and national newspapers. Others demonstrate, giving an hour or two of their time to take a stand for the sake of helpless, suffering animals.

Everyone should know that to become an animal rights supporter you don't have to be a vegetarian. Most of those who come through the doors at ARAN are meat-eaters. The move away from eating meat can take time. But there is no reason why that should be a bar to anyone working for the welfare of animals.

Who I am at the core of me

Deep down I am a decent person; someone who cares; someone who has a strong sense of injustice. That's me in a nutshell.

What life has taught me

Life has taught me to speak out against injustice so as to raise awareness. It has also taught me to push for positive change and to live somewhat responsibly.

The toll

The work I do takes a huge toll on me, so much so that I sometimes get to the point where I long to walk away from it. I tell myself that that would be okay, provided I continue to be as kind as possible. But then I think that my continued involvement is absolutely vital for the animal rights movement in this country, and that if I were to go in the morning, it would be a black day for animals in Ireland.

In my work I try to see the good in people. When that leaves me face-to-face with inherent badness and cruelty, I try to ignore that and concentrate on appealing to the goodness in the person in front of me. But sometimes I absorb the badness when I am trying to connect with the good, and that takes a toll on me, so much so that I need to learn to build a barrier around me; one that will protect me from absorbing badness like that.

The badness I encounter eats through me. It hurts me very deeply, and it makes me angry as well. What happens then is that the goodness within me kicks in to try and counteract the badness that I have absorbed. That's a process that both hurts and damages me.

My sensitivity is my strong point in so many ways, yet the downside of it is the depth of feeling I absorb from others. Because my sensitivity has led to huge positive change, I believe that my weakness is very much part of my strength. When I say weakness here I am referring to the fact that I absorb negativity very easily. The fact that I recognise this means that I have learned how to turn that around and use it in a positive way to bring good.

Religion

I'm not a religious person, but I would be very spiritual.

Reincarnation

I hope there is no such thing as reincarnation. After this life, I am done with this world. I am absolutely done. Whether there's a heaven or not I can't say, but I do believe there is life after this. This is something I came to believe in after my partner died. That loss made me aware that there's a spiritual connection between those who are living and those who have gone.

Looking back

In my life I have been an advocate for good. This was definitely a path that I was meant to go on.

One hundred years from now

There is a close connection between slavery, and the cruelty associated with that, and the way in which very many creatures are treated today. If we were to have this conversation a century from now, I believe we would be looking back at the way in which so many animals are currently treated in the same way that we now look back with horror and disbelief at the way in which slavery and race-based cruelty was so prevalent and so widely accepted and tolerated one hundred years ago.

The future

I won't always be doing the work I am doing now to the same extent. It has taken a toll on me, both emotionally and physically. I have great empathy and great sensitivity, and that helps me to bring about change in others, but it also means that I feel very intensely. Because of this I think that in time I will step aside and move in another direction – possibly into psychotherapy and counselling.

I believe that when you send out a message to the universe, a response comes around eventually. I have done that, so it's only a matter of time before the universe kicks me out of my current role and onto another path. I don't know what path that will be, but I do know that it will always be in my DNA to be kind.

The growth of ARAN in Ireland has largely come about as a result of our campaigning. We have always said that whatever one person can do to make a difference, however small, is to be commended. People are now opting to purchase products from companies that do not test on animals. Many people are opting to eat less meat, or buy genuinely free-range eggs from local farms. People are not nearly as likely as they once were to admire a new fur coat. Through these small steps, I hope that we will advance to a stage where a critical mass is reached, when widespread social change will follow. Our eyes may be on the prize of a cruelty-free world, but we always try to keep our feet planted firmly on the ground.

Austin O'Carroll

GP, campaigner and survivor of thalidomide

Rage and anger

When people don't believe in you, or don't believe in your capacity, anger can be a great driving force. Because it can also be a very positive emotion, I don't down it at all. What matters is how it's managed.

Anger is what has driven me most of my life. Most people who know me would be surprised by that.

I can remember feeling rage and anger as a 5-year-old child. I couldn't walk properly until I was 6 or 7, but before that I remember walking up and down really angrily, trying to show people that I could walk. Anger drove me to do that.

Today, when I want to achieve something, I tap into that space, feel the anger and use it to drive myself forward. If I encounter something that annoys me – and that 'something' may take the shape or form of a person or an institution – I try to defocus off the person or institution and keep the anger. I use the anger to drive me towards whatever course of action I think is necessary or appropriate.

The stoic approach to life

As a child growing up my legs were quite crooked, so I would have them broken, reshaped and put into callipers. Then, when I grew some more, they would become crooked again, so I would be back in for surgery again. I was in and out of hospital having my legs broken and reshaped until I was 13 or 14 years of age.

I remember climbing up our stairs at home one day. My mother was upstairs, painting, and I wanted to see her. I know I must have been younger than 6 or 7 at the time, because I was that age when I first walked. I fell down the stairs that day and broke both of my legs.

The experience of breaking or having my legs broken time and time again taught me to adopt the stoic approach to life.

As a young lad, when I'd be sitting waiting to see the surgeon I'd ask myself what was my worst fear. I'd say to myself: 'He could tell me that I have to go into hospital for more surgery.' I'd then prepare for that outcome so that if he said I was going back in to hospital I'd be ready for it, and if he said I wasn't, it was 'happy days'.

Ever since then, I always address my worst fear in times of crisis. I ask myself: 'What is the worst-case scenario?' and 'How will I manage this?'

As a GP, I find that approach useful when dealing with patients. When I am sending someone for tests and they are afraid, I ask what their worst fear is. If they say they are afraid that they have cancer, I ask them if they know what it means to have that. Then we discuss the fact that it doesn't necessarily mean death, and I tell them that the survival rate for cancer is really good these days.

When we have talked it through, I say: 'Well, you may not have cancer at all, but if the tests show that you do, then it's something we will manage as best we can.' The stoic philosophy is all about that.

Face your worst fear. Deal with your worst fear. Then you are prepared. I think that is a truly wonderful philosophy.

Fight, fight, fight

My mother was a 'get up and fight' type of woman. She'd never have wanted any of our family to sit around dwelling on our worries.

Her father ran a dairy. When he died at the age of 30, his partner ran away with all the money from the business, leaving the family totally bereft. My mother's family experienced real poverty as a result of that, and they had to find ways to scramble up out of it. They did, and as a result she's a real fighter.

I am a fighter as well. So many times she said to me, 'Fight, fight, fight.' And I did. When I was a young lad, I was often told by the various surgeons who operated on my legs that I wasn't to play football. After the visit I'd go home and play football. My mother would see me doing this and she'd give out to me. But while she could have stopped me, she didn't. I think she instinctively knew that it was something I had to do, so she let me get on with it.

Looking back, I wonder if my behaviour may have led to my having to undergo even more operations than might otherwise have been necessary, but if it did, it was worth it.

What I'm good at

I'm a good ideas person. I'm also good at getting a really good team around me – a team that will help me to succeed in whatever it is I want to do. They are my two chief skills.

Every ten or fifteen minutes in my practice I make a decision or I help someone else to make a decision. GPs are people who *do*. So I suppose I'm a doer as well. There are cons to that. My partner, Dorothy, often says: 'Stop giving me solutions. I just want you to listen to me.'

As a GP, I manage people every day, in so far as I give advice and try to manage how patients respond to that advice. Management doesn't come naturally to me, but I am working on being a good manager. I used to rely on instinct in choosing people and responding to their issues, but I now appreciate the value of learning about management theory and having a structured approach to management.

Something else I might have been

I enjoyed art in school, and thought about studying it in college. My partner, Dorothy, is an artist. When she first introduced me to the arts world I thought it was all quite weird. Artists speak a different language. They have a different way of thinking, of interacting and of being cool. Appreciating visual art is an acquired skill, and I had to learn how to look at a picture. After all, how is anyone supposed to look at a picture? I found it fascinating getting into all of that, and the more I learned about it through Dorothy, the more I realised that art was something I might like to have done if I hadn't opted for medicine. The creativity called me.

The best advice I ever got

The best advice I ever got came courtesy of a guy called Petr Skrabanek. I greatly admired him. He was a Czech intellectual who came to Ireland after the Czech revolution

– sometime after the Russians rolled in. He was a leading scientist and a professor of medicine.

Despite his brilliance, his 'across the grain' approach drove many people crazy. He was sceptical of many of the accepted methods of preventive medicine, and he constantly questioned medics about why they thought things were right. He questioned a lot of things, and I learned the value of questioning from him.

He questioned the value of screening for breast and cervical cancer. Most men wouldn't question that. They'd fear that they would be considered anti-feminist if they did.

Skrabanek asked: 'Is the evidence there to show that screening for these cancers works? Are we doing more harm than good in rolling out these screening programmes?' He would go into gynaecological meetings and argue against the flow. He would say: 'The reason you're arguing against me is not evidence-based, it's because you make money from thinking the way you do.'

Back in the 1990s I wrote an article in defence of women who bottle-feed their babies. I wrote it because I had seen numerous women who had become depressed because they had tried breastfeeding and didn't succeed with it.

In the developing world, breastfeeding protects babies. In the developed world, the evidence in favour of breastfeeding is much weaker than claimed by many of those in favour of it. While I am a fan of breastfeeding, I wrote that women who decide not to do that shouldn't be made to feel – as breastfeeding lobbyists suggest – that this makes them bad mothers.

Around that time I read an article that suggested that bottle-fed babies get more diarrhoea than breastfed babies. I saw the flaws in the article, and I spoke to Petr Skrabanek about it. He said that although the article was flawed, its conclusions were most likely correct. He then advised me not to let the fact that I wanted to make a point divert me from the truth.

That was great advice, and it always stuck with me. You can be set in a position. If someone then comes along with contrary evidence, you may try and refute that evidence or respond by looking for further evidence that supports your point of thinking. Both of those responses divert you from the most important task – that of looking for the truth.

Petr Skrabanek's message was: 'Be absolutely dedicated to the truth, even if the truth doesn't suit your position.' It's easy to get so caught up in a position that you lose your integrity because of it.

What most surprises me about people

What most surprises me about people is their resilience; the depth of the human spirit, the fact that people can endure so much. We often see this when we meet people who came to Ireland from Africa; people who have lost whole families in massacres. We also see it regularly where I work in inner-city Dublin.

I know many families who have lost several children to drugs and suicide. The loss of a child is the worst experience possible. I have seen people suffer in ways most of us cannot even comprehend when faced with this loss. Then I see them a little further down the line, and while they are still inherently sad, they are also empathic – they have that capacity within them.

I think what pulls most through is quite simply the will to survive. I think it's that, more than a wish to continue for the sake of others, that keeps them going.

While experiencing loss like that understandably makes some people angry, not everyone responds the same way. For others, the experience makes them more human-empathic. I'm not suggesting that either response is better than the other. Nobody should judge those who are struggling to survive loss.

I am always surprised by the fact that individuals can bear such loss at all, and that some come out of it, not necessarily stronger or warmer, but maintaining their strength and their warmth despite it all. Of course people are scarred and wounded by these experiences, but it is how they manage their scars and wounds that makes them human. In a way, that strengthens their humanity.

You get bad eggs everywhere, but the vast majority of those I've met really want to be good doctors who help people. Even so, I was greatly surprised by the very many young GPs who, because they are passionate about making a positive difference in the lives of the deprived and marginalised, signed up for our GP Training Programme.

Something that attracts me

I have often found myself admiring people who care, despite philosophical disagreements. On occasions, people with whom I agree intellectually come across as cold and uncaring. I have learned to distinguish between a person's philosophy and their humanity.

What attracts me is a humane person. I can be attracted to that part of the individual while disagreeing with his philosophy. Similarly, someone right-wing who has a charitable ethos may be someone I may not necessarily agree with, but I may still admire them as a person.

Social policy

Politically, I believe in rights, not charity. I'm a socialist, so I believe in equality. I believe in the Scandinavian model of economics and health care in terms of equal distribution of wealth.

In Ireland we live according to the social inclusion model. We give everyone free education and free health care, but we don't distribute wealth. That means that we still have huge inequality. Sure, you are allowed to get an education, and the thinking behind that is once you have your education you can then make your way up in the world, but that's not quite true, as that's not quite the way it works. Private schools ensure that the elite are kept separate from the non-elite, so there is still segregation, and the privileged continue to maintain power.

The American model is the underclass model. The thinking behind that is that people make their own beds. You can be anyone and still become the president of the United States, but even if you are the president, if you are also a junkie, your drug problem's your own fault.

In the American individualist system, those who are successful are perceived to be so due to hard work and ability. Those who are not are presumed to be lazy or less than able. It is not recognised that the unequal distribution of wealth and resources has a detrimental impact on the life choices of those living in poverty. More often than not, the poor are considered to be either worthless layabouts, or unfortunates requiring charitable support. While the latter is a more humane viewpoint, it carries an unfortunate subtext that links poverty with ill luck rather than inequity.

While I hugely admire many charities, I truly believe that charity, by its nature, diverts attention away from the truism that wealth distribution is the ultimate solution to poverty. Charitable organisations working to assist the impoverished would do more good if they fought for higher taxes and wealth distribution rather than working in a way that makes the wealthy feel good about being able to afford to give donations.

What matters most

What matters most to me is my own family and my wider family. Besides that, honesty matters most. I like to be honest and I like others to be honest with me.

Passion also matters to me, as does the ability to inspire. I love people who inspire me, and I love people who are passionate.

Fun also matters to me. You have to have a bit of craic. Fun encapsulates many things. Having fun with your family is more than just fun. But still, it's fun.

What gives me hope

The fact that things need to be changed gives me hope. If nothing needed to be changed there would be no hope.

What infuriates me

It annoys me when we, as doctors, in trying to protect our incomes, disregard our duty to protect the rights of our patients. We have to balance the right to earn an income with the duty to act ethically and professionally. GPs are fighting to maintain their income as the government has reduced their payments significantly. There has been a move, however, to charge patients for services that are not technically within the GMS contract. I have no problems with GPs fighting this out with the HSE, but it makes me angry when they charge GMS patients: the most vulnerable, most deprived group. Recently, a campaign by the IMO, where they placed posters in surgeries outlining how much GPs get paid per patient, infuriated me to such an extent that I resigned from the organisation. We should not use our patients as pawns in campaigns over terms and conditions. These are instances where we let ourselves down professionally. We should advocate on behalf of our patients and support their recognised right to free GP care.

What I fear

Most people fear death, and I am no different. Though I think about it regularly, the fear has diminished.

My greatest fear would be the death of one of my children. Having children makes us feel vulnerable. In fact, the first time in my life I ever felt vulnerable was on the birth of my first child. When she was born I knew instantly that I could never survive the loss of her or of any other children I might subsequently have. I am pretty sure I could survive anything except the death of one of my children. I have had that fear since my two children were born, and I have never been able to get over it.

Who I am at the core of me

I am not sure that there is a core in me. I think 'me' is made up of everything I do and the particular ways in which I act.

The features of me that are at my essence, that are essentially me, are hugely diverse. Everyone in my life knows different aspects of me. Some know the medicine side of me. Some know that I can be very driven, that I can have good ideas, that I can be very disorganised and that I can forget to follow through on things. Other people know that I can let them down. At home, some people know that I sometimes work too hard and that there are times when I need to be more available.

The reason why I think we probably don't have a core within us is that, if we don't, then we are free to evolve continuously. I used to label myself as 'disorganised'. These days I work hard at being more organised. If I were to believe that at my core I'm disorganised, then there would be no hope of my changing for the better.

Chaos

Chaos is something I really like. I like the chaos of inner-city Dublin.

As the youngest of six kids, I thrived in chaos; liked bouncing around in it. Maybe that's the reason chaos attracts me; maybe it's not. I don't know. I just know that I love it and that it excites me. Yet while I enjoy the fun part of it, sometimes in my role as GP I visit families who are living in chaos, and I see how terrible that can be.

Inner city

I have seen tragic plays about inner-city Dublin and concluded that the playwrights missed the point, because while there is a lot of tragedy in that area, there's great craic in there as well.

The tragedy is counterpointed by the humour and the fun. The tragedy is really tragic, but the fun is really fun and the humanity is immense. The sense of reality is so powerful that sometimes when I visit other places they don't feel as 'real' as it does in the inner city.

My social conscience

My parents did a lot of voluntary work for many different causes. My father did voluntary work for Sister Stan. I grew up in that environment.

I was part of the St Vincent de Paul society when I was in college in Trinity, and I worked in youth clubs and with youth projects around the inner city. I really liked being part of all of that. I got involved in the disability movement because I have a disability and because I am driven to make positive social change.

My work colleagues are equally driven. They input into my passions and they inspire me. We force each other further down the road towards the change we want to see. Our interaction forces that change.

Snippet from my bucket list

I want to see whales. I have done a lot of sailing. I have spent hours looking out to sea hoping I'd see some. I made 'looking for whales' an activity. But I never saw any. Instead, I saw loads and loads of dolphins and plenty of sharks. I will travel to Canada – maybe to British Columbia and Newfoundland – to see whales. I have always been fascinated by them.

My greatest source of solace

I am agnostic, so I never pray. I consider myself a humanist in so far as I believe in promoting values that are humane and values that make us work together. I genuinely believe that people inspire.

My deepest source of solace is my family, but besides them I find that cycling gets me into my own headspace. It's my way of taking time out to think.

I did a mindfulness course one time. That was really helpful as it taught me how to switch off thinking. Sometimes I switch off thinking, and other times I think things through. Sometimes, if someone or something is bugging me, and I just leave it and do nothing, I find peace with it in time. It's as though one day, out of the blue, maybe while out cycling, it all makes sense.

Reincarnation

Because I am a very logical person, I don't believe in reincarnation. I certainly don't believe I have been here before. That said, I would like to continue, and if I did have to come back again and I had a choice, I wouldn't mind being human again.

Some traits I admire

Honesty, passion and a questioning approach are just some of the traits I most admire in others.

A passion of mine

How to improve access to health care for those who need it is my biggest passion right now. The notion of equal access for all to health care in Ireland is a myth. In areas of great deprivation in Ireland, the ratio of patients to GPs is almost twice what it is in well-off areas. Add to that the fact that people living in deprived areas have higher needs, as they tend to get far more illnesses, and you get a truer picture of the situation.

Besides that, if you are a homeless person, a drug user or a Traveller, you will have problems accessing the health care you need in this country. Compare their opportunities to avail of the health care they need with people with health insurance, who live in well-off areas, and the difference between the two groups is huge.

Sister Stanislaus Kennedy

Visionary, social innovator, author, and member of the
congregation of Religious Sisters of Charity

Who I am at the heart of me

I am a child of God. I am made in the image of God. At
the core of my being, I am the living spirit of God. That is
who I am.

What most surprises me about people

I am always surprised at the kindness of people. There
have been extraordinary situations where I have found
individuals whose thoughts – while they were suffering
enormously – have been for others. That astonishing
thoughtfulness, that outward-looking goodness that people
have, even though they are in great distress themselves,
has always knocked me for six. It astounds me more than
the wrong that any of us do.

While I certainly look up to those wonderful and
astonishing people who show kindness in the midst of their
own suffering, my awareness of the frailty of human nature

and of the frailties within myself enables me to empathise with a lack of kindness in others.

The vulnerable

Very often the most vulnerable among us have the most insight. They stand on the edges, and from there they look in and see things for what they really are. They're more in touch with the things that matter most than are very many of the privileged.

When we allow ourselves to be vulnerable and to live with uncertainty we become more aware of the needs of those around us. When we do that we develop a better understanding of what matters most.

The brokenness within

I'm aware of all the brokenness within me. I know that I am broken in so many ways, and while that may not always be apparent to others, I am very much aware of it. That keeps me grounded. It keeps me close to the brokenness.

When we allow the brokenness of the poor, the homeless, the sad or depressed to enter into us, that brokenness makes us more sensitive. It changes who we are. That's why it's so important that we become aware of the brokenness within us.

It's the cracks we have to look at

The practice of awareness is a big thing. When we pray, a consciousness of who we really are comes to the surface. We see the things that we are good at as good, but we also see that within our strengths there are cracks. It's the cracks that we have to look at.

I am a good organiser. I recognise that. But I also recognise how easy it can be to be domineering and demanding while organising others. That awareness helps me to remain sensitive to the fact that I am at the service of those who help me; that I am their servant and that my role is to help them.

Just as our strength can bring out our weaknesses, our weaknesses can bring out our strengths. When I am working with the really poor and vulnerable, their hurt wounds me to the core. While that empathy is a strength, it's also a weakness in adversity. But that weakness is my strength, because it enables me to work more closely with those who are suffering.

It is possible to work all one's life with the poor, the oppressed and the marginalised, yet never be touched by them and never allow the vulnerability they encounter to touch our vulnerability. Only by doing that, though, can our weaknesses become our strengths.

When I see someone who drinks a lot and who takes drugs, I know it could just as easily be me. Because I have come to know the flaws in myself, I can easily identify with them in others – so much so that I know their weaknesses could easily be mine.

Sometimes it's okay to be weak

Many tell others that they must be strong in the face of hardship. I think that sometimes it's okay to be weak.

Racism

When I meet people who are very racist, I think there is something unresolved in them with regard to themselves and who they are. The same applies to those who are very anti the gay and lesbian community.

Getting to know ourselves

We need to get to know ourselves, but we also need to understand the nature of our relationships with others. We can ask: 'Who am I in this relationship?' and 'How is this relationship affecting me?' and 'How am I affecting it?'

Challenges and fears

I was told stories about rats and bats when I was a child, and I have been terrified of them ever since. But I have never been afraid of pain. I hope that if and when that comes, I will be able to accept it with an open spirit.

I have always worked really hard. For years I worked and worked non-stop, and then one day I became ill and I couldn't work any more. I was out of work for three months. That was one of the most difficult periods in my life.

Dealing with sickness is one thing. Not knowing whether you will recover is another. For me, the not knowing was scarier than the sickness. Living with the unknown is part of life. Living with pain and not knowing whether it will end is hard and frightening.

Over the years there have been times when following a religious way of life has been challenging for me. When I was younger I found it hard to be silent in the face of the things I didn't agree with. It was the structures and the systems that I found hardest to accept back then.

As time went on, my challenges came from within more than from any institution.

What I'm searching for now

I am searching for union with God. I try to find that through prayer and meditation, but I also try to find it through people.

God lives in people. He lives in the poor. He lives in the whole of creation. In all of my relationships, I strive to really get to know God, to love Him, and to unite myself with Him.

What life has taught me

The greatest lesson that life has taught me is that we are all one; that we are all basically the same as we have the same needs, the same hopes and the same fears.

Through my life I came to realise that even the most deprived among us; the people who are really in the gutter, are the same as me. All they want to know is: Does anyone care? Does anyone care that I'm sitting here? Does anyone care that I am lying here? Does anyone care that I have nothing to eat? Does anyone care that I'm thirsty? Does anyone care that I have no place to stay? Does anyone care if I die tonight? Basically, we are all the same.

When I started off, I saw myself as serving the poor. Life taught me to see it differently. I now see myself as being a servant of the poor.

Inequality

We have only a puny little notion of what compassion means. Because of that, when we think of world poverty and people starving and then compare that with the opportunities given to so many on this side of the world, we can only ask, 'Why? Why? Why?' Greed comes into it. It has to since so many of the causes of inequality are man-made.

When I think on these things, I remind myself that all of these issues are connected to me. Then I ask myself:

'What am I doing about the fact that there are awful things happening elsewhere?'

The violence in Syria is connected with the violence in me. Any good that's done elsewhere is also connected with how much goodness there is in me. We are all one, and in that sense I think of these issues in relation to myself. So, I ask: 'What does this teach me?' When I hear of violence, I ask: 'What violence is there in me?' When I hear of selfishness, I ask: 'How can I change for the better?' In the midst of all of this, I remember that somewhere within and above the interconnectedness there is a compassionate God.

Advice I give

Give time to silence every day. Be grateful. Develop your capacity for awareness and for compassion. Remember that because compassion is God's love within us, we all have an infinite capacity for it.

Feeling the presence of those who have gone before us

I believe that the people who have gone before us are around us. I sometimes feel the presence of those whom I have known and loved who are now gone.

Even though she was gone before I was born, I often feel the presence of Mary Aikenhead around me. I am very conscious of her life and her ethos and her extraordinary commitment. She lived and worked in Stanhope Street in Dublin, where I live and work today. Her Sisters worked in Grangegorman when it was a workhouse. I believe that her spirit is very much in the area.

We have set up a befriending system here at the Sanctuary. Young volunteers befriend local people who have a mental illness.

They are a small little group. We call them Friends of Mary Aikenhead. Those young people help to keep her spirit alive.

Feminism

I don't know whether I am a feminist. I absolutely believe in equality for women, and of course I will pursue that. But as to what feminism means, I don't know really as there are so many definitions.

What most delights me

I am always delighted by nature, surprises and the miracle of answered prayers.

What really matters

I have discovered in my life that it is the love of God within me that I love with. As I am only an instrument of God, my task is to allow God to love through me in this world. It is His love that matters. It's no longer my love of God, but God's love in me that really matters.

Abandoning myself to God

Several times a day I abandon myself to God. In this way I hand everything over to Him. The love of Christ urges me on. *Caritas Christi urget nos*. That is the motto of the Sisters of Charity.

Something I don't agree with

I don't agree with the Catholic Church's stance on homosexuality and contraception. It leads to the exclusion of both men and women.

Inclusion

One who very much understands the essence of inclusion is Jean Vanier. While remaining faithful to the Catholic Church, he welcomes everyone to L'Arche. Those who had no place in the Church are the most welcome: the people with intellectual disabilities, the gay and lesbian community, the separated and divorced. All of these had been made to feel unwelcome in the Catholic Church. When I went to see him in France earlier this year, he named these groups and he said: 'These are the people I am welcoming here.' At his core, Jean Vanier is truly Christian, and in my opinion, quite saintly.

Bishop Peter Birch was another very brave and wonderful man. He spoke out against capital punishment at a time when it was not popular to do so. Like Jean Vanier, he was opposed to exclusion. He not only gave people with mental disabilities communion at a time when this was not done in the Catholic Church, but he urged other priests to follow him. He took a risk in doing that, but he was always one to speak out against that which he felt to be inherently wrong, and he was never afraid to stand up and say, 'No. That is wrong.'

I learned a lot from working with him, and I did so until his death. After that I moved back to Dublin. That was a difficult transition for me, as I had grown used to working with him and I missed that when he was gone.

Kind of well known

When I was younger I used to be recognised when I walked down the streets. Of course, the fact that I used to dress in a full set of robes played a part in that. I never took the fact that I was kind of well known or thought to be 'great' with any seriousness. I just did what I did; that was all. These days, fewer recognise me on those streets and I feel much more at ease with that.

Never frivolous

I'm not at all frivolous. Not even with children.

Something I might have been

There was a time when I really wanted to be an actor. But I knew that even though I loved performing in school plays it wasn't something that I could have got into as the opportunities weren't there. But I also felt a stronger desire to work with the poor. All down the years when people would ask what it was that I really wanted to do, I'd say: 'I really wanted to be an actor.' I truly think that I'd have been good at that.

I don't know what attracted me to acting; it's so false-faced in so many ways. But there must have been something inside me that drew me to it.

The future of the Catholic Church – as I see it

Religious orders and institutions like them have a life-cycle of in and around 200 years. After that, most of them die and something else emerges. That's the cycle. That's what history shows us. There are exceptions of course – some institutions are reformed or re-founded.

Religious institutions were very important in Ireland in their time. Yes they had their limitations, and they made mistakes, but until very recently they also gave great service in many ways in different ministries.

When I go into old churches and old convents I think of all the people who must have prayed there, and I consider how times have changed.

I am absolutely certain that the fruitfulness of prayer and the great work done by the good people in religious orders will bear fruit into the future. We see this in nature: unless the grain of wheat dies, it will remain a grain of wheat. If it grows then dies and falls to the ground, it will grow again.

While I believe that the prayers said and good work done will be given new expression in the future, I think it will come about through people in the community rather than through any institution.

I really think that this is the kind of Church we need going forward: small groups of lay people who form communities around the Eucharist and prayer, but also around service, especially service to the poor, as the early Christians did.

The groups of lay people will be at the centre of these churches. Some may choose to live together, but that would not be necessary. Essentially, their mission will be to radiate goodness and love. They will be individuals who deeply respect the dignity of every human person. Leadership would emerge through these groups, and that will be important because so many people who want to live a good life and want to be part of the Church are not getting the leadership they need. That's what I would like to see in the future.

We have great young people who want to be of service and who are prepared to give their time to be of service to the community. In my work in Focus Ireland, The Immigrant Council of Ireland, Young Social Innovators and the Sanctuary there are many young people involved in community action. Besides our 'young befrienders', there are 'young social innovators' and community service volunteers who get involved in good work at a very impressionable age, and who are changed forever by the experience of being people who care about others.

While we have many young volunteers, we also need people to give witness and testimony. We also need leadership. What we don't need are the institutions and the hierarchical structures that we have today.

So, as to the future of the Catholic Church, I see the current structures and systems transformed, and I see it becoming centrally about Christian compassion and love. In my mind, that can only be good.

What it's all about

I attended lecture by Robert Kennedy earlier this year. He is a Jesuit priest and a Zen teacher. He has transcended religions and rules in so far as he is at one with God. He pointed out that so many of us get caught up in rules and regulations when all that matters is love, reaching out and having God in our lives.

I really believe in the Eucharist. I go to Mass as that is my way of offering myself to God and of uniting with all the people in the world who are doing the same thing. We do this so that His Kingdom may come.

Going to Mass matters to me, but I'm not saying that everyone should go to Mass every day. For those of us who really believe that Christ is God, it's a beautiful way of uniting with Christ, who gave himself totally for us. For us, the Mass is a way of offering ourselves to Christ to be transformed into Christ. In that way it has meaning for me.

I go to Masses in churches all around Dublin city centre. Very often they are quite empty during the week. Many are next to empty on Saturdays and Sundays. This is indicative of the void that needs to be filled.

I believe that if we had the kind of Church we have been discussing – as in small groups of lay people – many would come back to the Church as it would have more meaning for them. The Eucharist and service of the poor would be central, and all present would participate. It would not involve a man speaking from behind a table to individuals scattered across a large space. I never understood that sort of structure. In my view it should be about everyone participating.

Where the notion of confession boxes came from I don't know. But if the Church really was a community in which people came together in faith, offering themselves, forgiving and supporting one other, there would be a role for sharing confession; sharing the burden. I believe that we are better people after that sort of confession as it enables us to know ourselves and each other better.

Clerical child abuse

As a woman and as a nun I feel ashamed and let down by those in the Catholic Church who either abused children or helped in some way to cover up that abuse. I also feel very sorry for the good priests and the way this has impacted on them.

The whole thing has been disastrous, but in many ways I think the way the Church handled it was the worst part. That was shocking, disgraceful and wrong. What was done by people with power was awful; a terrible tragedy.

That said, the revelations have brought an opportunity for renewal and reform. That is of course if we take these opportunities. They have brought a real chance for all of us to get down on our knees and say: 'We are sorry and seek forgiveness.'

We must all seek forgiveness, and we must all go forward together.

Why so many reject the marginalised

Most don't engage with those who are begging or otherwise in the margins because they raise questions about who we are in relation to them.

I have been around for so long now that I remember the first conference on unmarried mothers that took place in Kilkenny in 1970. It was the first time ever that people in Ireland had gathered to speak about unmarried mothers and illegitimate children ('illegitimate' was the term used at that time).

A number of the delegates were opposed to the eradication of the terms 'illegitimate' and 'illegitimacy'. They feared that if those terms were eradicated, children of unmarried parents would someday have rights. They feared that they could one day go to their fathers (who may be married to someone who did not know of their existence), and they might look for their rights and inheritances. That was the view. In essence, the thinking was: if we change this for them, how will that change affect me? Their concern was for themselves.

At that time, the children of unmarried mothers in Ireland were considered by most to have no value, and they were demonised as a result of that. This made it possible for society to collude with their neglect, and ultimately abuse. Almost everyone colluded with this demonisation, not only of the mothers but also of their children. Back then there was no social welfare for unmarried mothers or their children, putting them in a particularly vulnerable position. Life for unmarried women could be could be extraordinarily difficult, and also for women whose husbands neglected, deserted or abused them. They had nowhere to go. It was truly a terrible time for many Irish women.

We campaigned for an allowance for unmarried mothers, and when that was introduced in 1973 it enabled many to keep their children. Later in the 1970s, the late Bishop Birch worked to bring about further positive change in this area. He established the Ossory Adoption Society, which placed pregnant unmarried mothers with families all around the country rather than in mother and baby homes. No money changed hands. The women had their own rooms in those houses. While they gave some help with the housework and the children, they were not there to work; they were there to be supported and befriended.

Mental health

Most of us have no idea how to help those who have mental health issues. We haven't a clue how to handle people who are living with depression. We are the ones who have to change. We have to allow the challenged and the marginalised into our lives so they can change us.

One of the most basic needs in all of us is the need to be recognised. Many who live or beg on the streets will say how hurtful it is to be made to feel invisible by those who won't acknowledge their presence, who won't look them in the eye. Naturally, the fact that we look away because we can't handle what they raise in us is of no consolation to them. Again, we are the ones who have to change.

Going back to God

I think that we are all put here for a purpose, and I believe that, just as we come from God, we go back to God after this life. I believe in life beyond time, fullness of life. I came from God and will go back to the fullness of life with God.

I think God's infinite and unconditional love will call me when I'm ready.

As to what happens at the end of this journey, I sincerely hope that I will meet God and that my spirit will unite with His. Because God is all love and all goodness, I believe that He will deal with everyone with enormous love, warmth and compassion. For this reason I have doubts about hell – I think we will be given every chance to reach perfection.

Reincarnation

I don't know whether this is the only journey we go on. I don't know because nobody has come back to tell me that this is what happens.

If I had the chance to do it all again

When I look back, I think that if I knew then what I know now I would probably do everything differently. I would like to think that I would be more aware and more attentive and that I would give more time to people. I'd also like to think that I would be more sensitive to others, and more kind and generous. Certainly, if I had the chance again, there would be less of the ego and more of the true self. I can think of lots of situations when I would have liked to have been more like that.

Catherine McGuinness

Retired judge and activist. Former barrister, senator and president of the Law Reform Commission. Also former judge of the Circuit Court and former justice of the High Court and the Supreme Court of Ireland

Who I am at the core of me

Who I am at the core of me has a lot to do with my upbringing. I was brought up in a Church of Ireland rectory by parents who had liberal, left-leaning ideas.

My father always liked things to be done decently and in order. I like things to be done that way too.

I am a practising member of the Church of Ireland and attend church regularly. Having been brought up on the liturgy set out in the Book of Common Prayer, I feel a lot more at home with a structured liturgy. While I am more liberal than conservative in general, I am traditional in that way.

My father came from Spanish Point; my mother from Tullamore. While I was born in Belfast, I went to secondary school and college in Dublin. For that reason I consider myself as coming from the whole of Ireland, from both sides of the border.

It was because I came from a liberal, Protestant Irish background that I was asked to chair the Forum for Peace and Reconciliation. My late husband Proinsias and I had fifty years together. He was a leading journalist, writer and political commentator. When we would get home in the evenings we used to sit down together and perhaps have a drink or whatever, and we would chat over all the gossip of the world. He was great at knowing where the bodies were buried. Of course, I too am very fond of that sort of information.

Proinsias was always very proud of everything I did, and because he was a brilliant writer and journalist himself he never felt put down when we received invitations that had clearly been sent because of my work. Instead, he would take up the invitation and laughingly declare: 'I see that I am being invited in my Prince Philip capacity.'

For me, family matters most. As well as that, what I'm most concerned with is the legal profession and ensuring that it retains a principled, ethical quality. Constitutional and human rights issues matter a lot to me as well.

Perhaps sheer obstinacy is what drives me. I like to be active, to be doing things. I am easily bored, and although I am retired (theoretically), I am still very interested in getting involved in public issues.

There was a time when I could get by on very little sleep, when I could stay up all night to complete a task. Now I feel that there's a limit to what I can do, but nevertheless I keep going. When I was a barrister I often worked late into the night. All barristers work long hours; those who don't work late tend to get up at an ungodly hour of the morning.

Courage, clarity and the ability to understand other people and to see their points of view are the traits I most admire in others. When I say 'courage' that sounds like a hard sort of virtue, but still it's something I very much admire.

I love to feed birds. I spend fortunes on food for them. The other day when I looked out the window, I counted twelve goldfinches hanging off the bird feeder all at once. That was amazing to watch. They were feeding on Nyjer seed, which is a great source of energy for them.

The garden is a comfort to me. It gives me hope. I really enjoy gardening and I always find that on a day when I might be feeling a little low, the garden cures me.

I sing in a choir. I've always done that. I'm a member of the Culwick Choral Society. When I was a student at Trinity College Dublin I sang in the college choral society. My mother was a very good singer. She would have been in the college choral society in her day, as were my grandfather and my two uncles. Her whole family was musical. I also sang in church choirs at home. When you are the clergyman's daughter you sing in church choirs. Singing can be very uplifting, especially for those who might be in despair.

Generally, I'm a relatively optimistic person, and because I don't really go in for despair, I take hope in general human nature. There are evil people about, but not that many. Most people you come across are well-meaning, although sometimes I think they are mistaken.

The journey

Going back to college the second time (this time to study law), getting into the Bar and actually making a career of it were the greatest challenges I have faced. At the time, people were telling me that it was unbelievably difficult to make a career at the Bar.

I was lucky in a sense, because I arrived at the Bar in the 1970s; a time when gender issues and women's rights were arising and when family law was changing in its entirety.

This was the period in which the Family Law (Maintenance of Spouses and Children) Act 1976 was introduced. By opening up family law, that statute created the opportunity to assist women and their children, particularly for lawyers who were working for nothing at Law Centres and for FLAC Centres.

Returning to college at a time when I had quite young children was particularly challenging. I had always been interested in law, and I had family members who were involved in the legal profession. But when I first graduated from Trinity in 1957, there was the idea that while a woman could practise law, she couldn't be expected to make a living from it.

Back then, I couldn't afford to sit around. I had to make money. So instead of studying and pursuing law, I did a bit of teaching and a bit of writing and a bit of this and a bit of that, and then I went to work for the Labour Party.

As part of that job, I wrote explanatory memoranda for TDs on the way in which Labour policy affected particular bills. I found that working on legislation increased my interest in legal matters. Back then, few TDs had an acute interest in the legislation end of things. They were more interested in looking after constituency matters.

After I left the Labour Party, I was appointed to the Adoption Board. At that time there were always two Protestants on the Board: one Church of Ireland and one Presbyterian. I was nominated by the Church of Ireland.

For some obscure reason, the Department of Justice was the controlling Department in charge of the Adoption Board. Their officials initially looked upon my nomination with some suspicion, but eventually they accepted my nomination. I think they decided that, since I had been nominated by the Church of Ireland, I must be relatively respectable.

One of my fellow members on the Adoption Board was retired District Justice John Farrell. He was a very kindly and considerate man, and I am sure he had been a very good District Justice in his day. He used to tell me that, since I was so interested in the many legal issues that came before the Board, I should go back to college to study law.

With that in mind, I approached a Trinity College lecturer I knew from my anti-apartheid work. When I told him I was thinking of doing the Bar, he said I could try it then devil for a year or so. He added that I would probably never make a living out of it. Despite that advice, I went back to college and entered the King's Inns.

I remember the day I was called to the Bar. It was 1977 and I was 42 years of age. Nine women were called in total that day. When Mella Carroll (who was the only female Senior Counsel in Ireland at the time) found us putting on our new, untried wigs for the call, she gathered us around her and said: 'Don't let people do you down because you're women. Don't let them say you can't succeed. Just keep working at it and you'll all be fine.'

Following our call to the Bar, one of the Irish newspapers ran a headline that read something along the lines of: 'Nine Portias Called to the Bar.' In those days, there was a lot of ridiculous nonsense written about any achievement by women.

Mella Carroll was definitely an amazing role model for me. She was a wonderful lawyer and a wonderful judge. Later, when I was appointed to the Bench, there were few enough women judges, but every month or so Mella would organise a lunch for all of us, from all levels of the courts. She was full of solidarity in so many ways. At that time she had headed the Commission on the Status of Women, of which I too was a member. She was wonderful at that as well.

Overall, the legal profession has been good on gender equality compared with other professions. Today, well over 30 per cent of Irish Circuit Court judges are female, and while an increase in the number of female judges appointed to the superior courts should not make any specific difference to the decisions made there, I think it is important that there should be more of them so as to achieve a better balance. It is notable that at present the four leading roles in the Irish legal system are all held by women – the Chief Justice, the Attorney General, the Director of Public Prosecutions and the Chief State Solicitor. This is very different from the situation in, for instance, the UK.

I am really pleased that there has been considerable progress in this area, and I am delighted that so many female judges are so admired for their work, and that my former devil Ms Carmel Stewart has now been appointed as a judge of the Circuit Court.

The work can be challenging. Making the transition from barrister to judge was certainly so, as it took me from one side of the court to the other. Instead of fighting for clients as I had been accustomed to doing, my new role was to make impartial decisions in accordance with the law.

In the early stages of my time as a Circuit Court judge I spent a couple of years in the Family Law Courts, where I tried to work out the best solution for families, many of whom were in situations in which none of the possible solutions was really satisfactory.

This was difficult, and there were cases that worried me, particularly access cases in which it seemed that the parent who was looking after the children was deliberately trying to stop them from wanting to see the other parent. That happens, and they are the kind of cases that are very difficult to deal with. I have met family law judges from all over the world, and every one of them says that these kinds of cases present the greatest challenges.

The most rewarding aspect of being a judge is finding a solution to a difficult problem or a difficult contest. What is frustrating sometimes is when people get themselves stuck into litigation to the extent that they are almost addicted to it, so much so that they refuse to settle their differences in situations where it would really be in their own interests to do so.

When that happened, like many judges, I used to say: 'I can see that this is a total waste of all of your resources. If I rise for half an hour, could you go outside and try to settle or mediate?'

It is frustrating to see people ruining their lives in this way. Some get to the stage where they can't even get a solicitor to act for them; quite often because the solicitor, who may not even be being paid for the work, can see that the case is a waste of time.

The law is a very interesting career. It's also dramatic in many ways because of the crucial nature of the decisions that must be made. Barristers and judges generally encourage people to settle their cases, or try to steer them towards mediation. But even then it's not necessarily straightforward. It's not uncommon for people to settle on matters of large sums of money, then sit arguing for hours over something as trivial as a set of saucepans. There have been occasions on which I have felt inclined to say: 'I will buy you a set of saucepans. Could we just go home now? It's ten o'clock at night.'

Before my time there was a whole set of judges who were nasty to counsel and to litigants. Of course I would never name names, but they existed. That has changed, and now the idea that everyone, including barristers, should be treated courteously by judges prevails pretty well.

Collegiality

There is very good and important collegiality among members of the judiciary. In my experience that was particularly noticeable in the Supreme Court.

However, you could feel quite isolated in the High Court when you would have a crucial decision to make, which could influence the law in the future. You could feel that you were on your own. It's different in the Supreme Court, where at least three judges are involved. Of course, the judges may disagree with one another and dissent is possible.

As it happened, the group that I was with in the Supreme Court was a united one. We got on very well with each other. Some of them were fond of gossip and chat as well, so there was always a bit of fun. The company of that group was something I really enjoyed, and missed terribly when I retired. I hated leaving, but it was an age issue so I had no choice. In Scotland they allow retired judges to come back to do individual cases, but you can't do that here in Ireland. I think that is a pity given the immense workload that the courts now have.

When I retired, I very much missed working in the Four Courts. It's a lovely building, and for so many years I had a kind of nest there, either in the Law Library or in my chambers. It was like a second home to me. For a while I would feel the loss of it every time I drove past it while travelling along the quays. But it has been a while now since I left, so I have got over it, and the parting was made easier by the fact that I was able to go from there to be president of the Law Reform Commission (LRC).

In my new position there, I had the most marvellous colleague in Patricia Rickard-Clarke. She is an absolutely fantastic person, and now that she has retired we have managed to tempt her onto the End of Life Council. I have great admiration for her. She was the backbone of the LRC, and her retirement was a huge loss to all there.

Change I'd like to see

We are still waiting for the Supreme Court hearing and judgment on the Children's Rights Referendum, which has been upheld by the High Court. I want that to pass and I want it to be taken seriously and I want it to be translated into improving children's rights. These things cannot happen soon enough. This is even more important now in the context of the establishment of the new children's agency.

What the world needs now is the willingness of people to sit down and think about things and talk about things rather than rushing out and killing each other. Meeting and understanding people who come from different directions and different cultures is important in combatting racism and in helping to build understanding and tolerance between people of different cultures. If people could get to know each other more, if they could better understand each other, they might hold back from going after each other the way they so often do.

Books on my coffee table

I like to read historical books. I love Hilary Mantel's work and I'm really looking forward to the last volume of her current series, even though her hero is going to be killed off by Henry VIII. I'm now looking forward to reading a new life of Jonathan Swift.

I also read detective books, most often those by Donna Leon, Ian Rankin, Michael Dibdin and Andrea Camilleri. I'm also a great fan of Jane Austin, and not just because she too is a clergyman's daughter.

My daughter gave me the beautifully produced and extremely interesting *The Martello Towers of Dublin*. Whenever I get a chance to sit down, I read about one tower at a time. I also have *Ireland's Coast*, which is another lovely coffee table book. My son's Christmas present to me was *The Church of Ireland: An Illustrated History* – another great book to dip into.

Language

The way in which I use the English language is coloured by the amount of biblical passages I learned by heart when I was growing up. I really love the language of the 1662 Book of Common Prayer. I love the way those prayers were written, I love the language. I particularly like the prayer that ends:

> And those whom we have forgotten, do thou, O Lord, remember. For thou art the helper of the helpless, the saviour of the lost, the refuge of the wanderer, the healer of the sick. Thou, who knowest the need of each one, and hast heard their prayer, grant unto each according to thy merciful loving-kindness, and thy eternal love; through Jesus Christ our Lord.

There are many who say we should put into modern English the words of the King James Bible, but I find this difficult to accept. We do not find it necessary to put Shakespeare into modern words. There have been quite a number of new 'versions' of the Bible, some rather more acceptable than others, but none of them has the same power of language.

The old prayers mean a lot to me, so much so that in a way I really find it difficult that people now ignore them and pray extempore, thinking up prayers as they go along. I presume that it is believed to be more sincere, and maybe this is so.

I am very interested in people, and I love listening to the way in which people speak. I love properly used English, and I pay attention to that when I am writing and reading judgments. For that reason, I always enjoyed reading Mr Justice Ronan Keane's judgments. His use of the English language was absolutely admirable.

I hate when people mess around with the English language. I remember seeing a notice in a shop that read: 'Ears pierced while you wait.' When you think about that, how else could it be done? After all, you can't leave your ears behind, then come back later to collect them. I constantly see notices and other public documents containing grammatical or spelling mistakes. There are also often irritating mistakes in broadcasts and journals – and 'business-speak' with all its clichés is pretty unbearable.

Politicians

People can be very scornful of politicians, but I have worked with them relatively often down the years and I would say that the vast majority go into politics with a view to making positive change and with the intention of looking after the

131

people they represent. They don't go into it because they think they will change the world, although I am sure that some of them may aspire to that. To a large degree, I think they are unfairly criticised. Our economic difficulties have played a role in that. While some politicians were at fault, they weren't intentionally so.

By and large, and by international standards, Irish politicians are not financially corrupt, but they may engage in the subtle corruption that we all go in for – the use of contacts, the acknowledgment that whom you know can be important. In most cases they have good relationships with each other, and while you might see them in the Dáil shouting and raving at one other, they get on well together on a personal level.

What I fear

Like most people of my age, I would be afraid of becoming helpless, partly because I am very independent and I like to look after myself, and partly because I think I would resent being looked after. For that reason I would be afraid of losing my mind; of being diagnosed with dementia or Alzheimer's.

There was a time in the period of nuclear stand-off in the Cold War when I might have been afraid that there would be a nuclear holocaust; that the world would push itself into that. But these days I am more concerned by the ways in which ecological change will impact on the world.

I have a feeling that the climate will be bearable in my lifetime, and that it will be my grandchildren who are going to suffer from more severe results of climate change. Right now, the scariest aspect of climate change is the way in which so many seem to be able to shrug off the topic, and the reluctance of so many to take steps that would help to remedy the problem.

Scientific manipulation that results in really elderly women giving birth to children is scary. Pushing nature too far is scary. Immortality is scary. The idea of being immortal would scare me rigid.

Shaw's *Back to Methuselah* is a book about the search for immortality. Of course, as a writer, he isn't fashionable at all now. He wrote this back in the 1930s. It's very long, and there are sections of it that are quite boring. It's based on the idea that the human race will develop to be born out of eggs rather than from people. On reading it, I got the impression that it would be ghastly to be immortal.

As a child

I was cheeky as a child. I went to Clergy Daughters' School, which was attached to Alexandra College. As it was run on endowments and charities, it enabled children who would not be able to afford to board in Alex to go there.

My academic school reports from the teaching staff at Alex were generally quite good, but the comment: 'Catherine is much too cheeky' was sometimes included on my reports from the housemistresses at the Clergy Daughters' School. That said, the comment: 'Catherine is much too talkative' was always included.

Source of my social conscience

My father was rector of Dunmurry, a working-class parish in West Belfast. The village at that time was very Protestant, although it would be mixed now. I went to the ordinary, public, primary school – the equivalent of a national school.

While I was there, I saw poverty around me. There were kids there who would come to school ragged and unwashed. They were obviously very poverty-stricken.

My father first went to Belfast as a curate in the 1930s. It was at the height of the Great Depression. Working-class Belfast suffered appallingly during that Depression. But the war helped the working class in Belfast by upping their standard of living. It did that by creating employment. Most of the girls who were at primary school with me went on at age 14 to work in suiting factories or at local laundries. When the war came, jobs became available at factories producing things needed for the 'war effort'.

Food rationing made a positive difference, as for most families the rationing was a rationing up rather than a rationing down. Better food led to an improvement in people's size and in their general health. It also led to a reduction in the incidence of rickets. Because the food rations were generally healthy, it became more common to see children eating apples rather than sweets, which in any case were strictly rationed.

I have always felt deeply privileged to have had such a strong educational background, and to have grown up with university-educated parents in a home that was full of books. We never really had any money, and I sometimes wore other people's cast-off clothes, but I went for scholarships and I got my education and that has been an enormous privilege for me.

Not everyone was so fortunate. Prior to the passing of the Education (Northern Ireland) Act 1947, children left school at 14 and went to work. The idea of that happening now is almost unthinkable, but many friends of mine who were very intelligent ended up in that situation. One particular woman who was very close to our family worked all her life operating a Hoffman presser – one of those very heavy machines used for pressing suits. That was what she did, and it was such a waste as she was a highly intelligent woman. Her story highlights the great importance of the passing of that Act.

Assisted death

The concept of the right to assisted death worries me. There is the concern that if there were such a right, it might encourage some people to say: 'I have become a nuisance to everybody. I have become a bad-tempered old crow and a burden, so why don't I just take steps to die off quickly?'

When people are very ill, and when they are in terrible pain, they may wish for death. We imagine that this might be so, and for a number of people we know that this is the case. But for all we know, if we were in that situation ourselves, we might not wish for death as much as we think we would.

I suppose, in a way, I personally would like to have the option to avail of assisted dying, but I would have considerable worries about playing a part in making it generally available. I would hesitate a lot about that. Having lived through the Hitler period, where so many people were slaughtered for falsely propounded 'eugenic' reasons, it would take a long time to persuade me that there ought to be a law to give people that right. So, that's my position, even though I understand the attraction of it personally.

Judicial appointments

I consider that judicial appointments should be made by an independent body. Since the recent referendum, judges' salaries are in reality controlled by the government, and other changes have to some extent reduced the true independence of the judiciary as provided for in the Constitution. We should no longer rely on a judicial appointment system that is in fact political.

The vulnerable in Irish society

The children of people who are involved in drug addiction and crime are among the most vulnerable groups in Irish society today.

I have a huge admiration for foster parents. As patron of the Irish Foster Carers Association I have learned a lot about foster parents. Many are amazingly good people who take on very difficult children, some of whom are hardly fit to go into foster care, and give them wonderful love and care.

The homeless young are also deeply vulnerable. Father Peter McVerry talks of the young ones who are wandering the streets homeless. Some of those may be 15 years of age, but even if they are, they are still children. They are deeply vulnerable because they have so few resources with which to protect themselves.

In camera rule

I have always advocated for change in the in camera rule, provided the details of individuals, and particularly children, remain protected. The fact that certain court cases are not open to scrutiny simply gives rise to misconceptions and exaggerated accusations. Openness is in the interests of truth.

What life has taught me

Life has taught me to keep going. It has taught me never to lie down when things go against me. Life isn't always easy.

When we were first married, Proinsias and I went through a period where we had absolutely no money, so we used to review books, then sell them to buy tins of beans. Of course, once hurdles like that can be got over, it's possible to win out in the end. For us, when we moved beyond that stage and finally got a house, that felt like a kind of triumph.

Life has also taught me that the people we think are our enemies are not necessarily so. Even those whom we may for a long time have thought of with dislike are often not half as dislikeable as we may think they are; particularly if we actually get to know them.

I have learned that there are very few people with whom you can't build some sort of a relationship. Therefore, I think that it is very important that instead of summarily dismissing people, we should first try to relate to them. That's not to say that I am not critical in my thinking and in what I say.

Given what I have learned so far, my advice to a young person starting out would be: keep hoping. Don't give up. Be prepared to work. Don't ever think everything is going to be handed to you on a plate.

Eavan Boland

Multi-award-winning poet and Stanford University professor

What life has taught me

It's certainly tried to teach me a lot. Whether I've always learned well is another matter. But it has definitely tried to teach me more patience. It's also taught me to live in the present. As you get older you lose a clear sense of a future, and I'm not sure that's a bad thing. And probably, most of all, it's taught me admiration for people that when I was younger I might not have seen as contributing so much. They might not even have been visible to me.

When you're young, and you want so much to write well, your values tend to be the ones you see as literary. That's a mistake. Later you see that the only values that really sustain a writer – or anyone else for that matter – are human ones, and that you share them with so many people who are doing what you're doing – and more than you're doing – but in different ways. Unfortunately, it can be a weakness of younger writers – it certainly was of mine – to think your writing separates you from other people; makes you better, more aware. In fact that's a really backwards way of looking at any art. And I'm ashamed to say I had to learn that. Any artistic attempt worth its salt should unite you with people, not separate you from them. It sounds like a trite thing to learn. But I still had to learn it.

Traits I most admire in others

Two traits above all: resilience and kindness. My mother was a very kind person. That one thing had a great effect on me as a child. As an adult, when I looked back on my childhood – which was a bit migratory and unsettled – I was struck by just how often my memories were of her acts of kindness: maybe just a small gesture, a passing conversation.

But those things stayed with me. She encouraged me to think about poetry, and when I was just beginning she gave me strong support. I'm not sure whether that was judgement or kindness, and at the time I wouldn't have known or cared which it was. But the fact is that one trait meant a lot to me. I found that quality again in my husband, Kevin. I look for it in people, and I'm disappointed if it's not there. And then resilience. I don't have to feel near to the person who has that quality to admire it greatly. People picking themselves up after some reverse or upset or loss. People persevering when everything's against them. People beginning again, even when they've failed at something. Resilience is a very moving quality to see in other people, as well as an admirable one.

My greatest source of solace

Probably a mix of conversation and poetry. For instance, talking to my husband, Kevin – we share a lot of common interests – and to my daughters, and to a few friends. When I'm on my own the main source of solace would definitely be poetry. I can get very involved with a single book by a poet I like and read it for weeks. And that's certainly a solace and a joy as well.

As a child

I was a fifth child – a fourth girl. Talkative, not really sure of my place in the hierarchy which is there in all groups of children. And I'm sure a great nuisance when I was trying to be included. I remember being left behind when I was 4 or 5 and my sisters and brother all got to go to the Sandford Cinema. I felt cross enough then that I remember it to this day. Of course it was a secure and helpful childhood as well. But I think I might have felt very pushed aside had it not been for my mother, who was very loving and encouraging and had a real gift for communicating with even young children. I felt she was very fair-minded, and she couldn't have had much time, but she still gave it freely. I did have my own space as well though. From fairly early on I wanted to write and read poems, and again I was very encouraged by my mother. I remember the thrill of getting a big, hard-backed and blank notebook for Christmas when I was about 10.

If I hadn't been a poet...

I have an off-the-track answer for that: I love computers and technology. From the beginning of the computer revolution I was somehow enchanted by this magical development – almost literally magical – that promised more control of the world. That was a first impression of course, happening years ago. There are all kinds of complicated aspects to technology since then, and concerns about privacy and so on. Nevertheless, I suppose I would have loved to be a programmer.

But this is not really an accurate statement about what I could have been. In fact, there's some sort of self-deception in it. I would have been a hopeless programmer. I don't have math, I'm not detail-oriented, and programmers need both.

They're a little bit like the medieval cathedral-builders who put one piece in place and then another. I don't think any of that would have worked for me. And I wouldn't have built a very good cathedral.

The poet's role

I think poets have a task more than a role. The task is simple enough. Poets just write poems. That's all they do. If they're public intellectuals or activists or politicians or whatever else, that's all well and good. But that doesn't of itself have much to do with writing poetry, although it might inspire it. It certainly doesn't guarantee the next good poem. So the task is a straightforward one: to write poems and write them the best you can. If you start inventing a role rather than just setting out to complete the task the best way you can, there's a real chance you could lose your way.

What it is in my poetry that stays with me

It's not so much themes in poetry that stay with me. I'm more or less a lyric poet. The life I live is always going to be a part of the text. I suppose as far as that goes, it's something of a consistent theme. But in terms of what stays with me, it's just the poems that I can look at again, with some hope, and think they work. If anything is close to me, it's that.

Making the past more visible

I've always seen a difference between the past and history. History feels to me like the official version, the last word on what happened. And yet it leaves so much out. I think the commonplace is right that history is written by the victors. And winners are few and far between, certainly in Irish history, and few of them were women. The past on the other hand seems like a place of whispers and shadows, and it's the place where so many ordinary people's memories are stored, from which they hand on traditions and stories to their children. That doesn't get into the history books. All those rich, surprising talks across generations about that Aunt who did surprising and unconventional things with her life, or that great-grandfather who ran away to the Crimean War, they're stories about the past. They become treasures in people's minds, and yet they're so often undocumented.

Some of that difference has really guided me as a poet. I don't think I could ever rewrite history; but maybe in some poems I could make the past more visible.

Experiencing anti-Irish sentiment as a child

It wasn't anything organised or malicious. But these were the early fifties. Ireland's neutrality in the war was still remembered. There were old frictions and sensitivities still around, though obviously as a child I couldn't see them. One day when I was about 6 I talked to a teacher in my new school in London. I said 'I amn't' instead of 'I'm not'. The teacher turned quickly to me and said – very sharply – 'You're not in Ireland now.' That stayed in my mind. It was a reminder that you weren't in your own country.

The poet as a sensitive observer

I'm not sure I fit into that description of being a poet. It's not sensitivity that starts a poem for me. It's not even sensitivity that factors into it. And though being an observer is important to any writer, I probably think of myself as writing poems just as much out of participation as observation. The poem that works is almost always some experience that's unfinished, that can only be finished in poetry, in language. It comes back to the fact that I don't really think of poetry as a method of expression. As a method of expression it has flaws, and all kinds of cumbersome customs and conventions. And I say that as someone who loves the formal aspects of poetry. All the same, it's not as direct as a play or a photograph. But if it has drawbacks as a method of expression, it has none as a method of experience. So I don't write a poem to express an experience but to experience it more. And that's where poetry really shines. You may feel that you know and remember a winter dawn when the trees were dark spikes; when the moon was falling out of the sky – the sort of dawn I saw when my first daughter was born around Christmas time.... You may think you remember the experience perfectly. But there's a difference between remembering an experience and living it again. And when you begin to write a poem about that dawn, when you reach for the language, you realise how well suited a poem can be to make that winter dawn not just happen, but keep on happening. But this time safely and securely in language, away from the risks of forgetting or erasing it through time.

Something surprising about me

It probably comes back to technology. I could build a computer in the early 90s – or maybe, to put it more modestly, I could assemble components – and would get very wrapped up in doing it. People can be surprised about that. I just don't think people associate poets with the right side of the brain. But I'm not so sure those worlds are as separated as people think. Poems circle around syntax. The original commands of the computer languages were all about syntax – it's just that it flowed into plastic parts and soldered pieces rather than into a poem.

If I had to be someone else for a day

I would probably like to be Grace Murray Hopper for a day. She was an American computer scientist, a rear admiral in the American Navy, born in 1906. She died in 1992. She was an extraordinary programmer who made a human interface between the machine and the compiler, which ended up with COBOL, one of the first usable computer languages. I wrote a poem for her called 'Code' – a play on the word 'ode'. I think for that day, if I were her, I'd be able to look out at the dawn of computing, the beginning of a whole new world.

As to who I am at the core of me

It's an interesting question, but hard to answer. The core of a person – I'll limit this to myself – is almost pre-literate and pre-language, and even pre-conscious. So it's very hard to define in words. But if I think of what I care about most – my husband, my daughters – then I answer the question by saying what matters most. At another level I've been shaped all my adult life by being a poet, by trying to put the life I live into the poem I write. As well as that, my experiences as a teacher over many years have mattered a lot. If the core of a person is something that can be educated, it's teaching that has educated me most.

On what it is to be a poet

I do believe that a poet is what you are, not just what you do. I don't think you stop being a poet when you stop writing a poem. It's an essence, not an activity. The issue about publication is something slightly different, but it's linked to this. I think for every writer who's interested in poems

– and I often see this when I'm leading a workshop – there's a mysterious distance between writing poems and being a poet. It's striking how often someone will bring a strong, moving poem to a workshop, or read it out loud, or even publish it. But they still won't call themselves a poet. Because they don't feel like a poet. It's a subtle, inward, complicated journey, that distance between writing poems and being a poet. Only you can give yourself the authority to be a poet, to feel that you are one. Publication can't do it. Recognition can't do it. But once you have that inner sense of being a poet – and for a lot of people it's hard-won – then that's what you are, not just what you do.

When my poetry is misinterpreted

I think criticism of all kinds – and interpretation comes into this – just goes with being a writer. I teach poems. I interpret them for my students, and I probably misinterpret them at times. When I see something about my work that I don't think I wrote or intended, I probably wish the writer thought differently. But I don't feel offended. It's an inevitable by-product of reading and writing about poems.

The greatest threat to the poet

I think the greatest threat to any poet is perfectionism. At all stages. A young poet can be so burned by their failures that they actually stop or interrupt their progress as a poet. An older poet can just give up on a poem from a later version of that discouragement. If you take a perfectionist view of a poem, and your writing of it, your disappointment will get to be toxic after a while. There's a big, inevitable failure rate in poetry. And it's the other side of the coin of what works well. The only way to press on, to get better and to have a sane attitude to your own work is to get some kind of balance about your own failures.

The perception that poetry is highbrow and elitist

I really do understand those feelings. I think I could easily have them about other forms and other arts. But I've seen so many people find poetry in the most unpredictable ways that I'm wary about predicting the barriers to it. People go to poems in unexpected ways, and it can sometimes actually be an elitist view to think poetry will be beyond them, or foreign to them. That being said, I certainly wish that in classrooms, in schools, even in homes, poetry could be made more approachable. And I know a lot of gifted young teachers are trying to do just that. If you go back and read novels from the nineteenth century – writers like Jane Austen or Charles Dickens, and if you think of Joyce, who wrote and sang poems – it's interesting to see just what a central part of people's lives poetry once was. People read poems to each another, remembered favourite lines, enclosed them in letters, felt comfortable exchanging them with friends. It was a normal activity, like pressing flowers in a book or playing some music.

We've lost a lot of that. I think it's easy to hand out blame. Some literary movements like modernism, which looked down on the popular reader, and some academic attitudes didn't help. Having said that, I'm often very touched but not really surprised at how much of the poet exists in a great many people who don't consider themselves poets in any serious way. Far more people write poems and keep poetry as a secret life than I think anyone knows. And nobody who turns to a poem in hurt or solitude and finds something there to remember or help them will ever think of poetry as highbrow or elitist again.

Sean Scully

Painter and printmaker,
twice nominated for the Turner Prize

Why I make art

I make art because I want to fight for culture. 'The world is a fine place and worth fighting for.' Ernest Hemingway said that, and I agree. The culture of the world is in my opinion the most important thing in the world. It's more important than politics.

When I first felt the artist within me

I was very young. I think I felt it when I was 6 or 7 years of age. I knew then that I was some kind of an artist.

Global attraction of abstract art

I try to spread art to other areas of the world, so when I have a show in a new country I'm very concerned with how my work can enrich that situation, and I want to be equal to the opportunity.

There's a lot of interest in abstract painting in China. That makes sense to me, because the development of the capacity for abstract thought is very much bound up with the future, and while America is quite twentieth century, China is very much twenty-first and twenty-second century.

As an abstract artist I have to think freely, so I don't tend to think about what the sky looks like in Connemara. It's not as though the goal is to paint a nice little picture of a fisherman's cottage. That would be very nineteenth century.

The idea of expanding structures, infinity and humanised infinity is very interesting to me. When you consider the free movement of human beings, the direction architecture is taking, the way cities are being built and the way the world is becoming globalised, there's a requirement to think abstractly, an obligation not to be bound up to a particular place, or to the idea of a particular place. I'm very invested in this and excited by it.

Of course abstract art is not for everybody. Many human beings are bound to the idea of place and to the story of that place. While I understand that, I am a person who is very much engaged in the future, and because of that it's absolutely crucial to me that I develop the ability to think freely, or laterally.

The ability to think freely is essentially what abstraction is all about. It's a bit like moving numbers or units around. Thinking about urban structures requires abstract thought. The same, of course, goes for philosophy. Basically, what you're doing is moving blocks around – which is what philosophers do. I know what philosophy is, and I am best friends with Jürgen Habermas, the world's greatest living philosopher.

My best work

My Doric series is, as a series, the work of which I'm most proud now, because I am doing it now. But I could just as easily say that I'm most proud of my *Wall of Light* paintings.

The Doric paintings in particular are an homage to Greece. They deal with the idea of classicism and poetic humanism within a single painting. The structures are profoundly classical, and are influenced by the Doric order, with the idea of the column and the spaces between the columns allowing for the possibility of questioning and the bringing of light into buildings.

The painting of them is, in my hands, to some degree reminiscent of Romantic nineteenth-century painting. You have on one hand classicism and on the other poetry, with the handling of the paint and the very subtle, sensitive calibration of colour.

Experimentation in the art world

It is the job of the art world to manufacture experimentation. That is its indispensible function in the building of any free-thinking open-minded culture. Of course this doesn't guarantee that all the results of experimentation are going to be worthwhile or successful, but that is really not the point.

People have to understand that while there is a lot to wonder at and to be moved by, there is also a lot to laugh at. Many artists laugh at themselves.

Artists are meant to be strange. They are meant to be experimental with themselves, and they are. The results may be pretentious, or may seem to be pretentious. But of course it's pretentious to make a painting in the first place because it's an utterly selfish act to make something that could be so difficult to understand for so many people. Again, it's not the job of art to explain itself. The importance of mystery and difficulty in life is self-evident.

I try to make my art as honest an expression as I possibly can.

How I know when a piece of art is finished

That's something you can never explain to anybody. It's a bit like trying to explain why you picked someone to be your husband. It's something you can't really do.

Explaining art

Whether you make stuff like I do, or whether you make images, including images of recognisable things, the art in itself won't explain what you have created, so it's worth explaining what it is and what it means.

An artist can explain the meaning of his art without suffocating his own creativity in the process. I'm often asked to explain my work. I do it because I see it as part of the package. I don't think I can walk away from it. Having to explain myself forces me to be more accountable. For me, that's not such a bad thing.

The superstar of art history

Pablo Picasso. Every other artist is beneath him.

I gave a talk in the Pablo Picasso Museum in Barcelona in June of this year because I have a painting hanging in relation to one of his in an exhibition of contemporary art. Picasso's ability to make a painting that is open ended and not brought to conclusiveness, yet still a great artwork, is one of his greatest achievements. He is able to make a painting that has the ability to convey several meanings simultaneously. I am doing this myself in my Windows Paintings, which are paintings within paintings, paintings with views to other possibilities, paintings with a double meaning. The most famous Picasso example is *Les Demoiselles d'Avignon*, where he painted the heads on top of the bodies much later, so you have this painting that contained a schism, yet is a very beautifully resolved artwork.

The life of an artist

An artist's life is both demanding and Darwinian. It is the process of selectivity taken to the most extreme degree possible.

What you have to be is suited for it, and I am extremely suited for it because I don't allow myself to be discouraged.

In order to succeed, artists have got to be able to live on basically nothing. Those who are overly dependent on higher levels of approval are in a sense doomed. They have to have a voice inside them that compensates for the criticism they might encounter.

I have encountered many such criticisms, some quite ridiculous, uninformed and bigoted. The ability simply to glide past that criticism, or somehow consume and use it, is vital.

The artist's life is lonely. Being a painter is particularly lonely. But I find that I am a very connected person, and I feel that I am well supported spiritually. I'm also pretty hooked up to the human race.

To be an artist, in the sense that one is a public, global artist – as am I – you have to be simultaneously massively sensitive and massively insensitive. You have to have this double capacity in order to make art that is interesting and be a person who can withstand the pressures and criticism that advanced art is bound to provoke.

My passion

I am utterly committed to art with all my heart and all my soul. It is our most divine creation.

The sort of man I am

In many ways I am a very simple person. I'm approachable and I have huge empathy for other people. I have always been that way.

As a child I spent a lot of time looking after wounded, injured animals. I have always had a deep sense of caring. I think I was born that way, but family and relations showed me how to care, and the surroundings in which I grew up nurtured caring in me.

I was brought up in Islington. Back then, it was in many ways a ghetto of Ireland, but there were a lot of wonderful people there who taught me about compassion. But I do see that empathy is a very real quality among the Irish.

My idea of beauty

That's very difficult to say, because one's idea of beauty changes all the time and because beauty cannot be defined. Also, what's beautiful so often comes as a surprise.

My kind of beauty is not easy, not facile. It requires some degree of brutality and spirituality, something that is very honest and deep. That's the sort of beauty that touches me.

What gives me hope

There are a lot of great people in the world. I concentrate on that. I also think that the world has improved. We don't often crucify people by the mile any more. That's not to say terrible things don't happen. They do, but we are more outraged when they happen now than we once were.

What I believe in

I believe in the great people in the world. I believe in a human destiny. I believe that we will all eventually reach the god inside us and I believe that I'm part of that struggle.

Personal traits that most define me

I have a tenacious intellect. I am very spiritually, almost religiously, driven. I am able to negotiate the world.

Who I might like to be

I suppose the second greatest person that ever lived was Mahatma Gandhi. If I had to be someone else I might choose to have been him. Also, I wouldn't mind having brown skin.

Jesus Christ

Jesus Christ is the greatest person who ever lived.

Feeling blessed

I feel I've been blessed as I think I've been given a lot of gifts and the ability to handle them.

Advice I'd give

If you love the world it will love you back. But you have to love the world first.

To my students I give advice made famous by JFK: don't think about what you can get out of it, think about what you can give.

Toughest time for me

The death of my son.

Sources of solace

My family and friends are my deepest sources of comfort.

What life has taught me

I guess life has taught me that it never stops teaching me.

What matters

I think the way we relate to other people matters. Not harming other people is very important to me, as is trying to help others whenever I can.

The Irish

My wife, who is of Swiss/Hungarian descent, is a big admirer of the Irish. She believes they're a truly benevolent Christian people.

I think there's a strong, spiritual, humanistic presence in Ireland. When asked for help, the Irish will always try to give it. They're approachable that way. As a people they have great empathy, but that's just part of the culture, part of the history.

People from many cultures have been brutalised, robbed, cheated and tortured. The Irish have had their share of trials, but the result was different for them, and in some ways that's linked to the fact that they have music and rhythm. That is something that has brought vitality, joy and an ability to overcome into the hearts of the Irish. They're a particularly positive people, and that's quite miraculous, given their history.

You would never imagine that the English had brutalised Ireland in the way they did if you travel around the country as a person with an English accent, like I do. People assume I'm English until they know my name. The Irish, even while thinking that I'm English, have always been amazingly kind to me and so nice. You wouldn't necessarily get that sort of welcome in other post-colonial countries.

What I fear

I would be disturbed if negative predictions about the future of the world were to come true. The idea of living in a dehumanised world scares me.

A future in which it would be the norm for human beings to be part-computerised would be a future that we should either resist or approach with great care – for ourselves, for what we are, because the whole point of being human is to have a soul, and also because there's the possibility that it would result in two layers in society – the workers and the queen bees.

In the future, scientists may download information from human brains to robot bodies, but there's no way they will be able to download the sense of morality, the sense of beauty or the sense of love that are part of being human.

While I am concerned with the future, I don't worry about myself very much. I'm more focussed on what's out there and what I can do about it.

Perfection

I'm not interested in perfection, and I think we should be less preoccupied by the idea of perfect human beings. Human imperfection is far more interesting to me. It's something we should embrace and love.

A trait I admire

I think it's important to always keep your word, because that's what you are. If you don't keep your word, you devalue yourself. This is something I teach my son.

What I want most

More than anything, I'd like to be a wonderful father. That is central to me – absolutely and profoundly central. I'm really heavily invested in that to my core.

Reincarnation

I don't know whether I've been here before, but I am open to the suggestion. I am a pretty open person so I don't discount any possibilities.

If I had to come back again, I'd probably come back as a woman. I'd like to try the other side.

Mark Patrick Hederman

Fifth Abbot of Glenstal Abbey, lecturer and writer

Entering the spiritual life

I do not remember entering the spiritual life. Like a ship in a bottle, I don't remember a time when I was not in a relationship with God. I joined a monastery because it seemed to be an appropriate place to cultivate that relationship.

Something I might have been

I wanted to be an actor when I was young. My father encouraged me to do so: 'Be anything rather than a monk,' he said. His thinking was that at least if you were an actor you would give some pleasure to people. Being a monk was a waste of life, in his view.

An Irish actor, Dermot Tuohy, visited our school on a career guidance course, and he advised me that under no circumstances should I ever become an actor.

What keeps my faith alive

Certain people who are Godbearers. My own personal relationship with God. Miracles that happen often enough to give me hope.

The Godbearers – what they do and whether I'm one of them

Every one of us is invited at each moment to become the mother of God. God has no hands but ours to reach out to others; no feet to walk with other than ours. We carry God to wherever God wants to go in our world. Like many other people, I do it sometimes and sometimes I don't. The only person who was a Godbearer at all times and for all her life was Mary, *the* mother of God.

Why I never had a crisis of faith and why I regularly contemplate leaving the monastery

I never had a crisis of faith in the sense that I might have doubted God's existence. I have always known (not just believed) that God was there and looking after me. I would say that I wonder whether I should leave the monastery, at least once a month, for the past forty years – you can never be sure that any place on this earth is the most appropriate one for connecting with God.

What matters most to me

Besides my faith, what matters most to me is finding out the meaning of our life here on earth.

Celibacy and theo-sexuality

Every religion that seriously proposes full-time contemplation as a way of life has identified 'celibacy' as an appropriate way of redirecting energy in the direction of the divine. Meditation techniques of various kinds, involving posture and concentration, have been devised the world over to help lovers of God to become in some way 'theo-sexual.' Just as it is possible for athletes and astronauts to train themselves to make their bodies perform in a way, to an extent and in a particular direction that seems impossible and unnatural, so the person who freely chooses to love in this way can focus themselves in the direction of the divine in a way that changes their total orientation.

A man (I cannot speak for women in this regard) who is sexually active is habitually directed towards and committed to the achievement of orgasm at least every three days. His body is then attuned to the recreation of this possibility by the refurbishment within himself of the testosterone expended in the previous orgasm. If one trains oneself to interrupt this cycle and to prevent its repetitiveness from carrying on this habitual and compulsive search, the need for such gratification decreases and the energy finds another direction. This has been identified, experienced and ratified in many religious traditions.

I believe in the possibility of celibacy and the condition of Christian chastity as fulfilling ways of being in a relationship with God, but I don't believe that everyone who wants to devote their life to God should be required to be celibate. These are very particular ways of being that require not just understanding and training, but a desire and a capacity to follow them as a way of life.

Prayer

Prayer is not our doing. It is not something that we do. It is not an effort that we make, an act of our will, a discipline that we impose upon ourselves, a series of exercises that we practice more or less faithfully every day.

When I get up in the morning do I say my morning prayers? Before I go to bed at night do I kneel down by my bed and say my night prayers? Do I say the rosary every day? All fifteen decades, with the extra five mysteries suggested by the late Pope John Paul II? None of these things are of any interest to God, unless they are useful to me. I might as well give them up completely and find whatever *is* useful to me and *does* bring me into contact with God, first person singular tense – me with God, now at this moment. Prayer is whatever works; whatever allows me to be present to God, who is always present. There are, we are told, seven billion people alive on this earth, which means that there must be seven billion ways of connecting with God. The only thing that matters in prayer is coming into direct contact with the living God. If that does not happen, then the prayer is useless.

When we pray we are not throwing out some kind of lines of communication as a fisherman might cast flies onto a river. On the contrary, we are trying to slow down, stop all our active faculties from racing around madly trying to achieve something, and allowing ourselves to sink back slowly into that cave within our hearts where the prayer of the three persons of the Trinity is already flowing through us like a murmuring stream. We have to incline the ear of our heart to hear what they are saying to each other, and to me, who has been invited to be part of their communication. So, rather than saying anything or doing anything, I have to stop doing anything, stop saying things, and allow myself to enter the diving-bell of prayer, which will carry me to the depths of myself where I can freely enter this conversation.

Every advertised exercise of prayer, yoga, transcendental meditation, rosaries (digital labyrinths to hypnotise the fleeting mind) are simply tried and tested ways of holding us down in the area of the heart where the agitated body and even more agitated mind won't carry us off into other areas of distraction. None of them is foolproof or guaranteed to achieve their purpose. Their only goal is to push you into position so that the Holy Spirit can pray for you and through you to the Father, and you can be aware of that breath of life moving through you.

There is really only one prayer: that taught by God among us when he was asked to teach us how to pray: Our Father. This prayer contains everything we need to know and everything we need to say.

I do pray for other people and for special intentions, but I always leave it up to God, who knows and cares much more than me, or anyone else, and who sees the bigger picture, as it were, to decide what is best. But we have been told in the Gospels to pray insistently, and even to persecute God with our prayers where necessary – and I have done this.

Monasteries and the future

The future, our future as a human race, is an evolutionary process instigated by the Holy Spirit, but implemented by ourselves. The Spirit can only travel at our pace. This future is, therefore, in our hands. Forging the future requires the right kind of relationship with the true Spirit of the living God. Without this, the future will be short-sighted, cramped and incomplete. There has to be a place where such inspiration can be received, distilled, distributed. Some bulwark has to be constructed that can shore up the game plan already accomplished and provide a runway for the next series of test flights.

Monasteries should provide such places. In Russia for instance, 200 kilometres south of Moscow, Optina Pustyn, the last great monastery of hermits connecting Russia with Byzantium, came to be regarded as a spiritual centre. All the great writers of the nineteenth century – Gogol, Dostoyevsky and Tolstoy among them – went there in search of the 'Russian soul'.

Monasteries should be dwelling places with listening ears for the world around, essential parts of any society, providing touchstones for our deeper selves, for nature, for God. *Ausculta*, the Latin word for 'listen', is the first word in the Rule of Benedict. Monasteries should act as beehives of the invisible, making honey that can be tasted out of otherwise unavailable nectar hidden in flowers designed to conceal it. Monasteries are breweries distilling wisdom from many sources, searching out new perspectives: ways of hearing, seeing, touching invisible life at every level.

Two presences are required to ensure that the form of the future is genuinely ours. The vast and increasing consumption of limited resources represents a mortgaging of the future, quick-fix solutions providing short-term satisfaction. Those with a deeper awareness of a longer-term perspective must offset the pragmatism of harried politicians. Artists and philosophers should be consulted about our future. Those who know about culture and understand its length and breadth, its height and depth, must combine with those who are responsible for decisions about what we shall become in the future. The line of history must connect itself with the well of hope. Two kinds of explorer must listen for the footsteps of the other.

Our future is spliced through the rope dangling between monastery and mountaineer.

The Catholic Church, betrayal and why we must insist on change

I was born into the Catholic Church, and I have had the good fortune of being able to study theology and the history of that Church for many years. I believe that this Church, whatever human beings may do to it, especially those who see themselves as being in charge of it, contains everything we need for allowing us to be disciples of Jesus Christ, whom I believe to be the Son of God, the Second Person of the Trinity come to Earth. He gave us His Holy Spirit and promised that this Holy Spirit would be with us forever until the end of time, and that not even the gates of Hell should prevail against us. That is all that matters to me. I have the Holy Spirit in my heart and that person will never desert me. The food and drink, which I need for the journey through life, is the Body and Blood of Jesus Christ, which he gave to us in the Eucharist at the Last Supper. 'Do this in memory of me,' he said. It is a deed that we do; not a dogma, or a book, or a set of concepts. Wherever this deed is done, indeed, wherever two or three of us are gathered in His name, He is there with us. We eat his body and drink his blood to give ourselves the blood transfusion that we need to swap our kind of loving for His kind of loving, to transfer from our own human energy to His Divine Energy. And this can be done in many ways. It matters little how we do it; what matters is that the deed is done in memory of Him and that we participate actively as often as we want to have the deepest communion with Him.

All the rest is secondary: what clothes we wear, what rules we obey, what forms of government and structures of community we adopt. If the whole world were to betray us the Holy Spirit would never do so. We need to cultivate direct relationship with the Persons of the Holy Trinity, first person singular, present tense. There should be no intermediaries, no third person, no go-between. Christ gave us the life and love of the Three Persons of the Trinity flowing in our own hearts; we only have to drop down there to bathe ourselves in this supernatural splendour. We don't need anyone else or anything else to access this privilege, which is our birthright since the time we were baptised. Of course it is a pity beyond all telling that we have been so betrayed by human institutions, but God never relied on any of these to speak directly to His chosen people. All we have to do is answer the phone.

Now I accept that being a male and a monk in the monastery of Glenstal Abbey make it easier for me to find a satisfactory life within the Roman Catholic Tradition, and I can see very easily how so many others are feeling alienated by the present structures of this institution. However, I believe that everything can change, and should change if necessary, except one thing, which is the love of God made present to us in Jesus Christ and the Holy Spirit.

It is up to us to insist on such changes, but for my part I do not want to invent a new Church, nor do I feel the need to abandon this one. And this one, for me, means recognising that Judeo-Christianity is one religion stemming from the revelation of the one God; that the break between Judaism and Christianity is similar to that between Protestantism and Catholicism, namely a family quarrel; that Jews and Christians belong to Catholicism, which stems from the God of Abraham (also recognised by Muslims) and Isaac and Jacob, and which (in our view) reaches its culmination and fulfilment of revelation in Jesus Christ (the Messiah that Judaism has announced through its prophets), who is God incarnate. The Church (the One, Holy, Catholic and Apostolic) must, as an organisation, embody the Holy Spirit of Christ. Until it does so, it remains human, fallible and faulty, not yet having reached its full potential. I believe in God and I believe that the Holy Spirit is gradually improving the mechanisms that might change the Church from being the fragmented, self-opinionated, thick-headed, sexist, male-dominated organisation that cultural forces in our patriarchal world have allowed it to become, so that it may eventually struggle towards being the transparent image of the God it was meant to serve. I shall work as hard as I can to remove such dross and clean these windows, so that all manner of things may be well, and that all may be one, without that meaning uniform. There are many ways of being Christian, and our union is one of love, not domination.

The servant Church as a domineering master

I would hope that the Catholic Church will never return to the status it had in the first half of the last century in the newly established Irish Free State, which saw an alignment of nationalist politics and the Roman Catholic Church. This allowed the latter to accede to a dangerous triumphalism. The servant Church became a domineering master. I would hope that we never go back to that.

The Catholic Church of the future, and what it might look like

The Catholic Church should be like its founder: a humble servant to the spiritual well-being of all. The two people in history who made the impossible become possible are

Abraham, our father in faith, and Mary, our mother in the Church. 'Be it done unto me, according to your word.' That is all we have to say; that is all we have to do. No one of us has the blueprint or the architectural plans for the Church of Christ in Ireland in the twenty-first century. These belong to the Holy Spirit. Each one of us has our particular job to do, and if we do it prayerfully and conscientiously then the Church in Ireland will be as it should be and will be renewed.

Why we will never be a godless society

I don't believe we are in danger of becoming a godless society. First of all, because it is not our love for God that is the most important thing, it is God's love for us. And God will never let us down. Secondly, the Irish people have a powerful and deeply prayerful connection with the living God, even if they do not express this or practise it in the ways that we used to regard as normative in the first half of the last century. I also have great faith in the young people of Ireland, and I don't think we should be trying to foist on them the ways in which we connected with God in the past. They will have their own ways of connecting with God, and they are far more concerned about our planet, our neighbours and the whole of the human race than we ever were. And I have no doubt at all that God will reveal Him or Herself to them in ways we could never imagine. They are also in contact with each other and with everyone in the world in ways that surpass all our understanding. So God is not short of ways to get in touch.

What I hunger for

Everyone hungers for the real meaning of life and eventually for real connection with the living God. They may call this by some other name, but in the end it is that real and fulfilling relationship between our deepest self and the God who is the most exciting partner anyone could ever hope for that is behind every hunger we experience.

How I spend my time

Reading and writing take up most of my time. Articles, books, conferences, emails, lectures, letters – mostly trying to understand and to explain and to share what I have discovered about the meaning of our life here on earth.

Why talk of hell and damnation is no good thing

It is a very good thing that there is little talk of hell and damnation nowadays. From the beginning, we have tried to make a monster out of our God. Heaven and hell were inventions of ours to describe how this God was going to deal with those he loved and those he hated. We even developed a theology to explain that the God who made us is a neurotic tyrant who has been so offended by our radical disobedience that nothing can satisfy his outraged self-esteem other than the blood sacrifice of his only son. This, we think to ourselves, is the only way God's anger can be appeased and the sins of the world expiated. The sadistic father requires the death-dealing punishment of his son, since no one else is important enough to act as proxy, to appease his terrible anger at our refusal to obey his commands. This is one of Christianity's major libels against God; but there are others even more derogatory in the history of world religions.

Nothing could be further from the truth. God has tried, from the very first revelations of his divine love, to persuade us that he is lovable, vulnerable, compassionate, and that he has this unbelievable obsession with us, which will never give up on the hope that we may love him back. Our problem is a complete misconception of God, from wherever we inherit it. We are unable for whatever reason to see God as a God of love, forgiveness, tenderness and compassion. This seems to stem from our own inability to believe and to trust that we are loved and valued in and as we are ourselves. The God revealed in Jesus Christ is nothing like the monster in the sky which we have insisted on trying to venerate; he is a God who comes among us in weakness and humility to stand with us in the midst of the created order. We cannot fit Christ into some previously established theistic understanding of the world. We have to move in the opposite direction, and this means that it is through Christ that we have to understand God and his relation to the world, so far as we understand those matters. Since the dawn of human consciousness we have been projecting our fantasies onto the screen we call God. We are called to love in the way that God loves. But we are free to become this or not to become this. We have free will. This means that there must be a heaven and a hell. Heaven is choosing to be with God in love for eternity; hell is choosing our own sweating selves. If there is a hell it is of our own making. Many know this from first-hand experience.

Why we're all à la carte Catholics

The word 'homosexual' is one of the ugliest we have invented. However, it is better than some of the other names we have used to vilify this very vulnerable section of our society. On behalf of the God who has spent so many centuries trying to prove to us that he or she is a God of love and tender compassion, I cannot understand how leaders of the Church, which was founded by Jesus Christ, can take it upon themselves to represent the wishes of such a loving saviour by making any such group of people feel unloved. We cannot allow any institution which, in the past, has vilified certain races, has condoned slavery and has refused burial in a Christian graveyard, or the consolation of a Requiem Mass to those who ended their lives by suicide, to prescribe for us who is, or is not, loved by God. If an institution like the Church, which claims divine guidance in its teaching and prescriptions, can be, for such an unconscionably long period of time, so wrong-headed in its judgements and so cold-blooded in its actions, then we have to be wary of ever again allowing it to take over from us our dealings with any of the most vulnerable and unique members of our society. Of course, God loves homosexuals and so should we.

As for contraception, it seems clear to me that people have made up their own minds on that score for some time now. This taking back to ourselves the right to decide about matters concerning our own lives as human beings was connected with education and understanding as these developed throughout the twentieth century. The decisive moment can be dated, in my view, to the Encyclical of Pope Paul VI, *Humanae Vitae*, which he promulgated on 25 July 1968. The reason why this particular encyclical at this particular time was the breaking-point was, in my view, that it did not simply reiterate the division between sexuality within marriage, which was lawful, and all sexuality outside marriage, which was sinful: it prescribed and proscribed for sexuality within the precincts of marriage itself. This was seen by many of the faithful as a step too far. The phrase '*à la carte* Catholic' probably now describes everyone in the Church, since no one has the appetite or the capacity any longer to order and to eat the whole menu.

Irish people too, in the meantime, have grown up and are not quite as biddable as they used to be, not quite as overshadowed by the father archetype. Contraception for most Catholics these days is not one of the articles of the Creed. Even our older nursery rhymes have adapted their endings:

There was an old woman
Who lived in a shoe
She didn't have any children
She knew what to do!

Humility

Humility has had very bad press ever since Charles Dickens created Uriah Heep in *David Copperfield,* whose cloying obsequiousness and hypocrisy, added to his endless references to his own humbleness, made most manifestations of this so-called virtue into a farce.

Such a stereotype is reinforced by contemporary culture's in-your-face self-aggrandisement and braggadocio. To be humble in our society means to be left at the starting blocks in the race for fame and fortune. However, I have no doubt that there should be a place for real humility in every generation and in every society, no matter what any particular culture may try to do to eliminate it. Real humility is neither a psychological attitude nor an ethical posture; it is a way of being. It is a way of being with both feet fully on the ground (*humus* in Latin means ground), taking a realistic appraisal of the world we live in and our exact place in that world. It also, of course, requires that we acknowledge the source of both our world and ourselves.

'Psychics'

People are alarmed, amazed and sometimes convinced by the accuracy with which their futures can be outlined and their personalities sketched by so-called experts or 'psychics.' Let us begin with a statement of fact: anyone who tells you what the future is going to be is telling you a lie. There is no future laid out like a map. The future is what we make it. Of course, we can be told, and some are better than others at surmising, what is most likely to happen if we go on being the way we are, and others around us do likewise. No one can foretell the future. It doesn't take a genius to know that people are going to die, fall in love, make fortunes, split up, move house or change job in every month of every century. People who predict such things have no vision of what is about to happen; they know that you are a human being, they sense your personality, they absorb your psychic energy, some more sensitively than others, and they 'prophesy' about your future. Whatever they say that has no relevance or doesn't come to pass is forgotten; anything that rings true, or that corresponds to what happens to you later, is often exaggerated and afforded significance out of all proportion.

There is a limited number of things which can happen to any or every human being in the course of any or every day of our lives: we are going to meet up with death in some shape or form; we are going to achieve some goal; we are going to 'fall in love'; we are going to have an accident; we are going to come in for some good/bad fortune. But when these inevitabilities have been predicted, they suddenly take on an aura of prophecy, especially when aligned with the particular unfolding of our ordinary lives. The normal becomes paranormal because it has been pointed out as predestination. People we meet are enlarged and invested with significance quite out of proportion to their actual reality. We become so determined to meet the person of our dreams that all our amorous juices are pumped into projectiles to be sprayed over the next person who happens to knock at our door. The future can only be shaped from whatever already exists, from the fairly predictable set of options that each one of us is.

My vision for Glenstal Abbey

What has become apparent to me is that this monastery of ours, Glenstal Abbey in Limerick, is being offered first refusal – and everything always depends upon the willingness of those who are approached – on establishing a three-ringed Community of the Holy Spirit in and around the present structure of the community here as it now exists. The outer ring of this community will comprise professional people (some married, some not), men and women who are interested in living the liturgical life of the core community and some of whom will be involved in the active life and professional engagements of the Abbey as a whole. The inmost circle forms the contemplative liturgical core: those who undertake to live the full schedule of Trinitarian life here on earth. In between these two there will be accommodation and space for a third party who might want to live with us for a certain time, at their own rhythm and to the extent that they find appropriate. This last group might be a few people whose interest in being in such an environment might be temporary and even sometimes quite tangential to the purpose of the whole.

Glenstal would offer initiation into a way of life that aligns the whole person, body, mind and spirit, with the universe as a whole, with those who are in it, and with the

Three Persons of the Trinity who have invited each one of us to share in their life. Taking our cue from Cluny, Glenstal can provide many people with an element and an atmosphere allowing them to breathe spiritually. Most people educated in the twenty-first century are blind and deaf to the symbolism of liturgy, the 'divine beauty' of nature, the language of art. Monks should provide for a world that has become blind, deaf and dumb to the language of symbolism, the meaning of life. Gifts of place, time and culture have been given to us as providential sources from which to provide 'the running streams' for which many (if not all) souls are yearning. And once we ourselves have learned and are living from this mystery, we too can provide small dwelling places on the land of the main house, which will allow as many people as possible to have, or to gain, access to these mysteries.

This means initiating people, starting with ourselves, to a new culture, a new alphabet, which is really the very old culture, the very ancient language of liturgy. But a language and a culture that helps us to become fully alive, with that fullness of life which the Trinity have always wished to share with us: resurrected life, the life of love with God. Providentially, it seems to me, the Holy Spirit has gathered together in this very beautiful and sacred place the people and the competences, the genius and the generosity, which could allow us to provide a well organised and effective oasis in an ever-expanding spiritual desert.

Contemplatives must preserve both the integrity of their loyalty to the invisible while at the same time working towards the emergence of the visible in the culture, the nature, the liturgy of the monastery as a place of worship. Such thresholds, where the very pores are kept open between the visible and the invisible, are essential to both a people and a culture; without them both perish in the reductive monotony of materialism.

What makes me happy

Knowing that what I am doing is the will of God for me. To quote Rumi:

> *The chess master says nothing,*
> *Other than moving the silent chess piece.*
> *That I am part of the ploys*
> *of this game makes me*
> *amazingly happy*

The deepest sources of strength on which I draw

The Eucharist, the icon chapel underneath our church at Glenstal Abbey and the Holy Spirit.

The phrase I use most often

Absolutely!

Challenges

I haven't really faced great challenges. Monastic life shields you from these for the most part.

Who I'd most like to be if I had to be someone else

Roger Federer.

My cures for the blues

Watching *Fawlty Towers*, playing tennis and cooking for friends.

When I'm at my most frivolous and carefree

Never.

Mary O'Rourke

Author and former Fianna Fáil TD and government minister, former member of Seanad Éireann

What life has taught me

Life has taught me my faults. One of them is that I am too quick – too quick in my reactions and too quick in my mind. It has taught me to weigh things up a bit more than would come naturally to me, and to be less quick to react.

I often think well of people when I first meet them, but as I have learned more than once that first impressions can be wrong, I am learning to be more wary. Now, I know it isn't a nice thing to be more wary, but sometimes it can be a good thing.

I am impulsive, so the question for me is whether to judge, embrace, or act on instinct. I have fair instinct. It's only the odd time that it lets me down. I want to keep a lot of the impulsiveness, as it's kind of fresh to be impulsive.

My life in politics has taught me that while 'always stick to your principles' sounds great in theory, it's not always practical, as sometimes it's necessary to compromise and to be pragmatic. It has also taught me that loyalty can be short-lived and that people can let you down.

Political life is certainly not easy, and anyone going into it has to be prepared to work very hard. Keeping faith with the people is vital, but with that it's important to make time for your personal life and to ensure that work is never allowed to rule your life or take you over.

For female politicians and other women who have both highly demanding jobs and partners, it's a good idea to get someone in to help with the home. I know this because I had a part-time housekeeper by the name of Mrs Samuels who stayed with me for eighteen years and who was a wonderful help.

Women have to stand up for themselves. That has been my experience, as in life I have found that I have had to stand up for myself, put myself forward and stand my ground. Conventions played a role. Going for them. Not getting them. Going again. Not getting them. All were defining experiences.

The assumption that women should be singled out for certain roles both annoys and disheartens me. This is how I felt on the two occasions on which I was approached with Women's Affairs portfolios. The first time it happened the approach was made by Charlie Haughey. The second time it was Albert Reynolds. I assume there was a civil servant behind both of those recommendations – someone who had that mindset about me, someone who, while deciding that I would be someone who would stand up for women, failed to consider my capacity or capabilities beyond that sort of position.

On each occasion I asked myself: is that all they see me as? A woman? Someone who would agree to be put into a corner? Someone who'd be happy to talk about babies?

I was a pure rookie in January 1983 when Charlie Haughey rang to offer me the Shadow Minister for Women's Affairs role, but even so, I declined. Something in my brain told me to do that. It must have been my intelligence or something that told me not to take that job – but there was no way I could accept it.

I felt the same in 2002, when Bertie Ahern asked if I would go around the country to seek council votes in a bid to be returned to the Seanad. My response was: 'You told me you would appoint me and you told me I would be the leader.' At this, he backed down, appointed me to the Seanad and made me the leader.

Looking back, I could say that, like Edith Piaf, *'Non, Je Ne Regrette Rien,'* but instead I will be honest. When I was younger I would say: 'Wasn't that terrible what happened?' 'Wasn't I wrong?' Now I say: 'I can't bring it back, but I can learn from it.'

Who I am at the core of me

At the core of me, I am very ordinary. By nature I am upbeat and positive, and because of that I try to perk up others when I think they need that.

I have always been a hard worker, and I have always been competitive. As a girl that showed up in netball and bridge, but as the youngest child in my family I was forever running to catch up. That process was hugely helped by the great convent education with which I was blessed.

The Loreto nuns could educate a goat in a field. Some were very brilliant, and I had a great mentor in Mother Benedicta Corless. She taught me Latin in boarding school. I was very fond of her and I admired her greatly. As she was a very hidden type of person, others didn't know why I liked her the way I did. But she encouraged me to do honours Latin in the Leaving Cert., and I did, and I got my honour. She nurtured a love of Latin in me, and under her tuition I learned that it's a great language for those who enjoy using well-chosen words.

Mother Benedicta used to say, *'Carpe Diem'*. And while I didn't have a motto when I was younger, I lived by that motto. Maybe that's why I have always loved the Robert Herrick poem:

Gather ye rosebuds while ye may,
Old Time is still a-flying:
And this same flower that smiles today
Tomorrow will be dying.

Isn't it lovely?

The Loreto nuns gave me a wonderful education, and when I think back on my boarding school days and I remember feeling lonely, cold and hungry, I think of the nuns and the way they would say: 'Always remember that you are Loreto Ladies.'

What matters most, and what has always mattered most to me, is my family. I have two sons. One came out of me and one arrived to me, but they are both my sons. I had a habit of saying 'our sons' until my late husband, Enda, was long dead, but now I've got used to referring to them as 'my sons.' I love them, their wives and their children. Nothing matters more to me than them.

I have been very lucky in life: I had a good husband and I have good children. I have friends who have not been as lucky. I got my work ethic from my father. He took a drink, but even when he did he would be up early next morning and he would turn up at work, shaved, and with a fresh hanky in his jacket pocket. He was a good man and a great worker. He taught me a lot, as did my brother Brian.

Charisma is something that Brian Lenihan Snr. and Brian Lenihan Jnr. had in bucketloads. In both, that was combined with a sincerity, a straightness in life and a determination not to be waylaid by anybody who might offer them anything.

'You are in politics to do your job; don't ever be waylaid by offers or inducements.' That was the message Brian Snr. and my father instilled into Brian Jnr. and me.

Jack Lynch was another man who had great charisma. He too was very straight in that he had a distinct honesty in his dealings with everyone. I have tried in my political life to follow a similar path, and I have always been someone who tells it as it is.

When I was asked in a live radio interview where I was when I heard that Brian Joyce [the then Chairman of CIE] had resigned, I replied that I was in the bath. That was my reply because that is where I was. It was the honest answer.

Similarly, while it might be expected that, as a woman, I would be in favour of gender quotas, I am not. I don't agree with them at all, and I believe them to be undemocratic.

These days, offers of inducements are made less often to politicians than they once were. But still it happens, and while I certainly have been offered money from time to time, I never in my life took an inducement of any kind from anyone. That's not the sort of person I am.

I'm optimistic by nature. I'm quite happy with my books, the radio and the TV. I like my own company. I'm not the sort who's always craving the companionship of others, although I so love the company of my grandchildren: having them here in my home – happy, healthy, pushing and jumping on my couch – the sheer unalloyed joy of them. Yet, despite all that, I can be lonely.

Sometimes it catches me when I hear a piece of music or a song that Enda loved. When that happens, I feel it in the pit of my belly. I feel the loss.

On the toughest days in life, I say to myself: this time is going to pass over; there are other days coming. That's one coping strategy for me. Another is sleep, or as Shakespeare put it: 'Sleep that knits up the ravell'd sleeve of care ...'.

I love my sleep and I love my bed, but I lost my sleep after Enda died, so my doctor gave me sleeping pills. They didn't give me sleep, and when they did, the sleep was distorted, so on the nights when I couldn't sleep I'd come out to the living room and watch TV.

Usually, though, I get great comfort from my bed and from my sleep. I can actually go to bed full of angst then wake up to find it has gone. That's wonderful. It's a God-given thing – or a somebody-given thing.

I never read in bed. I'd fall asleep. But I've lots of books on my coffee table: I have my autobiography *Just Mary*, and I have *Oscar's Books: A Journey around the Library of Oscar Wilde*, *Angela Merkel: A Chancellorship Forged in Crisis*, *William Dargan: An Honorable Life (1799–1867)* and Ann Widdecombe's *Strictly Ann: The Autobiography*.

I don't like fiction. I prefer real-life stories. Life is stranger than fiction.

In many ways I am most drawn to what's natural and what's real. My idea of beauty is water. Here in Athlone we're fifty miles from the sea, but we have the river Shannon, and once I'm within driving distance of water and I'm able to look at it and think about it, I'm happy.

It was the same when I was a young girl – I loved the beauty of the sea, the lakes and the rivers. Why that is, I don't know. Maybe it's because water is the staff of life and we can't exist without it.

The future

I'd love to see all of my grandchildren going to college and getting started in life. I hope that by then we will have a better Ireland.

I feel very sad and very downcast about the number of Irish people emigrating each week. My one hope is that when our emigrants have found out what life is like in New Zealand, or wherever they go, that they would have a wish to come back home, and that there would be a better Ireland for them to come back to – an Ireland in which there would be jobs for them, an Ireland in which their experience abroad would benefit them. I would also hope that their children would be educated here in Ireland.

I have a deep social conscience, so when I imagine the Ireland of the future I hope it will be one in which people have more regard for others than they do now. I hope there will be a more equitable society, one in which there is less poverty and less of the haves and have-nots.

I also hope that there will be more equality in Irish society and that there will be a better community life than there is now – one in which young people will be more involved; one in which people will watch out for one another more than they do today.

I hope it will be an Ireland where people will enquire after and keep an eye on the older people in their communities. I hope too that there will be far less seeking after material things. It's not that I want everyone to be spiritual; I simply hope that there will be less emphasis on material things.

Every now and again, when I think about the future, I fear getting really old, so old that I will not be able to get into my car and drive to wherever I might want to go. I would like to die in the whole of my health. And while that may sound stupid, it's true in so far as I would like to die with my mind and dignity intact. That said, it's not something I dwell on. I'm far more interested in and concerned by what's going on in the world right now. What's happening in Syria fills me with despair: the horror of children being gassed, the capacity of those who can kill in this way, the frightful destruction.

Right now, when I think of the future, I think of the book about my late nephew Brian Lenihan, on which I am working with two others, and I look forward to that being published.

What's surprising

While the emphasis that so many people put on material things sometimes surprises me, it's the fact that people can be so diverse by nature that most surprises me.

People are all so different: the good, the bad and the ugly. This difference is a good thing, as it would be awful if we were all like peas in a pod.

I've had the odd bad surprise when it turned out that someone I thought was a friend for life, or someone with whom I was aiming towards being a friend for life, felt I'd let them down, or I felt they'd let me down, and because of that the relationship didn't work out. When that happens I say to myself: 'Ah, the devil go with it,' as sometimes there's nothing more you can say.

Sometimes I can't get over the questions people ask. Matt Cooper, the journalist, once told me that in his view I was too easy on the people in my autobiography, *Just Mary*, and he enquired why I didn't ask Charlie Haughey where he got his money. I mean, really, can you imagine me walking into Cabinet and saying, 'Excuse me, Mr Haughey,' then asking, *lámh in ard*, 'Where did you get your money?'

Faith

I don't pray to God much, but I pray to Our Lady, and she is next to him, so he must think well of her. When I pray to her, and I often do, I say the Memorare. I have a great belief, a childish belief, in that prayer.

Yet, while I remember the 'Oh Angel of God,' prayer, I never think about angels.

I don't pray to the Holy Spirit. Nor do I ask him to guide me. But I can pinpoint things he has done for me. In fact, I can definitely pinpoint things that both he and Our Lady have done for me.

When I pray, I tell myself, 'Something will now happen.' And it does.

I believe there must be a God, because there has to be a higher being who is directing everything. I don't believe that God is a person; I believe God is more a force for good in the world.

The idea of those who have died lining up in their earth-clothes and waiting at the gates of Heaven for us when we die is not something I believe in. I really don't think that happens. Sometimes I think that when we die, we just die. After all, they have never interviewed anyone who had been to the other place.

But I like to believe that those we have loved and lost are in Heaven. I believe Enda is there as he was a good man and there could be nowhere else for him. What Heaven is I don't know, but I believe there is a place where good is expressed, so maybe that's it. Sometimes, after a person has gone, a feeling of good remains. That feeling is that person's goodness. I can't express it in any other way.

I don't believe in Hell. Most of the bad things people do are of a minor nature. Because those actions are tiny in the scheme of things, I can't imagine anyone being punished forever because of them. As for the really bad people, maybe they go nowhere at all after they die.

When Enda died, some people tried to console me by saying: 'Well, he is in a better place now.' When I'd heard that I'd get very cross, and I used to reply: 'How can you say that? That's not true.' The better place was here with me.

Conor Walton

Contemporary Irish figurative painter

Who I am at the core of me

I'm not sure that I have a core. I tend to see myself as a shell. While life experience imposes a shape on the character, I'm not convinced there's all that much left when you scratch away the various shaping influences such as family, language, class, culture and home place. It's possible that a will remains – that and an instinct to survive. But if there is, there's nothing unique about that.

I think of myself as a chest with a false bottom. When that compartment is opened, another is revealed beneath. In turn, that opens to reveal yet another, and so it continues. I imagine that, like that chest, people have no centre, no core. I believe that the further down you go, the closer you get to the species, to nature in general, rather than to any personal core.

As an intensely visual person, I sometimes think of myself as an iris. My physical capacities and training dictate the shape and size of the opening, and what can pass through in either direction. I want the iris to be as large and flexible as possible – this is my idea of 'genius' – but it's still basically a membrane with a hole in it. The hole is the important bit.

What life has taught me

To take nothing for granted. I'm still searching for the bedrock: something I feel won't give way if I step on it. If that sounds like I've suffered some great betrayal or disappointment, I haven't. Life has been good to me. I've been incredibly lucky. But I'm not secure in my own success, or the good fortune I see around me.

What matters most

What matters most to me is whatever I happen to be involved in at the time. I spend most of my life embedded in problems. To step outside of those problems in order to look down at them from a higher perspective is not something I try to do very much. Viewed from a high enough perspective, what I do or think or feel probably doesn't really matter at all.

The man I was

When I think of the person I was ten years ago, I think that person is dead. I don't remember half of what happened back then. We reinvent ourselves as we go on, or at least that's what I do, or try to do.

I try to be open to change, and unafraid of loss and inconsistency. I try not to obliterate or falsify my past. But those who know me may say: 'What a load of crap: you haven't changed a bit.'

The challenges

To keep painting and to earn enough from that to support a family have been the greatest challenges for me. Being a parent is also hugely challenging, as all parents know.

The mechanics of painting

Painting is an odd activity in this age of mechanical reproduction. To produce handmade images out of dirt and oil using sticks with hairs on the end of them is to use obsolete, almost prehistoric technology. Why bother to paint a realistic image when a camera can do it so much more easily, reliably and accurately? That's a question I have to answer.

The value of my work

It's possible today to 'paint' pictures on iPads, then produce billions of perfect copies. If you follow the logic of image-making in this age of mechanical reproduction, 'digital' is the obvious way to go. Every error can be corrected; everything can be manipulated down to the last pixel. The only way to compete with mass media and achieve cultural saturation – to become famous as an artist – is to get your image reproduced ad infinitum.

What I'm doing is almost the exact opposite: making each image by hand with almost Stone Age technology; confronting reality directly in an attempt to embody the most unmediated optical experience with no lenses or screens other than those provided by my eyes, creating my effects using a rich, viscous, sensuous medium that obeys its own laws and resists total control.

My own imperfection as a 'medium' is part of the mix at every level. The irony is that images such as mine continue to have a recognised value in our digital age. I think it's precisely because the digital image is so easy and cheap to produce and reproduce that it's so lacking in rarity and intrinsic value. So despite what I do being in a sense counter-cultural – an almost Luddite act of resistance

– there is sufficient appetite for what I do to enable me to make a living.

Overvalued art

The top end of the art business is completely overvalued. That a picture should sell for something like the GDP of a small African nation is monstrous; an obscenity.

This is particularly so in the case of contemporary art, which is basically trivial in so far as it's not going to change the world. Most of it caters to the status quo. There's nothing revolutionary about it. It's not going to open anyone's eyes to a better or truer reality.

Five hundred years ago, Leonardo and Michelangelo were superstars. Through their work, they opened up a whole new world. They explored and developed a realistic, naturalistic art that never existed before.

When Leonardo explored perspective and space to create a spatially coherent visual world, his work had implications for science and other fields. While I try to innovate, I am not contributing anything that will be of real interest to a physicist or to a mathematician.

Leonardo and Michelangelo lived in an age of exploration. For me, it's a case of: what do you do after all of the continents have been discovered? What peaks do you tackle once Everest has already been climbed? There are new things to discover, but I have to ask questions about what it is I am doing as an artist, and why I am doing it.

What I want

I want to paint pictures that people covet. I want buyers to really want my pictures for what they are rather than for what they might be worth. I hope that my pictures will become part of the cultural furniture of those on whose walls they hang.

My pictures reflect a good deal of cynicism and disillusionment. My hope is that they embody truths that people can believe in, despite their (and my) disillusionment.

My fears

I fear death. It's a pure animal fear. We're all implanted with it. Philosophically, that doesn't make any sense, as when you're dead, your worries are over. I don't want to die, but I can't see the point of sticking around forever either. Immortality doesn't make any sense to me.

I also fear failure as a painter, not being able to earn a living, not being able to support my children, global warming, the collapse of civilisation ….

Immortality

While I feature in my pictures, as do my family and friends, I'm not seeking immortality for any of us through my work. There is no such thing as reaching immortality through painting.

There are very few paintings that are more than 1,000 years old. They simply don't last that well. It's all relative, of course. My pictures will last much longer than photographic prints, which usually begin to decay within thirty years, and digital files, which are even more fragile.

They will also last better than most contemporary art because my concern for craftsmanship is unusual by modern standards. Most should last longer than I do, but they're still prone to accrue damage over hundreds of years, and they will eventually disappear. Nor would they survive any sort of major social catastrophe. We have no physical records of the pictures of the great painters of classical antiquity. The works of all the great Greek and Roman painters are gone.

I think of my pictures as being for immediate consumption. When our civilisation crashes, they will probably be destroyed, and if that doesn't get them something else will.

Perfection

Perfection is a long way above what I do. I am a messer.

The role of art in society

There's a saying by Fontenelle, which is something along the lines of: we're all basically mad, but not on the same level as those who are locked up because of it. Those shut up in a 'madhouse' are not concerned to discover the form of madness that afflicts the man in the neighbouring cell.

For the rest of us, it matters hugely that we have some insight into the strange and devious workings of other people's minds.

The imaginative arts, because they are constructed out of the inner workings of the human mind, are an invaluable aid for understanding each other. When it comes to certain forms of collective insanity and mass delusion, they may provide the evidence on which one might form a diagnosis. The contemporary art world provides us with so much evidence of collective insanity. It's invaluable in that respect at least.

Evolution

I was brought up in a fairly orthodox Catholic, Christian household, where evolution was treated with a certain amount of hostility. At home, we were asked: 'Why it is that the monkeys are still swinging through the trees while humans have progressed so far?' When I think about that now, I accept that that's a fair enough question, then remind myself that evolution is not about progress. But I suppose that's just part of the answer.

A crash is coming

The religion of our time is Progress with a capital 'P'. Things are supposed to be getting better. We're supposedly becoming more enlightened, more environmentally aware, getting richer, growing less prejudiced and more egalitarian. Progress is supposed to be the motor that drives our civilisation. The economy is supposed to 'grow'. When it doesn't, that's viewed as disaster. Of course, we do have progress in specific areas, but the idea that progress is a cosmic force that sweeps us forward – that's not what's happening.

Over the centuries, the life expectancy and the general health and well-being of the global population has improved. That's the justification for progress. But that trend won't go on forever. There are seven billion people on a planet that might sustain one billion living as we do. I believe there's a crash coming. My paintings give some indication of some of what I think we face. It's there in the background.

The opposite of art is nature

I am not afraid of ugliness. I don't try to paint beautiful pictures, and I don't try to be aesthetic, but I do try to paint meaningful pictures. It's a mistake to believe that art should be beautiful. So many go to galleries hoping to find beauty and come home disappointed.

To me, nature is beautiful and what is spontaneously generated is beautiful. There will always be something ugly about whatever requires calculation and artifice. The human-built environment seems ugly to me. When people produce things, they generally produce ugliness. Where nature is left to her devices the result is beauty. To me nature is objectively beautiful. Look at a leaf, a cloud, a starry sky or a sunset, and what you see is beautiful, full stop, and those who dispute that need to have their heads screwed back on.

In art, it's the opposite – what seems beautiful to one may seem ugly to someone else. Both sides are entitled to their opinion. When people describe my work as 'beautiful', I tend to disagree. I accept that some ugliness is unavoidable in what I do.

Describing in words what my pictures mean

I would hope that there are people who can get what I am doing without an explanation. But I think that in describing in words what my pictures mean there is a learning process for me, as well as for any viewer of my work, in that I often don't really know what I'm doing until after the fact. It has taken me a long time to explain to myself what I am doing and why I am doing it.

I think there has been great consistency in my work since I started painting. In the early days I worked more on instinct and denied the need to explain my work. But the more I do, the more I begin to see a pattern, and that's something that can be analysed. I have found it interesting to try and express through words what I am doing; to build an argument for my work through words.

I don't have a strong sense of self. But in terms of my work, I am a figure-head, so I have to justify what I do at some level.

191

Because every picture I do is 'a Conor Walton', I have to build some sort of argument about what 'a Conor Walton' is, about what that name stands for. That involves taking a very self-conscious stand on particular subjects in order to build an identity or a brand in which I become the logo.

I don't see that as contrivance. I'm not trying to say anything that is actually false. It's more like a more explicit version of what we all do when we construct a self. In the way that the hero of a novel might battle enemies and engage in small triumphs, we all build our identities in terms of a story. We all tell our lives as a story. What I find I have to do as an artist is write my story very deliberately. That can bring awareness, which can be a catalyst for change.

The telling or writing of a life story can be done with a level of falseness or deviousness if there's an attempt to hide something, or if there's an attempt to present a face to the public that is in some way inauthentic. But that is not my intention, and I don't see much contrivance in the way I tell my story.

I describe myself as anti-modernist. That is not a fashionable position to adopt. It opens me up to criticism and potentially to abuse. But I do say what I think, and while my beliefs may not always be politically correct or fashionable, and while many may not share my views on progress or on the less than magnificent future that lies ahead for our civilisation, then so be it, but at least the opinions I share are essentially mine.

Modernism

I take issue with three key aspects of Modernism. The first is its anti-nature agenda, embodied in the old Faustian idea that 'knowledge is power'; that we can use science and reason to conquer nature, giving ourselves almost limitless power. This idea goes back to the founders of Modernism; to people like Bacon and Descartes.

Modernism as an artistic movement is usually seen to belong more to the twentieth century, but to me this is because by then the campaign was thought to be already victorious. A conquered nature was no longer of much interest to artists, hence the emergence of anti-naturalistic art forms: cubism, formalism, expressionism, abstraction, conceptualism, pop. But while the full artistic expression of Modernism is a relatively recent phenomenon, its basic premises were expressed by the founders of modern science and philosophy five hundred years ago.

Now, I'm not anti-science or anti-reason; I'm delighted we have electricity, anaesthetics, antibiotics and all the rest. But at this point I think many victories in our 'War on Nature' are beginning to look a little hollow, and perhaps rather temporary. And as was intuited in the Faustian myth from the beginning, perhaps knowledge yields only so much power; beyond some point it may yield only the certainty of our inescapable doom.

The second aspect of Modernism that I take issue with is its self-presentation as a fundamental, irreversible break in our historical development – the idea that 'modern civilisation' is unique and uniquely durable, because unlike all previous societies it is based on rational principles and scientific techniques.

This idea was first expressed by Descartes, who dismissed tradition as a source of wisdom and regarded the study of history as pointless since it was little more than a record of people behaving foolishly. His modernity is supposedly enlightened, rational and free from the shackles of history, whereas the pre-modern condition is dominated by myth, superstition and irrational respect for tradition.

As a painter cleaving to an old, and some would say defunct, tradition, I have to take my place in this cultural battlefield, and stand with the primitive tribespeople, the peasants, the aristocrats, the religious, the endangered species, the unpopulated wildernesses; with all those who stand in the way of Modernity and Progress.

The third aspect of Modernism I take issue with is that which I think of as its anti-imagist agenda. This takes different forms. It may be the scientist who isn't happy until he has analysed a beautiful sunset into the refraction of white light through gases of different density. It may be someone dismissing my painterly skills as 'mere illusionism'. It may be Descartes wondering if the people passing on the street aren't people at all but robots; or Picasso not caring too much where an eye goes on a face. Modernists tend to denigrate face-values. The value of the face, and of the human image in particular, has come under sustained Modernist attack.

To me, it's vitally important that we have images of ourselves so that we can see what we are. A naturalistic human image tells us something different about who we are than the Modernist creed would have us believe. We are animals. We are a flesh-and-blood species. And we are dreamers. Every face reveals a dream. Each face betrays the flaw in the dream.

The struggle between the outward and the inward is always apparent in a face. You can be supremely successful in life, have an almost perfect public mask, but there is always some discrepancy between what's going on outwardly and inwardly. It may not be obvious; but it's always there – in the face.

When I drew pictures of people who lived in a shelter for the homeless, I worked with faces marked by deep emotional wounds. Etched on those faces was fallibility – their inner dreams and outer reality were at complete odds with each other. There was a world of tension and experience in those faces.

Because the human image is so important to me, I'm not interested in much of the modern or twentieth-century art that explicitly or absolutely eschews dealing with it. Artists who have taken the human image as a central concern of their work in this period have often produced unsettling, demonic images that give lie to our notions of enlightened rationality.

To some extent, I see Modernism as an artistic and philosophical movement tied to an industrial system: one that is stripping the planet; one that shows no respect for the foundations of our existence. Descartes famously distinguished between the self (conceived as immaterial rational intellect) and nature, conceived as matter in motion; a machine following rigidly deterministic laws. For him, nature is essentially dead, devoid of even the smallest spark of spontaneity, of 'anima'. Animals, he concluded, are simply automata. This kind of dualism ruthlessly mechanises nature, and in that sense underpins and justifies our industrial system.

To put all of that to one side, and to practise and adhere to something old and technically low-tech, is to make a small statement. It involves the preservation of traditional values and the upholding of ways that may ultimately prove more resilient than industrial systems or the machinery of mass production.

Wilderness

I enjoy being off-road, off-track. But there isn't much pristine wilderness to be found in Ireland; it's not easy to go out and get lost. That said, you can walk for twenty kilometres in the Wicklow Mountains without meeting another person. There are more than 20,000 deer up there. If there were fewer, more saplings would grow and it would be home to a wider species of animals and birds.

We have eliminated all of the large predators in Ireland. If we had more of them, biodiversity would explode. I think we should introduce wolves to the Wicklow Mountains. That would be brilliant as it would cut down the number of deer up there.

Sister Ursula

I spent time living in an Italian nunnery. It was run by elderly nuns. They didn't know I was pagan.

Sister Ursula was in her seventies. She tried to take me under her wing. She would shriek, 'Here's my boyfriend!' when I came through the door after a day spent studying in Florence. Then she'd grab me by the arm with a pincer grip and take me for a walk.

She ran a hospital in Rome during World War II. British spies operated out of that hospital, and paratroopers who were dropped into Italy hid there while identifying their escape routes. She was this Irish nun, secreting Jews, while working alongside the Red Priest, Monsignor Hugh O'Flaherty. Together they saved thousands from the Nazis, and in doing so; they got up to all sorts of hijinks together.

On being Irish

I don't see myself as an ardent nationalist or a 'Celt'. I never really bought into the drama of Irish history. My intellectual and artistic culture is European. Very few of the stereotypical markers of Irish identity apply to me. But Ireland is my home; my roots are here and I couldn't live anywhere else. I have tried living in other countries. In Italy, for example, I loved the visual and artisanal culture, which is so rich compared to Ireland's. But I still felt like an outsider. Being a 'native' confers benefits in ways that are often quite obvious, sometimes almost imperceptible.

I don't believe in creativity

I don't believe in creativity *ex nihilo*. I make things out of other things; I work and rework. It's recovery, salvage, transmission. Originality isn't important to me, except in its older sense of staying true to origins; cleaving to that which is basic. So when I paint a picture, part of me says: 'What will someone else make of this?' The aim is communication; sharing. It's not private. And you have to meet people halfway; to express yourself in a language that people will understand. So everything I do is intended to convince; to 'reach' the viewer. I try to be a 'medium', not a 'creator'.

When part of me is asking what the viewer will make of my picture, it pulls me back from getting lost in a merely personal fantasy. That's a good thing, as self-indulgence is always a risk for those engaged in the imaginative arts.

In one of his Salon reviews, Diderot wrote about the visit to Paris of British actor David Garrick. Garrick made the point that when acting the role of a madman on stage, an actor must remain sane and in control so as not to spoil the performance by actually going mad and having to be carted off stage. Diderot applied this idea to painting. He said every painting is a performance. I think he was right. So, when I find I'm getting lost in a fantasy or dream world, I pull myself back.

Along with being a brilliant actor, Garrick was an amazing self-publicist. I think he had about 300 portraits painted during his life. Gainsborough painted him. So too did Joshua Reynolds, who was a friend of his. But Reynolds suggested that Garrick always played a role when in company; he could only stop performing by being alone. So he often hid himself away from people to have a rest from being somebody. Reynolds thought Garrick had no core, no self.

Of course, Garrick is an extreme case. As an actor his great virtue was his ability to play any role. In this respect I'm not like him at all. So maybe I am in denial about not having a core.

Sarah Benson

CEO of Ruhama – an NGO that works nationally with women affected by prostitution and victims of trafficking

The battle against trafficking and prostitution

The battle against trafficking and prostitution may never be entirely won, just as the battle against murder and incest may never be complete. But that doesn't mean there is nothing we can do about it.

Human beings are often unkind to one another. Frequently, we are extraordinarily brutal. So, while I don't see the fight against trafficking and prostitution coming to an absolute conclusion, there can be no question of letting go of the objective to eradicate it.

We have to have ambition. If we say we want to cut trafficking and prostitution by a certain percentage, that is not inspiring. Zero tolerance for sexual exploitation is required. It is not all right to buy another person, or to sell another human being.

The need to find out what's really going on

Many believe that prostitution is okay for some women and girls (indeed a small number of men, boys and transgender women also, but the vast majority are female), but not for others. Some think that it's okay for those who are perceived as consenting to it, or those who are poor, or socially marginalised. The fact that the commercial sex trade is a fundamentally exploitative and dangerous environment is often not recognised.

Public attitudes need to change. The majority, who never think about prostitution because it never touches their lives, need to make an effort to become aware of what is going on.

How crimes are investigated

There was a high-profile international case recently in which a man who killed an Irish woman was caught. The murder was given high priority, and when the case was solved it was discovered that this individual had a history of serious violence against many women involved in prostitution. The risk this man clearly posed to women was not flagged as it might have been because, sadly, violence and abuse enacted on women in prostitution is often minimised and does not garner the attention and public outcry that the same crimes committed against others would.

Women in prostitution are the testing ground for abusers because they so often get away with perpetuating crimes against them. Women in prostitution are not some group that are somehow separate and different from other females. They are exposed to much higher levels of violence and abuse, and are much more likely to be murdered – partly because they are the most isolated; those least likely to have a network of support to reach out to. Women and girls, and some men and boys, fall through society's cracks into prostitution, which is the responsibility of all in society. No one should be left behind like this.

Silence

In another recent case, sex buyers became concerned about a girl who was underage. Their suspicions were reported to the Gardaí, who intervened. Sadly, very few buyers endeavour to help exploited women and girls in this way, so this case was more the exception than the rule. More often buyers write bad reviews about those they buy for sex on the websites that advertise prostitution.

Sometimes they write things like: 'Clearly didn't want to be there.' But often they are more explicit. This sort of thing makes disturbing reading. Because they are buying a fantasy, most buyers are unwilling to even consider these young women's lives. To know the answer would spoil their good time and force them to interrogate their own actions – which would undoubtedly be an uncomfortable experience.

Something I can never let go of

Something I can never let go of is the knowledge of how fortunate I am. I think of that every day, and when I do I remember how easily luck can change.

My sense of right and wrong is a compass that guides me

While I am not someone who comes from a history of personal tragedy, I know many extraordinary individuals who have. There have been times when I have met women who have endured such horrors and I wonder whether, in their situation, I would be as able to relay so articulately what

I had been through. I ask myself if I would have survived at all, and the answer that presents itself to me is humbling.

So many women fight through life in the face of persistent adversity. For some it is at times a case of existing from one day to the next and not looking beyond the next twenty-four hours. In these circumstances it's all too easy to slip, to go under; especially for those who don't have support or some sort of safety net.

Being entrenched as a survival tactic

The impact of prostitution, and particularly trafficking, is truly devastating. At Ruhama we encounter many who have been coerced into the most appalling situations and who have been deeply traumatised as a result. Sometimes it becomes apparent when we're meeting with a trafficked woman that she is not ready or able to exit; that she has no intention of trying to get out of that situation at that moment. When that happens it's usually because at that particular point in her life her best option for survival, from her perspective, is to stay with her abusers.

For these women, being entrenched is a survival tactic. There is a terror of the unknown. Their trust has been brutally betrayed before, sometimes many times. Unsurprisingly, they have no trust in anybody else; no trust that anyone else will offer something different; something better. So, until we can offer women like this a reasonable hope and earn their trust, they are not going to budge.

How women survive

There isn't a single answer as to how the women we work with come through and recover from such harrowing life events. For some, it's a core instinctual survival drive. Others say they take strength from their faith, or because they have to push on for the sake of their children. But there are also women for whom support from another person, even a stranger, who treats them with respect and kindness, is enough to trigger a positive change.

When a woman finds herself in a situation where she has been utterly ground down by her experiences, it means so much to meet someone who sees her value and reminds her of that. This is the case even if all that individual can offer is a kind and respectful listening ear.

By telling a woman who is involved in prostitution, and struggling with it, that it's not her fault, that she's worth so much as a person and that there are things that can change for her, we challenge the sense of worthlessness that she may have internalised, and we help to raise her self-confidence.

However, even with copious support there will always be a number of women who will continue to believe that, while a new way of life is within the grasp of others, it can never happen for them. We try hard to help women to change that way of thinking to a 'Why not me?' approach. When that works, change comes.

The structures and systems that work against women

The global environment is weighted against women and girls. Very many infrastructures militate against them – especially in the Global South. Often, the opportunities presented to men and boys (in areas such as education, employment, representation, bodily integrity, security) are greater than those presented to women and girls.

When you have this degree of inequality, women and girls can not only be damaged, they can be destroyed. We need to change the structures and systems that work against half of the population.

Further, no person in prostitution should ever be penalised by their own exploitation. I advocate a system that decriminalises those in prostitution. An attitude and approach that combines support to prevent entry into the trade by vulnerable persons, practical help when in prostitution and assistance to exit is the best way forward. This is what women tell us themselves.

This is an approach that refuses to accept complacency about the inevitability of prostitution for a certain group of people. Positive change is possible. Focus in criminal law needs to shift to the key drivers of the sex trade: the buyers and those who organise the trade should be the focus of criminal sanction. That's the only way that we can see actual systemic harm reduction. The more a State tries to regulate and control the sex trade, the larger the scope for exploitation, trafficking and organised crime to flourish as legitimate business; as we have seen from the devastating consequences of the failed legalising policies of Netherlands and Germany. You can't make this trade safer: it is predicated on harm.

The perpetrators

At Ruhama, we come across the victims; we don't as often encounter the perpetrators who are directly responsible for their exploitation – pimps, procurers and buyers.

As to whether a person who will exploit is born or made, the answer is probably a bit of both. Individuals who have lived in a certain environment or through a particular set of experiences may have a distorted sense of the world and of their entitlement to hurt others in order to make gains for themselves. Some pimps and traffickers may be sociopaths or psychopaths. For most, though, selfishness and greed are key motivators, and I think those are what most often breed cruelty and disregard for human dignity. Buyers are largely motivated by a sense of egotism and entitlement to have sexual satisfaction in a situation where the power dynamic is entirely in their favour – by virtue of payment for it; even if that costs someone else degradation, humiliation or pain.

In responding to the perpetrators of harm, it is critical that the victims are never taken out of the equation. Far too often I have seen individuals try to explain the perpetrator's behaviour in such a way that the victim becomes almost secondary. It's vital in considering the perpetrator's actions that the victim's rights and entitlement to bodily integrity, worth and regard are upheld.

While there may be a value in studying the motivations of perpetrators of abuse in the context of the sex trade and other areas, it is imperative that we don't minimise their responsibility for their actions, or forget the laws that they have broken.

The myth of the victim mentality

I worked for nearly a decade on the issue of domestic violence before my current role. During that time I often heard it said of women who were the victims of domestic violence: 'Oh, well, she had a victim mentality,' or 'She must have had low self-esteem since she didn't walk away the first time it happened.' Those who make assumptions like that do not understand.

In domestic abuse cases, it's common for female victims to be living with the perpetrator and for them to have children together. Some even have joint bank accounts. It's also common for the victim to have loved the perpetrator until, and even after, such time as he started to behave in a violent and abusive manner towards her.

These situations are so complex that they cannot be judged until they have been discussed and unpacked with the person impacted, and until such time as the context from their point of view has been fully understood.

While blaming the victim is common, it is deeply wrong, as it shifts the issue from the core concern, which is what he has been doing to her, to the substantially less relevant issue of why she did not leave.

Often, physical abuse does not occur until after a couple are married or living together. By then a commitment has been made. Sometimes the violence begins after they have had a child or when the woman is expecting a child. Abuse tends to increase when a woman is pregnant. Typically the mistreatment begins when the woman is, for one reason or another, dependent on the man.

Rarely is there a straightforward entry into physical abuse. Very often, the perpetrators have a history of putting their partner down and diminishing their confidence. Domestic violence is a hugely manipulative form of abuse. It is akin to grooming in paedophilia – so much so that it is astonishing the way it mirrors it.

Perpetrators build trust, then pull it away, then rebuild that trust then pull it away. They do this time and time again. In this way they create dependency. Isolating the partner by making her mistrust others is another tactic. The first slap happens in this whole context. It never happens in isolation. Evidence shows that if one incidence of violence goes by without reparation being made, the chances that it won't happen again and that the violence won't escalate are slim.

Witnessing domestic violence is a recognised form of abuse against children. Yet, while some women leave violent partners because of the kids, others stay because of them, or because they have nowhere to go.

Others stay because they are financially dependent on the perpetrator. They ask themselves: 'What can I do? Where can I go? Am I to pull the kids out of school? Are we going to move to a refuge?' The reasons for staying and going are many and complex, but the key thing is to refrain from blaming the victim and from underestimating the difficulty of the situations these women are in.

Reputations have to be guarded

There is a superficial perception that middle-class women are unlikely to be the victims of domestic abuse. The fact that their homes tend not to be close to those of their neighbours plays a role in fuelling this myth. Detached houses on large plots of land lend privacy in times of audible disharmony that paper-thin walls in terraced homes do not.

I had a conversation one day with a woman who was staying in a refuge. She drove there in a brand new Mercedes, which had been bought for her by her husband. Her car ran out of petrol about 100 yards before she reached her destination.

Outwardly, all was well in her world. Her husband had given her an expensive new car, the family lived in a fabulous house, the kids were in private education, and Daddy bought them everything they wanted. Yet, behind closed doors, when that woman needed tampons, she had to negotiate sexual favours so that her husband would give her the money she needed to buy them. Her car ran out of petrol the day she moved to the refuge because it was his habit to give her enough fuel to get to the supermarket and back; no more.

She didn't want to prosecute. She said that while the shame was one thing, so too was the fact that his reputation had to be guarded. If the truth got out, he could lose his job. That would impact negatively on all of them, particularly the children.

Physical safety is a critical factor for women in domestic abuse situations where there is physical violence; but emotional support is also essential to counter the dehumanising impact of psychological abuse. When people are continually treated like rubbish and told they are rubbish they can in time believe that they are rubbish.

The roots of my social conscience

I have always been aware of the people in the margins.

As a child I went to an Educate Together school. While I was there I learned about social justice and diversity, and I recognised that homogeneity is not necessarily a good thing.

Because there was a massive heroin problem in Dun Laoghaire in the 1980s when I was growing up, I was surrounded by people whose lives were falling apart. That made an impression.

My parents also played a role in fuelling my social conscience. As a family we had great chats around the dinner table. But one day, when I was 12 or 13, I called my sister a 'spa', as what I thought was a good insult. My dad overheard me and in response he called me aside, took out a medical journal and taught me the literal meaning of the words 'spastic', 'cretin' and 'moron'. Needless to say, I never used those words in a derogatory sense again. I went on to study English in college, and nowadays I try to be careful about the words I use.

Through my father's activity in the community, I became aware that terror of HIV very often led to those who contracted the virus being abandoned by those closest to them. This was back in the day when HIV was deemed to be a life sentence. I was hugely influenced by this catastrophe, and looking back I think it was the central reason why I got involved in the voluntary sector at an early age, and why I went on to do the work I do.

Before Mary Robinson ran for president, I had never thought about the fact that women were not proportionally represented in Irish politics. But my mother had, and was so enthusiastic in her support for the future first female president of Ireland that she displayed Mary Robinson stickers everywhere. I think it was her passion for equality that awakened me to the fact that women were not in fact equal in many respects. That really took root, and has influenced the directions I have taken in life and work.

Looking for good

Sometimes you have to go looking for the good. When faced with an incredibly dire situation you have to pluck out the small positives within and see those as significant. Ruhama's front-line workers do that every day.

Faith

My parents were both raised as Catholics, but when they lapsed they decided they would not baptise their children as they felt it would be better to allow them to make their own decisions about faith.

They did of course take care to impart many important moral messages to us to support our development, but this was done in a secular context.

A few years ago I did some voluntary work in Israel and Palestine. It was an interesting opportunity to see how the Abrahamic religions interact with each other. What I found really disenchanting was the fact that they espouse so many of the same core tenets, and yet there is such a bloody history of conflict, which has often focussed on perceived differences of faith rather than potentially unifying commonalities. And so, while I am aware that there are so many principles I live by that are similar to those adopted by others in the context of their faith, I have never felt the need to affiliate to any organised religion.

I would never say I am an atheist because I believe that it's possible that there is something broader at play. What that is I don't know. It could be nothing more than atomic dust. But it could be something more, and I remain open to that.

On practising mindfulness

I am conscious that we are all living together on one rock. While it is a speck in the infinite universe, it's the only home we have. For that reason, we all have to try and muddle through somehow. My way of doing that is to practise mindfulness at a personal level. I do that, but high, spiritual deliberations are not something I tend to engage in.

Mindfulness is my way of grounding and situating myself in the world. Sometimes things can seem overwhelming, but when that happens I remind myself that the only moment we occupy is the one in which we are living right now. That is a rather freeing realisation: it takes away the pressures of the 'what ifs' that can torment you about both the past and the future. 'What if I had done something different?' 'What if this happens?'

I don't have a spiritual guide, nor do I need one. I try to let go of things that I cannot control.

Feminist

Oh yes, I am a feminist. So many young women say: 'I am not a feminist, but ...'. They then go on to describe precisely what feminism is.

There is so much misunderstanding as to what 'feminism' means when really it's quite simple. All it means is the desire for equality for rights and outcomes between men and women. The word 'feminism' gets such bad press; it needs to be reclaimed.

If I could be someone else for a day

I am tired right now, so somebody on holidays might be good. Seriously though, it would be interesting to be a man for a day.

When I am in mixed company, and we start talking about violence against women, I am always conscious that no matter how supportive the men may be, their perspective may be coloured by the fact that they are never going to be at risk in the world in quite the same way that women are.

Obviously there are differences between men themselves, but, broadly speaking, life holds different sets of hazards for men and women, and also different opportunities and access to various environments. I'd like to be a man – any man – for a day to see how that feels.

Something that surprises me

Very many of those who wilfully perpetuate violence and abuse do not change, but sometimes they do. I am glad that after so many years on the job I still have the capacity to be surprised.

Something I want for my children

I have two children. I want to know that if their luck fails at any time in their lives, someone who is in a position to help out will be there for them.

What life has taught me

Life has taught me to take nothing for granted and to try particularly hard not to take the people around me for granted. It has also taught me that we are social creatures, and that besides actions, words and thoughts are important.

Who I am at the core of me

At the core of me is a very ordinary woman who has been very blessed. There is nothing extraordinary about me. There is no reason why many other women couldn't be doing the sort of work I do, if they were so minded – indeed many are.

What gives me hope

Change.

Those whose vested interests we challenge

Websites that advertise prostitution in Ireland make approximately ten grand a day – just from the ads. Pimps and traffickers make hundreds of millions each year in Ireland. Buyers want to be able to buy sex without criticism or scrutiny, but they are fuelling organised crime, and without them the trade has no economic base. There are massive vested interests at play, and many who want to see the sex trade continue, so when Ruhama's reputation is attacked from that direction, it's easy to see the motivation behind it.

When we are attacked, and attempts are made to insult and discredit us, I know we are doing something right – because if the vested interests weren't jumping up and down it would mean they didn't feel threatened.

Usually there is a deliberate attempt to distract from the fact that Ruhama offers an excellent, person-centred support service to hundreds of women in all circumstances in prostitution each year.

Ruhama's work may not be good news for pimps and traffickers, but we are good news for women affected by prostitution and trafficking. Fearlessness is part of the job description for this work.

Paul Cooke

Co-owner and CEO of the *Sunday Business Post*

From the *Star* to the *Sunday Business Post*

I joined Irish Independent Star as a founding executive in 1988, and became managing director in 2001. When I went in I was probably a little immature; perhaps a little shy. Anyone who knows me now would be surprised at me being shy. But the newspaper business is nothing less than a robust working environment, so when I resigned two and a half years ago I emerged confident, self-assured and not afraid of anything.

After that I spent five months working in South Africa. So as not to interfere with my kids' schooling, I travelled alone. The experience taught me that maybe I didn't really enjoy my own company; that my life's far nicer when at the end of the day I can go home to my family.

When I qualified as an accountant thirty years ago, I was offered opportunities abroad, but I stayed here because I thought that if I went I mightn't come back. I have no regrets about that, and the time I spent in South Africa confirmed my long-held belief that Ireland is the place for me.

When the *Sunday Business Post* went into examinership I saw an opportunity to acquire an iconic Irish media brand – in fact one of only a few Irish media brands into which I would consider investing my own money. I saw opportunity at a number of different levels, including cost reduction, which was well documented at the time. The real opportunity that I saw, however, was in the potential to grow revenues and establish 'Ireland's business media brand.'

What sells newspapers

Rupert Murdoch told a friend of mine that content and pictures sell newspapers. I might slightly disagree with that. I'd say it's content (stories) and marketing.

Human interest stories sell. The Joe O'Reilly story upped sales by 10 to 15 per cent in the *Irish Daily Star*. The fact that he brazenly went on the *Late Late Show* with the mother of the woman he murdered gripped the imagination. It was the same with the Madeline McCann story – that sold a phenomenal amount of newspapers.

Sophie Toscan du Plantier's battered body was discovered in the same week that a prostitute was found murdered in a flat on a Dublin city quay. Few members of the public know the name of the murdered prostitute, but Sophie became a household name. Some might say that was because of the power of the media, that Sophie's killing got far more coverage than that of the other lady. It did, and the reason it did was because Sophie was French and good-looking and her lifestyle seemed exotic. From a media point of view, her story ticked lots of boxes. Compare that with what most would perceive as 'just another story of another prostitute being killed,' and you have your reason as to why one story was so much bigger than the other.

Of course people care when others are murdered, but if you saw two newspapers and one ran a 'Prostitute found murdered in Dublin' headline and the other ran 'French film-maker's wife found brutally murdered in West Cork,' which newspaper would you pick up? Most would pick up the one with the story about the film-maker's wife. That's human nature. The truth is that people don't want to read about ordinary individuals or the people who live on the margins of society. They want to read about the people they see photographed in gossip columns.

Crossing the line

In my opinion, celebrities themselves are 'fair game' for media attention when in public places, as one of the ways they maintain their celebrity status is through being photographed for newspapers and magazines. To some extent, people who live by the sword must be willing to die by it. Of course, there are lines that journalists should not cross, such as photographing celebrities in a private context, or snapping pictures of their children.

Definition of a tabloid

A tabloid newspaper cannot be defined. A tabloid is a shape; nothing more. People say 'red-top' as if it's some kind of pejorative term. In my opinion, tabloids, by their very nature, get to the essence of a story much more quickly than other media.

Trial by media

In my view there is no such thing as trial by media. 'Blame the media' – that's something we hear all the time. But we don't create the stories, not even when we investigate something that isn't already 'out there'. The individuals that we investigate create the stories. If they weren't doing wrong there wouldn't be anything for us to investigate.

It's worth remembering that the ultimate sanction can be used against media; namely the threat of a costly libel action. Unlike a lot of other sections of Irish society, when we get it wrong we pay the price.

A threatened species

I don't think it augurs badly for the newspaper business that papers are not often read by teens. When I was 18 or 19 I wasn't reading newspapers every day. Nor was I consuming news. I think that as people get older they are more likely and inclined to consume news media.

The next generation may well prefer to obtain their news in a digital manner. For them, that's a user-friendly experience, and that won't change. However, at the end of the day what they're doing – albeit through a different medium – is consuming news. Obviously, as a man with ink in his veins, I would prefer if printed newspapers were not something of a threatened species, but that's evolution. I take comfort from my belief that the consumption of news media will continue in the future, and that the printed version of newspapers will be in circulation for the duration of my lifetime at least. And I do think that there will always be a place and a role for niche papers.

Why after 26 years I'm still a newspaper man

I am passionate about working in media. For me, the attraction never wanes. Its vibrancy calls me. I work with the people the stories are about, the people who get the stories, the people who write them, the people who sell the ads, the advertisers and the vendors. It's a people business, and people are always interesting. I think that if I moved to any other industry I'd be bored.

The lad at the back of the class

When we think of job creation in Ireland, we think technology and finance. But we have to remember the lad at the back of the class. He mightn't get one of those jobs, but there shouldn't be nothing for him. In my view we need to create a role for him and make him feel that he is a valuable part of our society. The construction sector fulfilled that task for the last number of years. The challenge now is to replace the jobs lost in the construction sector with something else.

What life has taught me

Life has taught me to be fair and to care about others.

Personal goals

Twenty-five years ago when a friend of mine outlined his career plan to me, I told him that I had no idea what I'd be doing the following week. I got the job at the *Star* through diligence and hard work for Tony O'Reilly at Dockrell's Builders' Providers. It didn't matter that what I knew about newspapers at the time would have fitted on the back of a postage stamp; I went in as an accountant.

I don't set personal goals, and until I left the *Star* I never did. At that time I proactively planned my next move. I resolved that, having been part of the team that built up the *Star*'s business from scratch to one that was generating profits of almost €4m when I left, I would in future business endeavours have a share of the action, hence my move into the *Sunday Business Post*.

Stress busters

In my opinion there are two ways of killing stress: exercise or go the pub. While I enjoy both, I think that exercise is the best. So, when I need to clear my head, I play football (yes, at over 50), cycle or work out at a gym. I also walk my golden labradors.

What I'm searching for now

I am searching for a secure future for myself and my family and a share in something that I have built.

Who I am at the core of me

I'm a bit sensitive, a bit religious and a bit shy; I'm also honest. I try to treat people in the same manner as I would like to be treated.

I don't believe in luck. When you work hard you make your own luck. The trick is to put yourself in situations with possibility, then work hard and see where that brings you.

I'm a hard worker with the ability to get on with others. I know instinctively whether or not I like someone and whether they're good or bad. I rely on my gut feeling. It rarely lets me down.

My business style is tough but fair. That's what I think. Others may strenuously disagree; they may think I'm a bollocks.

I am not a typical accountant. I shout and roar and look at things differently. I look beyond the bottom line. I am impatient. If I want something, I want to have it now. It annoys me when I have to wait for what I want.

I am not the sort of man who lies awake at night regretting things I have done. I never do that. I am not the sort of man who considers the meaning of life. But I might do that at 4 a.m. with plenty of pints of Guinness on board. I have very high energy levels, and an extremely high capacity for hard work. There are a lot of people who may have greater ability than I have, but it is my ability and my capacity for hard work that has got me where I am today.

Often very hard workers have problems delegating to others. I can be like that. I don't think things are right if I don't have control. Years ago I accused a colleague of being a control freak. 'I know you are,' I said, 'because I am.'

What surprises me

I have always prided myself on being a good judge of character, but there have been times when some individuals have behaved in ways I didn't expect or who let me down. I have worked with people who let me down, individuals I thought I was close to, had been good to and looked after, who then behaved very poorly and in a despicable manner towards individuals with whom I had been close. But more often I've been pleasantly surprised by people with whom I was never close; individuals who surprised me by so generously offering support when I would never have expected that of them. Fundamentally, I believe in the maxim that the penny is very round – what goes around comes around.

What most delights me

Sport is my greatest passion. Nothing delights me more than watching a race to see if my horse wins, or seeing Waterford win in any sport.

What I think about most of the time

I think about where I am and what I am at. But most of the time I think about money. When I say that I think about money, it is in the context of securing myself and my family's future.

Turning points

I've had five turning points: moving to Dublin from Waterford twenty-six years ago, getting married, joining the *Star*, leaving the *Star* and finally acquiring the *Sunday Business Post*. The latter has given me the opportunity of working for myself and shaping my own destiny.

Sources of solace

In times of trouble I confide in very few. I either work the problem out myself, approach those who might have a solution, or go to my closest friends and work it out with them. Only when I have a solution do I tell my family. That's my way of protecting them.

I don't tend to pray when I'm faced with a challenge. But even so, I sometimes look for solace in a church. My favourite time to go is when it's quiet and there's nobody there. It's becoming increasingly difficult to do that in Dublin, because the churches are so often closed at the very time I might want to go in.

What fills me with hope

Often I'd be hard-pressed to find anything that fills me with hope. That's not to suggest that I am despairing, because I am not. But in a climate where so many of us fear that our children will end up taking a boat out of Ireland, where can there be hope? Ideally, we feel there's hope for our kids, but at the moment it appears that most of us are just raising them to send them abroad to find work.

When I'm at my most frivolous

When I have a few drinks on me.

What matters most to me

Money and financial security. That might sound shallow, but it's not when you consider that the reason it's my prime concern is because if I have that, my family has it too. Really it's for them. I'm not one who sits in my counting house counting out my money; not at all. While I work hard, I also play hard and enjoy life. For me, in order to play hard I need to earn.

What fills me with fear

I'm not mad about hospitals. I was with my wife when she was having a scan while pregnant with our first child, and I nearly passed out at the experience. I'm not exactly looking forward to death either. I associate it with pain, suffering and the unknown.

Snippets from my bucket list

I don't have a bucket list. I never had any personal goals, and I don't have any now. But I'd like to own a horse that would win at Cheltenham, and I'd like to see a Waterford team win the Airtricity League and the Hurling All-Ireland. I'd be happy with that. I've no wish to climb Mount Everest or visit the Space Station. I'm not crazy about heights.

Advice I'd give to a young person

Cultivate friends, because in times of trouble you will need them. Work hard and play hard and be transparent to others. It's good to be a 'what you see is what you get' type of person.

Karma

Some people have wonderful lives, others don't – often, those who don't have tremendous strength of character. I have worked with people who seem to have faced a disproportionate amount of challenge in their lives. Why they have such a tough time I don't know. It's as if they picked a lotto ticket with bad luck as the prize.

I have been very lucky in that I haven't had many hard knocks in life. The biggest challenge I have faced to date was deciding on my next career move when I resigned from the *Star*.

I don't believe in karma. I don't think people get hit with challenges because of something they did in a past life. I don't believe in past lives. I don't believe in reincarnation. I'm not coming back as a pussycat anytime soon.

Christina Noble

Founder of the Christina Noble Children's Foundation

Singing and dreaming

Sings: *I had a dream, a song to sing, to help me cope* ....

In times of sadness I automatically sing. In my early days in Vietnam when I first set out to provide shelter, protection and medical care for children, I'd sing when the going got tough. It was a kind of therapy for me; it brought hope and inspiration and kept me on my path.

I also sing when I'm happy. When Mammy was alive we'd often jig around together at home. There was a road she and I planned to go down together. It was filled with music and dancing and song. I still remember how good that felt.

Living on the edges

I was 10 years of age when she died. Because of my father's problems with alcohol, the State took me, my brother and my two sisters into care. We were sent to three different orphanages. The parting was horrendous.

I ran away from the institution where I was being kept and lived rough in the Phoenix Park. While I was there, I learned that a smile from a stranger isn't necessarily a good thing.

There were many times when I thought I wouldn't survive, but I had a dream, and that kept me alive. I would keep my promise to the littler ones that no matter where they were I would find them and figure out a way for us to be together once more.

Living on the edges, as an outsider, I learned fast that society shuns those who have neither a home nor a family, and the pain of social exclusion I felt was intense. I felt I was holding a Niagara Falls of hurt deep within me. I held it there for years, believing that if I gave expression to any of it the whole lot would come gushing out so fast it would overwhelm and break me.

I couldn't take that risk, so I held onto the pain and kept going. Keeping that inside me, containing it, was not something to which I gave a lot of thought. It was there and I carried it, but mostly my thoughts were on keeping safe and surviving.

In the evenings I'd leave the lights of Dublin city centre behind and walk alone along the quays to Parkgate Street and on to the Phoenix Park. All the while I'd hold an image of my sisters and brother in my mind. That was what carried me; that and the companionship of the moon.

As I walked along the darkened streets, I'd never think of the damp, bleak hiding place that was my destination for the night. Instead, I'd succumb to wild imaginings: I'd look at the moon and visualise the surreally beautiful home that awaited me there. Then I'd pretend that that was where I was headed.

I'd tell myself that when I got home to this wonderful dreamlike abode that shone with yellows, reds, blues and gold, I'd be visited by lots of kids my age, all wanting to play with me. I'd imagine us laughing while eating cakes and sandwiches together, and I'd think how great it was that none of us would ever be hungry or lonely again.

That was as far as those imaginings would go, because then I'd think that maybe the other kids wouldn't come up to my magical moon house after all. Why would they, when they were all safe at home with their families?

As I continued to walk, I'd look up at the windows of the flats I passed, searching for the ones that weren't dark. Sometimes I'd catch a glimpse of family life behind the net curtains of a well-lit room, and I'd feel the deep loss of the siblings I'd loved and lost. I'd ache for them, and then I'd imagine how good it would be if we, like the families in the windows, were living together in a warm, safe home.

When I eventually found out where my sisters and brother were, I made my way there. Nothing prepared me for the reception I would get when I finally knocked on the doors of those sorry institutions. I was told that my journey had been fruitless as they were dead. I had no way of knowing that I was being lied to.

When the loss of my family threatened to dissolve me, I'd look to the moon to be there for me in the way my mam once was. On nights when I couldn't see it, I'd tell myself it was sleeping. I couldn't cope with the thought that it might never show itself again. It sustained me, as did the thought that my mam was in that magical moon house, watching over and waiting for me. Sometimes I'd visualise her gathering me in her arms and taking me back up there with her. Other nights, I'd imagine I was flying moonward; going home to her.

I often felt her presence around me. Occasionally I'd hear her crying and feel sure she was crying for me. One freezing cold night, when I was lying in the hole in the earth that was the bed I'd dug for myself, I got the feeling she was trying to cover my legs with something; trying to warm me. I knew she was doing that to mind me, but because I could feel something covering me, and I couldn't see what it was, I was afraid.

Then I felt a cobwebby sensation on my face. I thought there might be spiders, and that scared me. I tried to wipe away whatever was on me, but found there was nothing physical there. I relaxed then, and when I did I felt my mam's touch all over my face. I knew it was her, that she was with me, that she was trying to comfort and protect me and that she really wanted me to know that I was not alone.

When I think back on that, I feel lucky to have been able to feel her touch. It reminded me that in many ways I was blessed as a child, given the great love and companionship I had known at home.

Childhood

My childhood was tough in that my family was desperately poor, but it was in no way horrific. Very many children grow up with no great or even good childhood memories to draw on. I was not one of those. While there were some painful memories, I never dwell on them. I prefer to remember that I had good parents who took the time to teach me right from wrong, who taught me never to hurt, disrespect or make fun of anyone, encouraged me to do the right things in life and to ask God to help with my worries.

My mam was always fixing me up and taking care of me. When she was around, there was a certainty that nothing bad would happen to any of us, as she would keep us safe. I remember the delight we all felt on nights when the whole family would gather around the fire and my dad would take out his mouth organ and play 'Danny Boy', 'The Wild Colonial Boy' and 'Paddy on the Railway, Picking up Stones'.

My mam showed her love for me and my brother and sisters all day, every day, but I particularly remember the frock she made for me when I was about 7 years of age and in hospital awaiting surgery. It was two shades of green, with tiny red butterflies. It had a little belt and puff sleeves and a Peter Pan collar. The time and effort that went into creating that was a complete act of love for me. I thought I was the bee's knees.

These were the wonderful memories that nurtured and kept me strong when our family fell asunder. They were a source of guidance, comfort and support, so much so that they played a central role in my survival.

It's because I know first-hand how vital it is to have good childhood memories that I so often say that it is our responsibility as adults to ensure that every child has them.

Poverty

I was brought up in shocking poverty. I was also brought up with a 'you have to do whatever you can to stay alive' attitude. But from an early age I knew that there were values and principles we lived by, and there was the word of Our Lord, so we knew that there were limits to what we could do to survive. I knew that no matter what, I couldn't go out and rob or steal or do anything like that, as that wasn't allowed and that was wrong.

The Ten Commandments meant a lot to me. I can't say I stuck by all of them, but I obeyed as many of them as I could. I never did anything seriously bad, but I broke the Eighth Commandment (thou shalt not steal) a little bit the time I took my mammy's one-and-six to get my hair cut like

Lily Walsh. I did it again, at the age of 8 or so, when I took the money that had being given to me for bagpipe lessons and spent it on myself.

I did that because I just wanted to get away from the madness of Daddy's drinking. I was constantly in the middle of that. I was the one trying to fix it all the time. That job fell on me because I was the one with the sensitivity to deal with him when he had been drinking, and I was the only one who was able to get him to be quiet.

My father was in the habit of going straight to the pub as soon as he was paid. On the evenings when he didn't come home, it was my job to find him and bring him home. I never felt annoyed at being sent to find him, probably because I was so used to it – it was a central part of my childhood – but I'd be upset that he couldn't come home sober like other fathers.

'Why can't you just stop?' I'd ask while leading him home. Sometimes I'd tell him that if he didn't change I'd go into the pub and tell everyone that while he was spending his money on drink his family were hungry at home. He'd always respond that he'd give up the drink, but he never did.

He used to be noisy after a night on the drink, so I took on the role of keeping him quiet. To do this, I'd listen to him when I didn't want to. Or I'd pretend to be listening when I couldn't stand to hear him repeat the rants I'd heard so many times before. Sometimes he'd ask me to sing for him, and I would. Then he'd join in and we'd sing together. I did that not because I wanted to, but to keep him from driving the rest of the family mad.

My father was a really good man when he was sober. He truly cared about us. He also cared about the old people and the poor who lived around us. Sometimes he'd say with compassion: 'Ah they're very poor – I don't know how they manage at all.' He seemed to have no realisation that we were every bit as poor, and that it was because of his drinking habit that we often had very little food at home. Of course, parents have to provide more than food: kids need their souls to be nurtured as well.

But the fact that we were no strangers to hunger and cold didn't worry us half as much as our mother's worsening health. We could see that the strain of living in such deprivation was taking a massive toll on her already failing health, and we became increasingly terrified that she would die. So when I'd go out in the evenings to search for our father, I was hugely motivated to bring him and whatever was left of his money back home. I knew that would lift some of the burden of worry from our mother, and I desperately wanted to do that.

While I have had many challenges in my life, it wasn't all bad. There were some good times as well. In many ways, my life has been a great learning experience. What happened made me stronger. But not everyone is so lucky. Hardship and hard knocks can have terrible effects on young people if they don't have whatever it is God gives us so we can cope in difficult circumstances.

I had a natural instinct as to how to protect myself as best I could. I wasn't able to do that all the time, but what happened to me when I was unable to protect myself could have been a lot worse.

Where home is

I was born in Ireland and I spent seventeen years here before moving to the UK. I lived there until I moved to Vietnam and Mongolia. As to where home is, I think I belong to the world.

I have always felt that my place in this world is to help my own family and as many others as I can. When someone is getting hurt or being attacked, or is in danger of that, the heart works with the soul to send a 'get in there and help' message. When that's heard, there's no stopping to think – we spring to action. There's an element of brainpower involved: we have to use our heads to make sure that while coming to the rescue we don't get killed. Dead heroes can't help anyone.

In Vietnam, I sometimes tried to watch a video in the evenings to take my mind off the pain, sickness and suffering that was so much part of my daily and nightly work. I say 'tried' because, more often than not, the video came to an end midway through the movie or thereabouts. This is something that happens a lot with rented videos in Vietnam. It is something I've grown used to.

Mongolia

When we went into a children's prison in Mongolia and saw that the children were freezing and that they had hardly any clothes, the first thing we said was: 'Okay, guards, I am going to be back in one hour. Turn that heating on. I am going to pay for it so you turn it on.' Then we went to the market to buy warm clothes and boots for the kids, and then came back to dress them. We then got builders in to build showers, toilets and a kitchen. We got this done very fast because we wanted to bring positive change for the kids very fast.

Then we brought in our own teachers. We made sure the kids followed the normal school curriculum while they were in prison, and we taught them English. We then worked with the government to ensure that they were allowed to study for and sit university exams.

We then set up a bakery. By having professional bakers teach the kids how to bake their own bread and cakes, we ensured that anyone who might like to work in that area when released will have the necessary skills.

We tried hard to get on with the prison governor. We sent very many prison wardens on yoga courses in the hope that it would help to prevent them from losing their tempers with the children. Working with them on a spiritual level benefited them, but much more importantly it benefited the children.

A Palestinian camp

I have worked in several Palestinian camps where the doctors had nothing, not even medicine. The first thing we bought for one of those camps was a music box. Noticing the long electric cable that circled the camp, I asked whether we could rig the music box to that so that everyone in the camp could have their spirits uplifted by the music. This was done to a great cheer.

We then brought in lots of food for the camp, and masses of toys for the kids. Then we went to the matriarchs who were in charge of the individual families and said: 'Here's some money. Buy whatever you need.' We then distributed board games among the men. That helped to keep them occupied and to bond over play. When people have little to do and they spend too long idly vegetating around camps, hatred starts to breed.

The children in our care

Loving isn't something anyone can do half-heartedly. Individuals either love or they don't. Where children are concerned, those who love them should love them with all of their hearts. Those who don't should leave them alone.

There is only one way to bring up children, and that is the right way. Children have to be raised with love and respect and dignity. We have to treat them as we ourselves like to be treated. While they are in our care, we are the most precious people to them, so there is a huge responsibility to do right by them.

I never consider the children I work with to be 'my children'. Every one of them has or had a mother and a father. Sometimes the parents are no longer around – they may have died, or abandoned the child. Either way, the true identities of each of those children are linked to their parents.

Even though they're not my children, I love, respect, care for and worry about them as though they were. I would fight for them in the very same way as I would fight for my own, and I would never ever allow anyone to hurt any one of them.

I often become sick from holding ill children, but I don't mind at all, as there is no way I wouldn't hold and comfort and care for a child who was physically in a bad way. We are there to help children to get better. That's what we do. If they are infested with something, our only thought is to wash that away; if they are ill, our only thought is to help them to heal.

The first thing I notice when I meet children for the first time is their spirit, never their physical state. When we hold children, we hold their spirit. That's really strong and lovely, no matter what the circumstances.

Keeping children on the right path

I have been deeply blessed with the family I have. Every day I feel very grateful that my children are well and good. But I am always aware that when it comes to young people – whether our own or anyone else's – we can never be sure that they will stay on the right path.

The fact that pornography is so easily accessible is hugely challenging, given the horrors and the disrespect for other human beings that these sites contain. CNCF is very strict when it comes to implementing a ban on accessing material like this. The children we work with are taught that it contaminates, that it is forbidden and that this is one line that they must never cross.

I have worked with very many troubled children over the years, kids who have lost their sensitivity and done things that led to their being put into detention centres. Others hurt other people and end up in prison for twenty years. Because they're often very angry and hostile, change doesn't come overnight. There are ways to turn young people around. It's our role to love and help the children in every way possible, but when they are older the task of making the necessary changes is theirs alone. We are the tools, but they have to do the work.

There is a debate as to whether some people are born with genes that lead to them becoming serial murderers. Their crimes are so evil. Are they genetically born evil? Is there some genetic chain there that causes them to be as they are? Are they psychologically ill? Psychopathic? I don't know because that's not my area of expertise, but I really don't believe that people are born bad. I can't look at a newborn and say: 'Her mother and father are no good, so she will be the same.' I can't do that. Nobody can.

I think it's more about environment. Kids raised by parents and extended family who have gone through the mill sometimes go down the same roads because they don't know any different. It's a 'follow the leader' kind of thing. Some kids make different life choices, and they're the ones who get out of that scene. But the notion that it's in someone's genes to be bad, the 'you're a bad bastard, that's who you are' school of thought, that is wrong. I don't think Our Lord allows any child to be born bad.

Advice for young people

There is no formula to advising young people. You have to know the children and understand the areas in which they're strong and not so strong. I usually begin by talking with them about their strengths, and then try to give guidance on the areas in which they struggle as individuals.

I would then say something along the lines of: 'Love yourself, like yourself, respect yourself and avoid putting limitations on yourself as you are more than capable of whatever it is you want to do.'

I would talk with them about good and bad, and I would remind them that they will constantly have to choose between remaining good and doing the right things, or doing the opposite. I would tell them that if they respect others they will get respect in return.

I would say: 'You have to keep your eyes, your heart and your soul open. You can't walk away from reality or close your eyes to it. Try hard to keep your vision and your third eye open.' Then I would give them a hug.

No child is safe

No child is safe in the world we live in. No child at all. The ordinary people know to some extent what is going on in the world of child trafficking, but they don't know the depths of pain, despair and filth that that involves.

Some look away when they know a family member is abusing children. Others dismiss it by saying that that individual was a good father, uncle, mother or whatever, and by insisting that what happened is past and the victim should let it go.

We portray ourselves as civilised beings. We think we are rapidly evolving because we have become so technologically advanced. We make robots that can look after human beings, yet I can't imagine a time when the vulnerable will not be preyed upon in this world.

In relation to those who prey on children, the situation is getting worse, not better. The trafficking of human beings across the world is big business. There's huge money in it, and that money buys drugs. Human flesh is the biggest export trade in the world. It's scary.

Good and evil

There is good and there is evil. Good people are a big problem for evil, particularly good, strong people who stand up to evil and fight it. When that happens, evil tries to find a way to break them.

Why some hurt others

I think that those who inflict hurt on others are quite lost really. I think that there must be something missing in their souls. That is the only explanation I can think of as to why they are the way they are. There must be some need in them that they are trying to fulfil, and they must have gone through some pain or experience that created that need.

Something I'd like to do

I would love to help the kids in Gaza as so many of them are living in terrible poverty. I would fly there tomorrow if we had the money and resources to help, but we don't, and there would be no point in going without that.

Karma

I believe in karma. I think it's possible to meet people and feel bad karma straight away. I also believe that if you do bad things here on earth you definitely pay a price. It comes back on you.

Spirit

I have seen spirit. I saw the spirit of an old lady coming out of a cottage on the Old Lucan Road. I felt rather than heard her say, 'This is my house' before vanishing back inside. She appeared in misty, partly transparent form. I know what I saw. She was definitely spirit.

One night I saw tiny pink objects floating in my bedroom. Candyfloss-shaped, they had tiny little lights on them. There were cerise-coloured ones on the far side of the room, and they were all sparkling. No words can properly describe the experience, but somehow there was something deeply relaxing and reassuring about their presence. It brought me sleep.

When I woke, I was upset to find that they had gone. But then I realised that I felt different: all the stress I had been feeling up to that point was gone. I was at peace.

Divine intervention

A few years ago, I underwent chemotherapy for foot disease, but the treatment had little impact. One night I prayed for relief from the horrific pain I had suffered for the past four years. When I woke next morning my feet were completely healed. When he saw them, my doctor said that could only have come about by divine intervention as the malady I had was incurable.

Reincarnation

I believe that reincarnation is a possibility. It could be that those who learned so much and gained so much awareness as earthly beings are sent back again to help others.

What life has taught me

It has taught me everything that is good and everything that is bad.

There was a time when I trusted everyone, when I believed every single person who stood in front of me. Maybe I was naïve back then, or maybe that's just the way my soul is. I don't know. But I used to think everybody was great, and even when people would warn me to be careful, I'd say, 'Ah, don't say that – she's a lovely girl.'

I have learned to be more cautious. I have to, as I don't want anyone to destroy the lives of the children we work with. But while being more cautious, I try hard not to be judgemental, as I sincerely believe in giving people a chance.

An angel in my life

I have always been able to identify earthly angels really fast. Some tell me to 'fuck off' when I tell them that this is what they are. But that makes no difference, as it's something I just know.

There is no human being on this earth who doesn't sometimes need someone to lift their spirits. My great friend Jean Murtagh does that for me. Smart and clever, with incredible humility, she not only has great empathy for those who suffer; she has a way of taking pain and stress away. Jean is a gentle but strong character who doesn't have to shout and bawl as I sometimes do. She truly is my earthly angel. I feel that deeply, even though trust doesn't come easily for me.

If I had to be someone else for a day

I am so glad I am me. I would never want to be anyone else. Not even for a day.

Who I am at the core of me

I am an ordinary woman who was an ordinary child and an ordinary girl, with a great gift of love. When I am alone, I often speak to God and the Holy Family. I also speak to my mammy.

I carry a heavy weight on my shoulders. Keeping the Foundation [CNCF] running is my top priority, and it's scary never knowing where the next tranche of money is coming from. Our Foundation is excellent. It's also absolutely massive. It's our job to support children all the way through their education and beyond. That's a mammoth task. Our buildings are top quality, as is our team. It took years to get it all right. It was difficult in a politically sensitive climate.

I have always had great passion and compassion for others. Growing up in poverty instilled that in me. But I was always particularly sensitive to the suffering of children. There was lot of polio in the inner city when I was a child, so it wasn't unusual to see children wearing built-up boots and leg irons on the streets and to hear someone shouting 'gunner eyes' in their direction. That was really horrible. I felt deeply saddened every time I heard that said, and whenever I was tap-dancing I'd think that while I was having so much fun there were children in my neighbourhood who struggled to walk.

Very often I know what children need just by looking at them. I know when people are sick, even when they mightn't know it themselves, and I know there's trouble ahead, even when there's no obvious sign of it. Sometimes I feel sentiment so deeply it makes me shake inside.

I remember listening to Edith Piaf's '*Non, Je ne Regrette Rien*' on an old Bush radio at home when I was very little. I couldn't understand the meaning of the French words I heard, but I felt every bit of it. My father heard me sobbing and asked what was wrong. I told him I had heard 'the foreign woman' singing and her voice made me sad.

God

There is a stronger spirit than all of us. There is a greater energy above us. That is true whether we like it or not and whether we believe it or not.

Life

I never think life is too hard. The most beautiful thing in the world is to work with children and young people and to see them grow and develop because of that. It is so wonderful to look at the little faces and see the progress that is being made. At the Foundation we have worked with almost one million kids. You have to get to know them to see the power of their determination to express their potential fully. This is so deeply inspiring to witness. It is beyond what you can imagine in the world. They paint, draw and perform music from the earliest ages. Very many of them have won international awards.

Life has helped me to understand who I am. I can sit here today and say I love me and I like me and that I would never want to be anyone else. I have to say that because I feel that, in giving me the life he did, Our Lord has given me something beautiful and something for which I am very grateful.

To be the person that I am today, I had to go on a very long journey. I imagine my journey as a trip along the Amazon; one that has pushed me up tributaries to show me what's there. It has been an incredible journey.

Would I want it any other way? No. To be who and what I am today, to live my life the way I do, to feel the way I do about humanity, to feel happy that I have been given this life, I had to have the experiences I did.

Am I happy with the world? No. I am not happy about what is happening to the children and to the people. Because of that I think that, when I die, I will say to Our Lord: 'Will you let me go back down again, to carry on the work?

Joanne O'Riordan

Student, campaigner and writer, born
eighteen years ago with tetra-amelia syndrome,
which means that she has no limbs

What's fun

Looking at old photographs, I realise that I've had lots of
hair colours over the past few years. I am a natural blonde.
Some say I'm closer to ginger. I tell them I'm blonde.

When I was in Junior Certificate someone asked me
if I was going into third class. I decided immediately that
the blonde had to go. So, off I went and dyed my hair this
horrific reddy browny colour. Good god it was horrendous.

At the moment I'm a brown-haired girl. But I'm going
blonde soon, so I can dye my hair a light tint of pink. I
think bubblegum-coloured hair will suit my crazy, insane
personality.

Party animal

I'm a bit of a party animal. Sometimes it frustrates me
when people say I shouldn't drink alcohol or get drunk or
whatever. I'm nearly 18, so I decide what's for me.

I've decided that the night of my eighteenth is the night I'll let loose. That night I'm going to go for it. I'm 'gonna YOLO' (you only live one) – cringey as that may sound.

Obviously, I'll regret it the day after. But to be honest, it will be the one night I get to enjoy chilling with my friends without having to speak soberly with the people who come up to me asking for a photograph.

My big softie side

Tom Petty's 'Free Fallin'' really gets to me. I don't know why that is. Maybe it's the 'good girl loves bad boy' aspect of it. My big softie side comes out when I'm watching *Toy Story 3*. I cry at that, even though it's a kids' movie. Now *that* is sad. It also comes out when I'm playing with my three dogs: Doug, a King Charles spaniel; Rocco, a Pomeranian; and Sally, a shih-tzu.

Sally is definitely my baby. We nickname her 'the dog nobody wanted' because she was passed from house to house. I always joke that I'm going to take Sally to my debs. Like every teenager, I imagine myself living alone with my sixty dogs. It's a teenage thing, I think.

YOLO pacts

For fun, my friend Claire and I do these YOLO pacts where we do stupid things in honour of the YOLO pact.

Because a YOLO pact isn't considered fulfilled until both parties do something stupid, Claire might have to add someone she fancies to Facebook, while I'd have to text the guy I like. I know that might sound weird, but honestly we think the things we've done are hilarious and we have created many great memories. I recommend these pacts to all teens, because, let's face it, there is no greater satisfaction than texting a lad you like and getting a reply. YOLO pacts aside, my friends and I *are* quite normal. Trust me.

What I am passionate about

Like every teenager I'm passionate about everything: music and sport, GAA, county finals, stuff like that. I'm also passionate about human rights and sticking up for people. When I met Enda Kenny while he was campaigning ahead of the 2011 general election, he said he wouldn't reduce disability funding if elected. I get really fired up when I feel that people with disabilities are being treated badly. So, after the election, I wrote an open letter to him asking that he reverse the cut to disability funding his government intended to make. That letter helped to bring about a U-turn on the cuts.

A poem I like

I love Derek Mahon's 'A Disused Shed in County Wexford'. To me it's about people with human rights problems; the voiceless and how we must help them. I particularly like the line:

> *They lift pale heads in gravity and good faith*

That's kind of cool because it shows that even though these people are down in the dumps, they still have a glimmer of hope that things might work out eventually.

What matters

As a teenager, loads of things matter to me. My own personal self – that I am healthy, happy, positive and confident – most of the time anyway.

Mental health is hugely important to me. We did an experiment in school that showed that if you push down on someone's outstretched hand when they're in an upbeat mood, their hand won't budge. But if you do the same thing to that person when they're feeling down in the dumps, their hand will collapse straight away. That shows that when we're feeling low our negativity impacts on our physical body, causing it to be more prone to collapse. I can relate to that. If I'm in a bad mood or feeling down, my muscles become weak.

I am lucky in my disposition, because I don't often feel sad, and even on days when I'm fit to tear my hair out, I always know there's light at the end of the tunnel.

What surprises me

Some doctors make their patients feel as if they mean absolutely nothing to them, as if they're no more than part of the daily routine. Empathy, both in the way medical news is delivered and in the relationship between the doctor and the patient, can make a big difference to how the patient feels. While we expect medical professionals to have empathy, some don't, and their manner can be hurtful. It can even be cruel, especially when they seem to show blatant disregard for the person sitting in front of them.

Now I understand that it wouldn't work if doctors were to bring emotion into their everyday work. Even so, they're supposed to be caring professionals, and they should know that it makes a positive difference when they show compassion to those receiving their care.

I have met many doctors whose concern for their patients goes beyond merely helping them to heal. They invest a huge part of themselves in helping them to cope with their challenges and to become better people in the process.

We share a common humanity

Recently, a woman who was sitting next to me on a train turned to me and asked if I needed any help with the bag I was carrying. She herself had heaps of bags, but her thoughts were for me. The fact that she asked me, a total stranger, was very nice.

We hear every day about gangs killing one another, and, while that's terrible, this woman and others like her restore my faith in humanity. All she did was ask if I needed a helping hand. But that's all any of us need in this life. We are all the same in that way. We share a common humanity.

What the world needs now

The focus is always on the great men: the Bill Gateses, Mark Zuckerbergs and Brian O'Driscolls of this world. From a woman's perspective I believe that the world needs more powerful women. We have female role models like Mother Teresa, but we also need more women from the fields of enterprise and sport who young girls can look up to.

While male rugby finals will usually be televised, Irish television stations tend not to bother filming ladies' finals, even when they take place at the same venue on the same day. Because that involves a decision to switch off the camera, it's as if there's a denial that the ladies' events actually occur. To me, that's outrageous and it needs to change.

We also need more access to the wider world for people with disabilities. Many small villages have lots of humps and bumps in the footpaths. That causes people in wheelchairs to jiggle up and down as they manoeuvre over every stone. Given that the pavements in big cities like New York are so smooth, flat and such a pleasure to travel, I wonder why it can't be like that in my local town. Of course that's not to say the facilities couldn't be better in New York for people with disabilities. While there are over two million apartments there, only 1,000 or so are wheelchair-friendly.

In 2012 I delivered the keynote speech to the United Nation's International Telecommunication Union in New York. It was the week of my sixteenth birthday, and I had amazing fun. But more importantly the trip left me with a great sense of empowerment.

I met many of the world's leading experts in technology – an experience I never thought I'd have the opportunity to have. I spoke about how technology improved my quality of life, and how I hope it will continue to do the same for others. The speech went down really well, I think; probably because those I addressed were all technophiles like me.

Because I sincerely feel that technology is the way forward for people with disability, I set my audience the challenge of making me a robot that would give me independence in my life. There is great potential for robots to improve the lives of very many individuals in different circumstances. If there were personal robots available to individuals who live alone in rural Ireland, and who for a variety of reasons may have very little contact with the outside world, those robots might enable them to get on with their own lives without being dependent on the services of organisations such as the HSE.

Gadgets and devices

Like every teenager, I am obsessed with Twitter and Facebook, and I love nothing more than texting and calling my friends. But while I am very attached to my phone, my wheelchair is in many ways one of my BFFs (best friends forever), because it helps me to go out into the outside world.

A battlefield

Sometimes the world feels like a battlefield, especially when I'm liaising with government officials in an effort to get some of the things I need in my life.

When I had my last operation in June 2012, I needed a back for the seat of my wheelchair, as without that I couldn't get around. For some bureaucratic reason, that couldn't be organised, so even though I had completely recovered from the surgery, I was left waiting for six days in a bed that would have been better used by someone who was ill. At that point, even though the wheelchair part had still not arrived, I went home without it.

As I couldn't use my chair, all I could do was sit on the couch or lie on my bed. This made my father so upset that he decided to take on the task of making my chair usable. To do this, he used the leg of a chair to make an armrest, and some memory foam to make a back for the seat.

Sometime afterwards, staff at the clinic I attend berated me when they saw my now functioning wheelchair – the one that their colleagues failed to equip, even though it was their job to do so.

When dealing with situations like that, it can seem as though life is essentially a battle, so instead of dwelling on that I try to remember that every situation has a positive aspect.

When I was in the hospital bed waiting for my wheelchair to be made ready, my mother told a woman she met in the smoking area what was going on. When she heard, that woman insisted on giving my mother a memory foam mattress so my father could use it to make the chair-back I needed. Thanks to her kindness and his, I have been using that seat ever since.

What life has taught me so far

It has taught me that there are very many obstacles to be overcome – especially for people with disabilities.

Looking forward, I hope that I will go to college and become a journalist. That goal motivates me to work, study hard and try to do well in my exams. I get so excited when I think of the prospect of going on to third-level and starting a new life for myself. But then I remember that I am not like most other students. I can't just take a room in any house and throw my stuff down there in a casual way. I have to find somewhere that's wheelchair-accessible; somewhere with doors that I can go in and out of without problems. I also have to know that I have access to twenty-four-hour medical care. Wherever I am, I need that. So when I consider my future, I see obstacles. That said, my experience in facing and moving beyond them has taught me to be motivated and determined, and I am both.

When faced with a challenge I say to myself: 'Right, let's get over this obstacle.' To do that, I visualise myself as an Olympic hurdler jumping obstacles in the 110-metre hurdle race. I see life like that. For sure it's a bit longer than 110 metres, but even so, it's all about jumping hurdles. Of course we might fall or trip over some of them, but when we do we still have to get up and get back in the race.

What I'm like

I like to think I give great advice, but my friends might beg to differ. I am a complete and utter chatterbox, so much so that it's a problem. Friends say I'm wild, crazy and talkative. My true friends see my serious side.

My mantra

Work so hard that your signature becomes an autograph. That's a quote I found on Google the other day. I feel it's going to be my new mantra in life.

While it might sound corny, I've always dreamt of being famous. If I had to be someone else, I think I'd love to be Beyoncé. I'd love that kind of fame. I'd love to walk into a club and have a VIP area designated for my friends and me. It's just something I have in my head.

My main goal right now is to work hard. Hopefully, one day, when this book is fifty years old, I will read back on this chapter and say to myself: I made it!

Richard Kearney

Philosopher, writer and Charles Seelig Professor of
Philosophy at Boston College

On philosophy

Philosophy is a very simple thing at one level. It's not about
highfalutin ideas. It comes from the quotidian; the everyday.
In essence, it's quite simply the making explicit of the things
that go on all the time in our lives.

In his book *The Myth of Sisyphus*, Camus said of the
absurd that you come across it sometimes – as you would any
philosophical idea – in a swing-door. It can strike unexpectedly
when perhaps you are simply going in or out of a door.

I began my philosophical studies at Glenstal Abbey
by learning about Heidegger and the existentialists, and
ever since I have felt very drawn to both. Even though
philosophy wasn't on the curriculum at the time, Patrick
Hederman, Andrew Nugent and other monks taught us
about Sartre, Camus, de Beauvoir and more through the
study of French literature. I discovered then that I had a
great love for philosophy.

There's an idea in existentialism that the moods that we
have, about anxiety, wonder, fear and joy, raise and respond

to philosophical questions, the most basic one being: to be or not to be? Now, that is a question about being and nothing, and Heidegger would argue that that comes, not from some great metaphysical revelation from beyond, but by simply experiencing – as everybody does at some point in their lives – real moments of angst and of nothingness, where everything slips away: all meaning, all value, all sense of self-identity.

In those moments of what we might call existential depression – not clinical depression, but being in a very strange, dark mood – somebody may ask: 'What's wrong with you?' And in response, the individual who appears depressed might reply, 'Nothing.' That in fact is the truth: *nothing* is what's wrong; there's no cause for it. There's just this gap, this emptiness, this absence, this nothing. As Heidegger and the existentialists said: that's the beginning of philosophy – the experience of nothing, when you no longer take everything for granted and then suddenly, through the experience of the nothing, *something* emerges as important.

Wittgenstein said: 'That the world is; *that* is the mystical.' Suddenly you marvel that something exists. This 'mystical' or 'metaphysical' experience has been formulated in different ways by Aristotle, Plato and philosophers right down to Heidegger and Sartre, but it begins with that existential, ordinary mood of just not knowing anything any more. We usually fear this mood and flee from it, particularly in contemporary society, where there is really no language for it, and also in many of our western secular cultures where, for many, religion no longer answers the question: why is there something rather than nothing?

That question is the first question. Yet, it doesn't begin as a silly question like something from a pseudo-intellectual dialogue in a Woody Allen film. It is something quite basic. For the Greeks it was the very beginning of philosophical wonder (*thaumazein*).

There is a certain kind of folly to philosophy. After all, 'Why is there something rather than nothing?' is a crazy question. And in a way, when one experiences the mood of anxiety or wonderment, one is kind of mad; there is a moment of folly that takes over. *Idiōtēs* (as in 'to become an idiot') was the word Aristotle and the Greeks used to describe the act of becoming mad.

Socrates made the point that philosophy is accompanied by a certain *mania*. He himself (and Plato describes this in some of his dialogues) fell into these moods. Suddenly, he would stop still at a doorway and his friends would be looking at him while he was off somewhere in his thoughts – 'off with the fairies' as we say in West Cork. He was somewhere else, being visited by gods and demons. Socrates actually spoke of a special *daimon* existing within the psyche, a mysterious double of the self, an other within us that puts us into question and invites us to think beyond ourselves.

The Greeks use the word *enthousiasmos* (literally: to be one with the gods) as a way to describe that. Idiocy is another way, as is mania or madness. So philosophical 'enthusiasm' means 'to be visited by the divine'. *Ex-stasis* is a term Heidegger plays on, meaning a form of 'ecstasy' where we stand outside of ourselves. It is as if to say that the beginning of metaphysical questioning is a certain moment of hysteria –tears, laughter, wonder – where we find ourselves beside ourselves and so put ourselves and everything else into question. Heidegger says that the human being is the only being whose being is at issue for it. Animals and plants don't interrogate themselves, don't go to psychoanalysis.

Hysteria was a term originally used disparagingly to describe the madness of women. The Greeks used the word *hysterium* to describe the womb – that part of the female being that was inhabited by the other. Hence, women were 'hysterics' because they were not themselves; they were beside themselves in their moods. That view was accepted for thousands of years, until psychoanalysts like Freud, Lacan and Kristeva came along and disputed it. They said that hysteria was not necessarily a pathology, but part of the human psyche in its more transgressive and creative modes. They also said it was something that belonged to men as well as to women. They de-stigmatised it. Even so, it's still regularly used in disparaging terms, as are the 'crazy moods' of ecstasy, enthusiasm and mania.

Sartre defined the thinking self as a being who is what it is not and is not what it is. In one sense, that is what it means to exist in time: it is to be what you are *no longer* (that is, your past), and what you are *not yet* (your future). So, before we even hear the word 'philosophy', we are all inhabited by the double 'not' – the 'not' of both past and future. This informs and splits the present moment so we are never totally at one with ourselves. We are beside ourselves, outside of ourselves, strangers to ourselves, inhabited by otherness. Rimbaud famously wrote: *'Je est un autre'* (I am another). It's thanks to this that we can, as Heidegger puts it, be the only beings who ask the question: what does it mean to be? We only *ask* that because we *don't know* what it means to be. We put ourselves in question because our very being is in question. From the beginning, our existence is in issue and at issue for us, because it's not a presence that coincides with itself.

In many respects, prayer, yoga, being one with nature, alcohol and food can be different ways of responding to the gap; bringing ourselves back to a certain kind of presence. Sex does that too, in so far as it's about being totally and immediately there with the other person. Ideally. Supposedly. There's an attempt to be present in the present moment, which is actually impossible, existentially, because we are always shadowed and ghosted by a 'no longer' and a 'not yet.'

It is sometimes thought that one of the purposes of meditation and silence is to become almost animal-like or plant-like. Some say: 'Oh, you happy carrot.' They say this because a carrot doesn't worry about the question: what does it mean to be? In that sense, Heidegger or Sartre would say it does not exist. It 'is', but it does not 'exist'. To exist is to stand out and apart from – *ex-sistere*. The animal does not do that, and that is the beauty of the animal, and one reason why we relax with animals: they calm us and bring us back to earth, to basics, to peace and quiet. Think of a purring cat or a sleeping dog.

In many religions, the same applies to the mountain, the river and other natural things. In the Celtic religion, it applies to stone. We see that in stone circles, such as the one we have in Drumbeg in West Cork. Those circles remind us that a stone is a stone is a stone. It endures. It is itself. Rest in peace. Look at tombstones. Burial mounds. Newgrange. And that is true of certain animals too in places like India, where the monkey and the cow are worshipped. They are sacred because, unlike us, they are at one with themselves. They don't even have to meditate and stand on their heads in order to 'cease the fluctuations of the mind' (as Patanjali prescribes in the Yoga Sutras). They simply *are*.

So philosophy is not a thing for animals, plants or minerals. It is about no-thing. And that is why, at one level, it is a sort of pathology. All humans are a little diseased, and so a little philosophical by nature. We are born philosophers before we ever know we are. But the positive side of our being philosophical is that we don't take things for granted – we can begin anew, from nothing, start all over again, rewrite our history and our story, be surprised by joy and wonder. Life as an endless journey of questioning and questing.

At one level we are all philosophers

There are lots of philosophers here in West Cork who don't have PhDs or MAs or BAs. I recently had a great conversation with a farmer who is a neighbour of ours. I met him about a year ago when I was trespassing on his land, and he drew up beside me in a tractor and got out.

I said: 'I hope you don't mind me walking through your field.' To which he replied: 'No, not at all. Sure, you must be one of the Kearney family. I heard you and a brother of yours on the *Miriam Meets* radio show. One of you was very good; he believed in God and works with Jean Vanier and the disabled. The other, who was discussing his new book, seemed very confused. Which brother are you?' To which I respond: 'I'm the one who is confused.'

After that, we had a great conversation about God, God after God and God after the death of God. As we spoke it struck me that this man was totally philosophical, even though he didn't have an academic degree.

So, at one level, we are all philosophers, but at another I would say that our society is one that prefers to deal with 'problems' rather than 'mysteries', and given that problems are generally and necessarily the domain of science, technology and commerce, we sometimes lose the dimension of mystery and enigma that philosophy fosters.

Slowing the mind

Every morning I try to take an hour away from technological devices to read, think and meditate, and when I do I can feel my hand reaching out, like an alcoholic for a vodka, for the tab or switch. The pull of virtual communication is amazing, but its rapidity and velocity comes at the expense of meditative thinking and questioning.

If I don't take that hour free from technology in the morning, I switch on and get into a very rapid way of working. A real buzz, a fix stronger than five cups of coffee. If I want to read or write properly, I have to slow down. I never read from electronic texts in the same way that I deep-read from a book. I never grade work on an electronic medium, because if I did I would read the text so quickly I'd miss half of it. I sound like a Luddite, while in fact I am for an ambidextrous approach – namely that while we need access to online information – who can live without email or Google? – we also need material books to take it down a notch, to go gently, to attend.

There's nothing like the smell of the page, putting a hand on it, turning it, making notes in the margin and a little personal index at the back of the book, maybe opening it at the wrong page, finding an idea you weren't thinking of, then putting it back in the library, and as you're doing that suddenly finding another book with another unexpected, unsought idea. There is a happenstance about the embodied world that we can lose with the pseudo-immediacy of the virtual world.

Wisdom

While I think I have done a pretty bad job on myself in terms of gleaning wisdom in life, I do hope a little comes from the study of philosophy and from thinking about things. I certainly hope that when I teach philosophy, some of my students acquire some wisdom.

An occupational hazard

I am very high-energy, but I have very low dips. I have learned to manage those over the years, but I have had to be helped by spiritual disciplines such as prayer and meditation, and there were times when I needed to take Prozac, sedatives and therapy to get through depressions. So I am a great believer in all of those ways of coping.

In some ways philosophy can go hand in hand with a certain type of melancholia; it's almost an occupational hazard – we need only think of Sartre and Heidegger. Existentialism, going back to Nietzsche, deals so much with dread, anxiety, depression, melancholia and emptiness because that's part of the philosophical, and maybe the artistic, imagination too. There are highs and lows – certainly Socrates suffered from them, and when he talked about mania, enthusiasm and so on, that in itself was 'high-energy'.

When I write a book, whether fictional or philosophical, I work non-stop. I write maybe one hundred pages in a week, then spend months going back over it. But the initial run is always manic, mantic, enthusiastic; hysterical even. For me, the challenge is trying to find the balance between being one who is high-energy and one who experiences the void that follows. That is why in my second novel, *Walking at Sea Level*, I was trying to find a balance between the highs and the lows.

Deepest source of solace

I am very, very close to my family. While my wife Anne and I live in Boston, our two daughters live in New York. My happiest times are spent in West Cork with them. I come from a big family. There are seven of us. We all congregate in West Cork at Christmas and in the summer, and that is a huge source of comfort and solace for me. Whenever I am low, that's where I go.

In tandem with that, I spend a lot of time in the garden. I have taken to growing trees and crops in our little garden in West Cork. I go out fishing every day. There's a rhythm that goes with that; a feeling of getting back to nature that's very good for keeping my mood in balance. Nature – both sea and land – keep us at sea level, and that's a source of equanimity. One of the reasons I also love living in Boston in winter is that I need only walk out my back door to go cross-country skiing. I find that very meditative. I spend an hour at it every day.

I also make time first thing and last thing every day for yoga, meditation and prayer. And I spend time with animals. Ever since I was a child, I've had a dog. We've always had dogs and cats in the house.

An abuse of power

I was very fortunate to have met many good, spiritual people growing up in Ireland, given that many others met very bad spiritual people who beat the hell out of them. I was particularly fortunate in terms of my Irish education in so far as I wasn't physically abused. Now, I don't want to be down on the Christian Brothers, because some of them are great, but I saw a lot of beatings when I attended a Christian Brothers' school in Cork, before I went to Glenstal. That's the sort of behaviour that puts people off religion, or off an ecclesiastical form of institutional religion, for life.

The child abuse scandal also turned many away from religion. Power was at the core of that. The abuse of power was a sickness in Ireland, and the Church was sick because of the collusion with the State (and the Vatican wasn't much better!). I abhorred the appalling interference of Church power in Irish society and in Irish politics. The ongoing revelations of mistreatment of women and children are a case in point. But there are now signs that people have had enough. The old system is beginning to collapse. As Nietzsche said, 'When something is leaning, give it a push.'

Glenstal Abbey

I was very blessed to have parents who were extremely devoted without being devotional. They were really good, spiritual people who practised their Christianity in the most tolerant way. They were tremendously inspiring in so far as they never pushed religion at us, never interfered, never said we had to go to Mass. They had an enlightened approach, and I was influenced by that, as I was by the monks at Glenstal Abbey.

One of the reasons our parents sent us to Glenstal was that they were very unhappy with the fact that beatings were happening at the school we attended; they just didn't want us to continue in that environment.

One of the first classes I had at Glenstal was taught by a monk by the name of Andrew Nugent. He walked into the classroom, and the first thing he said when he addressed the class was: 'Put your hand up if you believe in God.' Every pupil in the class raised a hand. 'We'll see about that,' was his response. Then he introduced us to the arguments *against* the existence of God. We read Bertrand Russell's *Why I am not a Christian*, Friedrich Nietzsche's declaration of the 'Death of God', Sartre's *Existentialism and Humanism* and Simone de Beauvoir's writings on God as the oppressor of women – all of which were incompatible with the thesis of God. When we had read all of these and more, he asked: 'Is there a Christian left in the class?' Not a hand went up. 'Right,' he said. 'Now we can begin.'

That method of teaching kept me open to all that is good in Christianity, particularly the monastic and mystical traditions. It also kept me open to the practical side of Christian faith, as in the service to the poor. I was greatly influenced by the social activism of Sister Stan, Jean Vanier, Father Peter McVerry and Dorothy Day, and also by my mother, who did a lot of voluntary charity work in Cork.

These were the sides of Christianity that greatly influenced me. Therefore, even though atheism is sort of mandatory in academic circles, I keep myself open to the spiritual, the sacred and the religious.

What drives me

Freud suggested that to be healthy is to love and to work. Or more exactly: 'The communal life of human beings has a two-fold foundation: the compulsion to work ... and the power of love' (*Civilization and its Discontents*). I really love writing and teaching philosophy, and if I wasn't paid I would pay to do it.

For about ten years after I went to the States, I stopped doing media work and went silent. I didn't do any work for the National Public Radio, TV shows, writing for the *New York Times*, or anything along those lines. Now I'm coming back to that again. I recently did radio series for CBC and ABC, and I'm writing more popular, accessible books – of the public intellectual type.

While I enjoy philosophical work that engages with political, ethical and artistic issues, I also love the solitary, monastic, meditative side of philosophy, where days on end can be spent thinking, writing and walking. So, I am motivated by both the public and meditative sides of thinking.

Then, going back to Freud's definition, there's love. I am also motivated by love; anything to do with love. I love people. I love my family, my students and my friends, and that's a very passionate commitment. So, the two big things for me are love and work.

On being labelled 'a brilliant intellectual'

I really don't consider myself a brilliant intellectual at all. I always feel as though I haven't done any real work yet; that the real work is still to come. But maybe that's not being sufficiently grateful for the work I've been able to do.

Looking back, I remember Micheal O'Reagan, a wonderful Dominican therapist I used to attend in Dublin. He would say to me: 'Richard, sit back and enjoy the fruits of your labour. Be grateful for what you have already done.' But because I am so highly strung, driven and hyper-motivated, I'm always thinking of the next thing to do. When my first novel was published, I had no interest in talking about it. It was the next book, the one I had yet to write, that I was already fixed on.

Certainly, I don't consider myself a great philosopher, like Heidegger, Sartre or Ricœur. Nor am I a great scholar. I don't have the patience or the depth, the skill or the attention to detail that is required for great scholarship. But while I don't consider myself an original philosopher or scholar, I hope I am at least a sort of 'thinker'. I make a distinction here between philosophers, scholars and thinkers.

Who I am at the core of me

I asked my wife, Anne, once, whether there was anything she liked about me. This was after a row. 'Three things,' she replied. 'You make people laugh, you love children, and you love life.' Certainly my being a thinker didn't feature on her list, but I believe that, had she had time to reflect, it would have, as she admires the fact that I work hard and that I try to think things through. I hope there's some kind of gift or virtue in that.

I am a very happy person most of the time. When I have my dips, however, I am singularly unhappy, but that's the price to be paid.

I am a person who loves to think. I love philosophy: talking about it; talking to you about it. But for me to say 'I am a philosopher' sounds a little bit pretentious. I don't think I am there yet. At one level, there have been relatively few philosophers in the history of the world; at another, everybody is a philosopher. But the word 'philosophy' can be a bit intimidating. So I find it easier to say: 'I try to think; to be a thinker' than to say: 'I am a philosopher.'

I am quite interdisciplinary in my work. I like thinking across disciplines in an interdisciplinary way. I do a lot of work on the realm of narrative imagination and trauma. I am very interested in psychology, psychotherapy, psychoanalysis and in the philosophy of religion. Some of my most recent work, particularly *The God who May Be* and *Anatheism: Returning to God After God*, has been about the latter.

So, in saying that I am a thinker I mean that I try to think aesthetically, politically and theologically outside of the box. In some circles – particularly in analytical philosophy circles in North America – philosophy has become very much a specialist discipline. In those circles, any kind of interdisciplinary work would be deemed a compromise. Pure, abstract, technical thinking is what is preferred.

I try to bring philosophy out into the street. Socrates did that. He brought it into the agora – the marketplace. Because I very much believe in the benefit of that, I greatly support Michael D. Higgins's attempts to develop a 'presidency of ideas'.

A retreat

I was really glad to move from Ireland to Boston when I did. Not just because I like moving on and being on a journey, but because, as mentioned, I had been suffering from very severe depressions. I think the fact that I was over-extended played a part in that. At the time I found it difficult to say 'no.'

At one point I was a member of the Arts Council and of the Higher Education Authority. I was also chairing the Irish Film Centre building project, running the Irish Film School at UCD, running UCD's Philosophy Department (rotating with my colleague, Dermot Moran), teaching in Boston College and the Sorbonne as visiting professor, holding a lectureship under the Erasmus exchange and hosting a TV show.

Then something snapped, and I felt a need to go underground for a while. So, while it may seem strange to go to Boston to go underground, that's what I did. While there, I worked slowly and patiently on my trilogy: *Philosophy at the Limit*. Out of that came *On Stories; The God Who May Be; Strangers, Gods and Monsters* and eventually *Anatheism*.

To do that work, I needed to be away. I don't think I could have done it had I remained in Ireland. I was too busy in Dublin; too over-committed. In Boston I discovered a sort of anonymity. I was nobody there. I could and did retreat. The silence of the phones!

Now I am feeling, rightly or wrongly, that it may be time to come out of the woods again, so we'll see what happens.

Change

I love change, but for me it's change in stability, in the sense that West Cork always remains an anchor for me. No matter where I may be working or travelling, that's my real 'home'. Our house near Union Hall is off the beaten track. There isn't a hotel for thirty or forty miles. We are right out on the coast. When there's a storm we can see the islands being lashed by tidal waves. The roads around us are unpaved and rocky. I like the inaccessibility of the place. It saves me from my social instincts.

What most concerns me

At a personal level, what most concerns me is the happiness of my children and the well-being of those I love. That concern should and does also extend, of course, beyond family and friends. When she used to pray, my mother – and she was no craw-thumper; no sanctimonious beater of the breast – would always pray first for the family, then for the community and then for those suffering elsewhere in the world. Her prayers were like the extending circles that Stephen Dedalus talks about in *A Portrait of the Artist as a Young Man*.

Those extending circles of concern kept me open to an authentic potential within religion – that the religious imagination was at best an empathic imagination that never got caught up in itself, but was always concerned with others.

In India, a Benedictine Sister once said to me: 'I am here not to convert, but to listen and learn.' That seemed right to me: that the religious imagination should ideally and authentically be an attentive imagination, an acoustic imagination, an auditory imagination – one that listens rather than preaches. Patrick Hederman has spoken often about that.

Each trip I have made to India has been both a return to the heart and a return to the body. There, I learned how to breathe again, how to be in the body again, how to climb a mountain and see its sacredness and that of the rivers, animals and birds. The extension of the sacred to include the animal, vegetable and mineral worlds is not apparent in our western Christocentric culture. I say that with no offence to Christ, because he probably did love animals, plants and things. But, apart from what we know of St Francis, it has not been a side of Christianity that has been celebrated.

It is the reverence for all sentient beings in Hinduism, Jainism and Buddhism that I find important as a supplement and complement to Christian humanism.

The perception of what it is philosophers do

My wife, Anne, has often heard the remark: 'It must be very interesting to be married to a philosopher. What kind of conversations do you two have?' Her reply is always the same: 'We rarely talk academically.' There is a general perception that she and I regularly have profound discussions about great metaphysical themes like being and nothingness, being and time and the God who may be, when the reality is that most of our conversations are very ordinary, but never boring. Like 'pass the salt'. I love salt!

What scares me

I am not a person with a huge amount of fear. I don't fear death. Nor do I fear physical danger. Maybe I am a little reckless at times – my wife would say I'm pretty fearless. At least of the sea.

I fear the potential within certain human beings for gratuitous evil. Human evil scares me. I fear cruelty. The fact that people can torture gratuitously is terrifying to me.

What most surprises me about people

I am also astonished at how impossibly good people can be.

Religion for me is as much about the community of saints as anything else. Most saints were never canonised – they are people like Jean Vanier, Sister Stan, Stanislas Breton, Sara Grant, Chökyi Nyima Rinpoche and people like that. I have been lucky to have met some of them in my life. You know when you are in the presence of really holy people like this. They are full of love, full of joy. They are never sanctimonious; never take themselves seriously. There is a simplicity about them that is almost childlike or animal-like.

Stanislas Breton, a great teacher of philosophy and a friend of mine, used to get down on his knees and laugh like an animal to amuse my daughters, Simone and Sarah, when they were little. There is something in the presence of Chökyi Nyima Rinpoche that reminds me of the essence of a deer or a llama. When I met him, the Dalai Lama was scratching under his arms in monkey-like fashion. I am always struck by the inconspicuous simplicity of holiness; the fact that so much goodness can inhabit such embodied human beings.

I have been blessed to have met very many good people in my life. Why I have met them, I don't know. Maybe I seek them out, because very good people bring hope in the midst of what is a pretty dark world at times. And while they bring me hope, so too does the impossible love that people can have to overcome evil and to forgive enemies. Hope in the impossible is an inspirational and motivational force. Prayer is the attention of the soul.

What life has taught me

I am a very impatient person. I always have been. I hate to wait. But life has taught me to be patient, to listen. Attending is literally tending to, caring for someone or something that is there; someone you normally take for granted or pass by. Patience has passion (same etymological root: *patio-patire-passi-passum*) in it, but it also has suffering, as in the Passion, as in suffering little children to come unto you, as in letting it happen, letting things be. It has that sense of suffering; of acknowledging the pain and woundedness that is within all of us.

It's important that we learn how wounded we are and to work from that, as that awareness helps us to become more empathetic with others. Having experienced my depressions I have learned to live with suffering and to be much more sensitive with others than I might otherwise have been. If someone is behaving really badly, I ask myself what pain they're coming from, what wounds are behind the violence or meanness.

I think our woundedness helps us to be more human – as in *humus*, from the earth – more earthy, more humorous, more incarnate. Probably the best thing we can learn from philosophy is to laugh.

Seán Donlon

European Bank for Reconstruction and Development (EBRD) board member

Childhood

I am the second eldest of thirteen children, born in Athboy, County Meath and brought up in Athboy, Drogheda, Cavan, Ennis and Dublin. The frequent moves were a consequence of my father's career, initially as a primary school teacher, then a schools' inspector and finally as the Director of *Instituid Teangeolaíocht na hÉireann*, a State-funded research institute with a focus on methods to enhance the teaching and speaking of Irish. We were an Irish-speaking family, and that, combined with our frequent moves, made us in many ways double outsiders when we arrived at each new place. I have happy memories of all the places we lived in, especially Ennis, which in the fifties was an unusually vibrant place with Shannon Airport nearby, more secondary schools than comparable towns and a lively young crowd.

The size of the family required that we compete for scholarships and probably instilled us from an early stage with a spirit of competition. Hardly surprisingly given that Irish was the language of the home, the first prize I won was for Irish conversation, at Drogheda's *Feis na Boinne* in 1943 when I was 3 years old. The prize was a biography of Pádraic Pearse, an extraordinarily rabid, militaristic account of his life and times. I was not, however, allowed to read it for years because my father rightly felt it was unsuitable. I enjoyed competing. It was probably a big family thing. My oldest sister, now a distinguished Loreto nun, recently drew my attention to the fact that she had beaten me in the final of a national spelling bee competition run back in the fifties by the *Sunday Review*. She took the winner's cup with her name engraved on it down from a shelf, just to remind me!

Education was a big factor in the family. My father was educated on the scholarship route, my mother successfully competed for a civil service place in the early thirties and many of my eight sisters have made their careers in education. At one stage Áine was Professor of Education in UCC, Máire (a Loreto nun, Sister Rionach) was Principal of Loreto, St Stephen's Green, Maeve was Principal of Coláiste Iosagáin in Stillorgan, Éilis was Principal of St Louis High School in Rathmines and Deirdre, having taught for twenty-five years in the Presentation Primary School in Terenure, went on to follow in my father's footsteps and became an Assistant Chief Inspector in the Department of Education. Family gatherings, especially when my father was alive – he lived to the age of 92 – were dominated by discussions on education. I listened, said little and used my Foreign Affairs skill to pour the wine.

In 1953 I won a Cavan County Council scholarship and spent the next five years in St Finian's College in Mullingar. It was an all-boarding minor seminary for the Meath diocese, and our teachers were almost all priests. My abiding memories of those years involve GAA football and music. Father Jim Deignan, a veteran of great Cavan teams, coached football and

Father Frank McNamara taught me the piano and organ and produced the annual Gilbert and Sullivan opera. Finian's went on to develop a *Schola Cantorum*, a specialist music department set up by the hierarchy to which musically gifted boys from all over the country were recruited, mainly in the hope that they would eventually contribute to raising the standard of music at liturgical ceremonies. I became the school organist for my last two years, a position rewarded with two slices of fried bread at breakfast, the reward also given to boys who had become prefects or sacristans. The real heroes, however, were the boys who made it onto the senior football team, which competed against teams from schools like St Mel's in Longford, Ballyfin in Laois, Belcamp College and St Joey's in Dublin. These were the nurseries that produced many of the players who went on to become the GAA stars of the sixties.

Maynooth

In my last year in Finian's I entered yet another competition, this time for a place in Maynooth, then the national seminary for the island of Ireland. Each diocese had a limited allocation of places, and there was far more demand than there were places available. I had been steeped in the hyper-Catholicism of the time, and had served as an altar boy from a young age, participating in many ceremonies including the blessing of a GAA pitch, a commemoration of the Battle of Benburb, Corpus Christi processions where the Army had a central role, weddings and funerals where we made some money and, unusually and incomprehensively to me at the time, the churching of women after childbirth.

My application for a place in Maynooth had, in retrospect, at least as much to do with entering and winning another competition as with a firm commitment to the priesthood.

To be ordained a priest in those days was a sought-after prize. Indeed, the class I joined in 1958 went on to become in 1965 part of the largest group ever ordained in Ireland, a grand total of 462.

After two years, however, I left Maynooth. It became clear that while I had no difficulty with the vows of poverty or obedience, lifelong chastity was not something I was prepared to commit to. Bizarrely, in Maynooth in those days we almost never saw women. There were no women on the staff, and the kitchen and dining room staff were all male. If your sister came to visit, you went to see her in the gate lodge where she would be well hidden from the other students. If on the other hand your brother came to visit, you could walk him around the magnificent grounds and introduce him to your friends. The theory apparently was that if we never saw women we would be less tempted to succumb to what were referred to as sins of the flesh.

Many of my contemporaries in Maynooth went on to senior positions in the Catholic Church in Ireland, including Cardinal Seán Brady, Archbishop Dermot Clifford and Bishop John Buckley. Bishop Michael Smith was a contemporary in Finian's, but he studied for the priesthood in Rome. There were also many contemporaries, like myself, who did not make it to ordination but with whom I subsequently became involved in a professional capacity. These included Minister for Foreign Affairs Michael O'Kennedy, and the Nobel prize-winning Northern Irish politician John Hume.

Public Service

Immediately after graduating from UCD in 1961, I joined the Department of Finance as an Administrative

Officer. Competition for these jobs was not as tough as it subsequently became. To attract suitable candidates, the salary was high (£780 a year) and we were guaranteed promotion to Assistant Principal within seven years. My immediate boss was the poet Tom Kinsella, and in the two years I spent there I had some interesting work, but I found the atmosphere somewhat monastic and the system very rigid. When positions were advertised in the then Department of External Affairs, I competed, yet again, and joined that Department in 1963. After a year I was appointed to the Embassy in Bonn, Federal Republic of Germany, spent five years there and somewhat to my surprise was appointed Consul General in Boston in 1969 at the age of 28.

Boston

The Northern Ireland Troubles were at an early stage, but the interest and involvement of Irish America was intense, with a strong inclination to support violence as the only way forward. Divisions at home within the Fianna Fáil government were such that we seldom got specific instructions on how to respond. Well-known friends of Ireland, some of whom had been involved in de Valera's visit to Boston in 1919, offered funds, and in one case guns, for the IRA. Publicly asking people to refrain from supporting the IRA did not endear us to Irish America, with whom there was already a divide because, on instructions from Dublin, we had in the sixties opposed any move that would make it easier for Irish people to emigrate to the US. A rational decision taken to discourage emigration because of the rapidly declining population had unintended consequences in the US.

Northern Ireland

In the summer of 1971 I was asked by the Department of Foreign Affairs temporarily to leave my post in Boston and spend a few weeks in Northern Ireland. The job there was to establish with as much hard evidence as possible the circumstances surrounding the introduction in Northern Ireland by the British of internment without trial. It involved a lot of travel around Northern Ireland, a place with which I had no previous familiarity, and establishing contact with reliable solicitors, doctors, community leaders and others who were in a position to give details of the torture and inhuman and degrading treatment to which many of the internees had been subjected. Because of the Maynooth background I was able to knock on almost any parochial house door and be sure of any introductions that I might need. I also reconnected with John Hume, who not only introduced me to others in the newly formed SDLP, but also to Unionist political leaders with whom from the beginning of his political career he had established working relationships. John became hugely influential in my professional and even in my personal life from then on.

Even though my assignment to Northern Ireland was intended to be short-term, I ended up working on that issue full time for the next seven years. Initially, the focus was on what became the *Ireland v the United Kingdom* successful case at the Commission and Court of Human Rights in Strasbourg, but my role was significantly expanded, particularly when Garret FitzGerald became Minister for Foreign Affairs in 1973. The focus became monitoring and assessing the political situation and reporting to the minister and the taoiseach. There had been an extraordinary gap in the Irish system up to the early seventies. No government department had the responsibility for following the Northern Ireland situation, despite the fact that it was the major issue both in domestic and foreign politics. In contrast, the British had quietly opened an unmarked presence in an upmarket suburb near Bangor and staffed it mainly with MI5/6 operatives, whose focus was partly political, but mainly security.

My seven-year stint included the Sunningdale conference in 1973 and the subsequent loyalist actions that brought it down. The whole period was dominated by bombs, bullets, death and destruction. I was lucky not to have been caught up in any of the bombings or shootings, and when I reflect on it now, particularly lucky not to have been kidnapped or worse by one or other of the nasty factions in both communities. I travelled throughout Northern Ireland, usually in a Dublin registered car, and frequently stayed at places like the Europa Hotel in Belfast, which were used by media people and their contacts from both the political and paramilitary ranks. I should have taken more security precautions, not least because I now know from British official papers that I was regarded by them as the head of Irish Government Intelligence in Northern Ireland, a description that would have made me a target for many.

It is difficult now to realise the threat that Northern Ireland posed to the stability of the Irish State in the seventies. The IRA campaign was at a vicious peak, north and south. Dublin and London took very different approaches, which could not be reconciled, and it is now a matter of public knowledge that a Harold Wilson-led government contemplated complete British withdrawal from Northern Ireland. Governments under the leadership of Jack Lynch and Liam Cosgrave managed a potentially catastrophic situation with courage and skill. There is little doubt that a unilateral British withdrawal would have led to chaos on the island of Ireland, and the creation of a Lebanese type of disintegration.

Back to the US

In 1978 I was appointed Ireland's Ambassador to the US by Jack Lynch's government. In making the appointment he gave me a very clear brief. First, I was to do everything possible to cut down support among Irish-Americans for the IRA, and second I was to assist the IDA in attracting US investment to Ireland. The first of these tasks took up most of my time. The IDA was very professionally run, and other than lending my presence at their functions and hosting dinners to which they would bring target investors, there was little I could add to their work. Together with my colleagues in the embassy in Washington and the consulates general in New York, Boston, Chicago and San Francisco we tried to get across the complex message of no violence and the need to bring all the people of Ireland together in agreement and with consent. It was not an easy message to convey, especially when faced with the simplistic 'Brits Out' slogan of the IRA supporters. The task was further complicated by the frequently insensitive and counterproductive British policies in Northern Ireland.

We were fortunate, however, to have a number of well-placed, powerful allies. We had the Four Horsemen – highly regarded Irish-American politicians, Tip O'Neill, Ted Kennedy, Hugh Carey and Daniel Moynihan – and they persuaded successive presidents, notably Carter, Reagan and Clinton, to become involved. With the help of these people it was possible to reduce popular US support for the IRA, but equally importantly they became key figures in supporting negotiations involving Dublin, London and Northern Ireland politicians, which eventually led to the peace process and the structures of government now in place in Belfast.

In 1981 I left Washington to become Secretary General of the Department of Foreign Affairs in Dublin – a post

I held for seven years under two Taoisigh: Haughey and FitzGerald, and three Foreign Ministers: Dooge, Collins and Barry. The highlight of that period was to be involved in the negotiation of the 1985 Anglo-Irish Agreement, which secured for Dublin for the first time an internationally recognized role in the running of Northern Ireland.

The Private Sector

In 1987 I resigned from the public sector, and since then my activities have been mainly in the private sector, with the exception of five years as Chancellor of the University of Limerick and Chairman of its Governing Authority. This was a part-time and unpaid position, but gave me an insight into academia and education as well as giving me a topic for discussion with my father in his last years. In a sense it brought me back to the family mainstream!

There are of course major differences between working in the private commercial sector and the public sector. The public sector necessarily takes account of the whole community and the national interest. The private commercial sector has the narrower function of looking after the interests of its stakeholders, with particular reference to making profit. I was fortunate that my first experience of commerce was with Tony Ryan, the inspirational aviation entrepreneur, and working with him and his very able team at GPA in Shannon was a great and generally positive experience. There was undoubtedly a thrill in negotiating and closing a deal, but it was a very different thrill to doing something in the public sector that was likely to have an impact, hopefully for the better, on the lives of a large number of people. When GPA was taken over by the US giant GE in 1994, I returned to the public sector to work with Taoiseach John Bruton until he lost the election in 1997. Since then I have worked as a non-executive director with a number of companies, private and public, in the financial sector in Ireland, the US and the UK. Recently I became a resident director of the European Bank for Reconstruction and Development in London. The bank is owned by over sixty governments, including the Irish government, and it functions in every sense like the major international banks, but has in addition a political mandate to foster transition towards open-market-oriented economies in former Communist countries and in the Arab Spring countries. I have been given a particular responsibility, inter alia, for Kosovo, a small country that was part of the former Yugoslavia. It is recently independent, and in many ways like Ireland in the twenties, struggling to get international recognition and to put its economy on a solid basis.

On reflection

It is not possible for most of us to set a road map early in life, which we then follow. I have been fortunate in the many positions that I was given, and I continue to enjoy working in my seventy-fourth year. I have been inspired and supported by many people along the way, including my parents, colleagues in Irish and other diplomatic services, very able colleagues in the GPA and elsewhere in the private commercial sector, and political figures such as John Hume, Jack Lynch, Liam Cosgrave, Garret FitzGerald, Tip O'Neill and Ted Kennedy. I have learned from all of them. But whatever I have done, I have, as Frank Sinatra sang, done it my way.

Marty Morrissey

Sports commentator and TV and radio presenter

As a child

I grew up in an extremely close-knit family; sometimes maybe a little too much so. I wasn't spoilt, that's for sure. I was an only child, as were my mother and father, so I have no aunts, uncles or first cousins. That dynamic fostered both dependence and independence in me.

Not having brothers or sisters meant that from an early age I had to go out and make friends. I didn't know any different, so it didn't bother me. But there was always the feeling that I was on my own, that the onus was on me to get out there and mix. This stood to me, as I made really good friends down the years and I am still in touch with every one of those.

As a kid, the only time I thought about my being an only child was Christmas; when Santa Claus arrived, I was kind of on my own. When visiting friends' houses over the holidays I'd see the fun they had with siblings, and I'd be conscious that I didn't have that at home. But I didn't miss out, as I always felt I belonged with their families as well as with my own. I was always included.

A vivid memory

As a kid I used to help my grandfather on the farm. Well, I thought I was helping, but I was probably more of a hindrance. I remember the 'trams' or 'cocks' of hay as they were called. We used ropes to pull them up on the back of the horse. Then my grandfather would put me up on top of the tram; the smell up there was amazing.

That is one of my most vivid memories. When I recall it, I feel transported back to that time and place. I clearly remember the sound of my grandfather's voice, the horse's hooves on the ground and how everything felt, looked and smelled.

I feel very close to nature. I went out for a cycle the other day and really enjoyed the fact that the bees were buzzing around me, the birds were singing and there was a great smell of the countryside.

Rural Ireland

When I was growing up in Quilty, County Clare, we had a pub. That was a very sociable environment in which to be raised. Rural Ireland has changed hugely since then. It has been desolated. You don't actually notice when you are living in the cities how hard the recession has hit, but when you are down in the country it's very apparent. Every night when you go out in Dublin or Cork, you see crowds. That is not the case in rural Ireland or even in the major towns. The over-forties very rarely go out socialising. They can't afford to. And where is there for them to go? Once you go past 25 or 30, the nightclub scene is over. They can go to pubs, but the pub business has been badly affected.

When we had the pub, it was the epicentre of the village and the parish. Before we bought it, it was a dance hall, so you can imagine what it was like – a big barn. It was always mobbed in July and August. Crowds came in their droves to hear The Bannermen and the The Kilfenora Céilí Band. They would come early and stay late. The men would get so hot from the set-dancing, jiving and waltzing that they'd bring a change of shirt. I was one of them. I never drank, but I would dance till my shirt needed changing, then dance some more. It was crazy and wonderful stuff.

I am a countryman at heart. I enjoy the values of rural life, but I also enjoy urban luxuries like the twenty-four-hour shop and the late-night cinema.

Fan mail

Most weeks I get a letter or two ... or three. Most are male sports fans who want to give their view on a game or controversy. To be honest, I get a few letters from females as well. I don't know who they are. Some send photographs. I never reply. I'm not sure why they contact me, but I think they're attracted by the banter and sense of fun – it certainly isn't my body or face that interests them! I think most people go for good personality; someone who makes them laugh. Most of the letters are normally quite complimentary, thankfully, and want to discuss some recent controversy.

The power of the microphone

Given the job I have, I'm acutely aware of the power of the microphone. I feel honoured to be given that power, and when I am, I'm conscious that it must be used in a fair and equitable way. Everyone I mention on air has a family; people who love them. So whenever it's necessary to level criticism, I try to do so fairly.

Fame

So many are searching for fame. But fame is a whimsical thing – not something to be pursued for itself. To achieve something meaningful, you have to love it. You have to be in it for the marathon, not just for the 100 metres. You really have to want it; to be really passionate about it.

Anonymity

At this stage, nowhere in Ireland offers me anonymity. That doesn't bother me too much; people are very kind and mannerly. Usually, the only time I enjoy total privacy is when I'm abroad. Even then, I am sometimes recognised. This happened a few years ago when I was walking around Cardiff with my then colleague and now RTÉ Sport boss Ryle Nugent. We were near Cardiff Arms Park, walking down the street after a Six Nations Wales v. England game, on which he had commentated. He was slagging me that at least we could have a bit of grub together in peace with nobody asking me for a photo or who would win the All Ireland! Almost on cue, a group of lads from Longford roared from across the road: 'Jaysus, Marty, how's it going?' They started singing: 'Marty, we love you'. They were on a stag weekend in Wales. Ryle rolled his eyes to heaven. He couldn't believe it because these were all GAA lads at a Wales v. England match! We laughed at that.

Nowadays, with social media, you really have no privacy at all. Within minutes of being somewhere I read about it on Twitter ... that can be both laughable and very annoying!

Behind it all

The general public has been very good to me, excellent in fact. I can't think of a time when someone has been outright rude. That said, I would never go into a pub on my own – ever – not even to meet friends, if doing that meant I'd have to walk through the pub on my own to reach them. This is not because people heckle me; they don't. But I wouldn't be the bravest of the brave in a situation like that. I give the image that I am, but I'm not. Behind it all I'm a bit shy, and some might be surprised to learn that I am not in Copper Face Jacks (nightclub) every Friday night. I am not a clubber at all. Although, they very kindly sent me a Gold Member Card recently!

Criticism

Criticism is part of the business I went into. It's as common to get knocks as praise. Sometimes broadcasters have habits or phrases they're not aware of. Being made aware of that is helpful, constructive and positive; the trick is to accept that and take it on board.

Something I struggle with

Time management. But I am improving ... slowly.

Something I dread

I go for a full medical check-up every year. I know I'm fine, health-wise, but when waiting for the results I feel apprehensive, as I remember the many I've met who thought the same thing when they were anything but. I think we all fear bad news. It's only natural, and it's the main reason why I wouldn't go to a fortune teller. I have an open mind about those who claim to be able to tell the future. I don't doubt that some have the talent to 'see'. I never knock what I don't know or what I don't understand.

The other side

The closest thing I have ever experienced to the 'other side' is something that happened two or three weeks after my father died. I had a dream in which he and my mother's mother were in my sitting room at home in West Clare. When I asked what they were doing there, the reply was that they just came to say hello and to let me know they were happy. That was an unusual experience for me, not just because of the content but because I tend not to remember very many dreams.

I felt reassured by that 'experience'. I felt the same when, shortly after my father died, I got the scent of roses in the house – and this on a day when there were no flowers nearby. In response, I said to myself: where the hell did that come from?

I am open to suggestion. I like to believe in an afterlife, and I do believe there is one. I don't believe we can be such vibrant and energetic beings, then disappear after death. The energy has to go somewhere, and the essence of the person has to be somewhere. Where that is, I don't know. Some call it heaven. Maybe that's what it is. I imagine it's a place of total happiness, so 'heaven' is a good word for it.

What I fear

I wouldn't be a fan of death. In fact, as I get older, I think I probably fear it. It's the notion of whatever we have inside us stopping, the not knowing what that is like. I'm in no rush to that destination, in no rush to find out. I love life and would not want to die. I feel frightened by the thought of serious sickness and impending death. I think I could deal with anything other than that.

Faith and prayer

While I am a Catholic, I would consider myself a Christian first. That said, I wouldn't be over-religious. I have been disappointed by some of the things that happened in the Catholic Church. I didn't know Bishop Eamon Casey, but I always appreciated his kindness and good work. In falling in love with a woman he did what comes naturally to men. I thought he was badly treated when news of that relationship emerged. I know he probably did wrong, but I always thought he was a good man. And he did put his hand up. It was a difficult problem for the Church, but I think it was handled badly in so far as the response was to hide him away, move him to somewhere else and make him somebody else's problem.

When I go home I cycle a mile and a half to the local church in Mullagh or Quilty. I like to pray there when there is nobody else around. My dad is buried in the graveyard at the back of Mullagh Church, and it's a beautiful, peaceful place with panoramic views that stretch from nearby Mutton Island along the coast to faraway Aran Islands on the horizon to Mount Callan to the east. I visit him there because that is where we put him to rest ten years ago this Christmas. I don't think of him as being buried, because I don't like the word 'buried'. I prefer to think of him as he was, not only because of my fear of death but because that gives me some sort of solace.

When I pray I thank God for my life, for giving me the chance to do what I do, for giving me so much. I also pray that I never do any harm to anybody. That's important to me, as is not talking ill of others. I try not to do that.

What fills me with hope

The goodness of people. Their determination to overcome obstacles. The human spirit. The courage of some to deal with the breaks of life that I would find difficult.

What fills me with despair

Bureaucracy. Negative thinking. The political correctness that we are now so obsessed with. Not being allowed to say the things I want to say, because if I did there would be consternation. The refusal – particularly in broadcasting – to allow individuals to freely express themselves. Those who work in the public domain can be muted a little bit, and that's the way it should be when it ensures that comment remains neutral and balanced. One mistake, and it's on YouTube within minutes. In my work I have to be 'extra careful' about what I say, all the time. Sometimes I want to rant a little to get something off my chest. When that involves fair comment on sensitive issues, it can be frustrating when it's not allowed.

Greatest passion

Family and friends. After that, I would be passionate about West Clare. Growing up, there was so much I loved about the county, but mostly I felt drawn to the people and their passions, be it sport, music or pride of place. Even though I lived in New York as a kid, and only came to Ireland for holidays, I always felt that Clare was my home; that that was where I belonged.

Because West Clare's my home turf, and a naturally beautiful place with exceptionally lovely people, I have always felt that the roads should have been improved there and that those that could should have given more industry to the region. It has always annoyed me that public representatives didn't do more for the area. The strip from Killimer to the Burren is a little goldmine. It can be somewhat desolate, wild and raw, but that's the splendour of it. On Christmas Day I walk in those places and it's simply fantastic.

When travelling to Castlebar to cover matches, I've seen what became known as the 'the Padraig Flynn roads' that brought tourists to that town, and helped to develop the area. You could only admire the man for having achieved that. I think the Wild Atlantic Way as a marketing strategy is both a good and a beneficial one with huge potential, while the people in Shannon Airport are doing a wonderful job in re-establishing Shannon as a major hub.

Technology

Mobile phones are deadly. People are obsessed with taking photographs. Some take mine without first asking if that's okay. They're the smart alecs, and they're in the minority. Most ask first, and when they do I always say it's no problem.

Like many, I'm obsessed with my phone. It's a desperate way to be. I'm not on Facebook any more, although I think somebody may have opened a page for me. I am on Twitter, and have almost 35,000 followers, which isn't bad considering that I don't regularly tweet. I have to be on social media in some shape or form because of my job. I have to know what's happening, and Twitter plays an important role in that. The people I work with say I'm so attached to my phone that when I die it'll go with me to the grave. I like that idea.

Advice for a young person

Keep at it. Never say never. And smile ... it is your greatest asset.

Turning points

When I was 10 years of age, almost 11 and living in New York, my father bought a pub in Quilty. If he hadn't done that, we might never have come home to Ireland. I was the reason why we came home. My parents didn't want me to go to an American high school.

Quitting medical studies after three years changed the path of my life. I left to do a science degree with the intention of returning to medical studies after that. But after I did the science degree, I decided to do the H.Dip. instead.

Given that the next turning point was leaving that teaching job after three years and moving into broadcasting, it may be high time for another.

RTÉ

RTÉ was where I wanted to be. I did an awful lot of travelling as a child, back and forth from New York to Ireland, from the age of two weeks to eleven years. When we came home and Dad bought the pub, we put down roots. For a while, I didn't want to return to travelling again, especially as I was so into sport, especially with my club, Kilmurry Ibrickane, which I love and feel very proud of. Thanks to RTÉ I have worked at three Olympics: Athens, Beijing and London, and commentated on

RTÉ Radio 1 as Katie Taylor won her gold medal in London. It was an incredible, joyful and proud experience.

Time for change

A bit like Fianna Fáil, I have done a lot but I have a lot more to do. This is probably the longest time I have spent at a job – over twenty years – and I think the time is coming for me to do other things. If that means moving from TV to radio, or going to Africa for a year or six months, I might do that. I would be open to change.

I thought ten years ago that maybe I would like to work abroad in another network for a while – even if only in wintertime – but family commitments kept me in Ireland. I don't regret that. It was a choice I freely made. And to be honest I love RTÉ – it's a good place to work, with great people.

Over the years I have often felt that I should move, but each time I suppressed it as I was enjoying the journey I was on. Even so, the desire for change niggles, so much so that I now know that I really need to move forward again in my career; that I can no longer suppress that need. I need new challenges, whether that's in TV or radio, in Ireland or abroad. Who knows? Time will tell.

If I had to go back in time

I would like to be 20, 21 or 22 again; finished college and playing inter-county football and hurling. The facilities today are so much better than they were in my time. We used to tog out in the back of a car, throw the boots into the boot and run down through a meadow and onto the pitch. The whole culture of sport is so much better now than it was in my time.

When I was young I played, and I wasn't bad. I played inter-county football for Clare minors, under-21s, and I was on the Clare senior football team for a while. I played hurling and football with St Flannan's, and I played for UCC.

Would I do it all again? I would. And I probably wouldn't do anything differently. I figured that if I was going to get into RTÉ it would have to be through sport – because that was the subject about which I was most passionate. That happened, and I spent decades there. Over the years, RTÉ management have been very good to me, but I might still be knocking down the door … again!

Dissatisfaction

When I first graduated, I went teaching biology and maths in a secondary school in Spanish Point in West Clare for three years. At the time, Paddy Hillary, the former president of Ireland, was our next-door neighbour. While I loved the academic side of it, and the students were fantastic, I knew I didn't want to be doing that at the age of 65.

I trained football teams after school. We won a Munster Colleges title, and with my own club won Under-16 and Minor Championships. That gave me a buzz. Each of my career changes and pathways have all happened by accident really. I applied to RTÉ, and was rejected many times. Had that organisation offered me work from the outset, I might have wanted it less. But that didn't happen. The response was repeatedly no, and the more they rejected me, the more I wanted it and the more I pursued it.

Greatest challenge

I literally started on the back of a tractor and trailer in West Clare, doing my first ever commentary for a video for my club, and ended up commentating on All-Ireland Finals in Croke Park, gold medal victories at Olympic games and international sports events in Australia, Russia and the USA.

So ... getting to where I am in my career today was the greatest challenge I have faced. What got me there was a number of things, but pull or influence wasn't amongst them. I had no pull. But people in RTÉ have been exceptionally good to me, and had faith in me. For years I wrote and made phone calls to RTÉ in Dublin. Determination, persistence and passion for the job got me into something I loved.

Something I might have been

An airline pilot. I got a gift of flying lessons a few years ago, and I've a friend who has a flight simulator, but I have yet to give it a go. I am fascinated by planes and aviation in general. My late father was a travel agent in New York, and I spent a lot of time with him in Kennedy or LaGuardia Airport seeing clients off on their various journeys.

Who I am at the core of me

I don't like hypocrisy. I live my life trying to be as good as I possibly can. Many believe I get up to more devilment than I do, and I am happy to let them believe that if they choose, but the reality is that I lead a relatively quiet, but enjoyable, life. Loyalty is very important to me. I give total loyalty to my friends, but I expect it back as well!

I am a kind person. I hate selfishness and meanness with a passion. I really hate it when people are mean to others. Being fairly sensitive, the last thing on my agenda, ever, would be to hurt anybody, whether that might be someone I care deeply about or a total stranger.

Because I would be aware of the sensitivities of others and their apprehensions, I try to avoid passing flippant comments. If somebody is critical of me, or a bit mean in some way, I would be a little bit upset by it. I'm not talking about being slagged – I don't mind that. But if it goes deeper, I would be a little hurt by it.

I'm meticulous in terms of what I want to do. If I'm doing a minute-and-a-half news report for RTÉ, I want it to be the best minute-and-a-half it can be. I'm someone who likes to be given scope to experiment. That suits me. I thrive on it. I appreciate what I have, my colleagues and friends.

As for my greatest strengths, I'd say it's my sense of fair play, my temperament – I'm very seldom in a bad mood – and my being a glass-half-full rather than half-empty type of guy.

What life has taught me

That life is good. That the gift of life is one of the great mysteries and one of the greatest gifts of all. That life is tough for a lot of people. That some are continually hit with health or personal tragedies. That others are born in the wrong place at the wrong time. It has taught me to thank God for my life and my health, and to be glad to be Irish. The beauty of us Irish is our great sense of fun, and our tendency to live life to the full.

Life is sometimes not fair, but I do believe that, no matter what, if you have a dream you should follow it. I have had to work at everything. Nothing came easily for me. You have got to realise and accept that you are going to get knocks. Sometimes you won't get the gig you want, and sometimes you get what you want and others are disappointed. It's life. You have to accept the complexities of life, take it for what it is and ignore the negativity. You have to be positive and live life to the maximum. I have been lucky enough to find myself in a career that I really love.

I thank God for that. But on the journey there, every time I got a rejection I went at it again. I hope I never crossed the line and became pushy. But you can never give up. Quitting is not an option. Getting to where you want to be in life is never an easy ride. But hey, if it were easy then everybody would be doing it, and that's what makes each and every one of us special and unique and our lives so compellingly different and exclusive to us. Now isn't that amazing when you think about it?!

Rebecca de Havalland

Model-agent and TV presenter, first transgender in Ireland to have a full sex change

A female, modern-day Oscar Wilde

In some ways I feel like a female, modern day Oscar Wilde. While he was imprisoned for being gay, I was the first person in Ireland to have a sex change. At the time I didn't realise how huge that was or the impact it would have in this country. It still has an impact today. I've been a role model for the many young people here who have gone on to have hormone replacement therapy. I'm really glad to be getting a taste of that legacy while I'm still around.

On being Eamon, Ross and Rebecca

I think Eamon (the person I was when I was born, and who I was growing up) and Rebecca (the woman I am now) are two people in one. Eamon and I are the same person, but Ross was someone else. He thought he could do it all. He never cared much for anyone or anything. If I met him now,

I wouldn't have anything to do with him. When I stopped being Ross and became Rebecca, I got all the qualities that Eamon had. That was a gift.

I had some really good times as Ross. I hung out with the Rolling Stones. I worked on the Eurovision Song Contests. Even in my early days as Rebecca, I was working in Madame JoJo's in London. I think that's because, back in the early Rebecca days, there was still a huge injection of Ross in me.

Ross was hugely indestructible. As Ross, there were so many high highs and low lows. I wouldn't want to be him again.

Rejecting the Catholic hierarchy

My passion is Our Lady. I adore her. I do. I get people who tell me I'm 'so Catholic,' but I'm not Catholic at all. While that might sound confusing, it's not. The way I see it, Mary and Jesus lived on this earth. He believed he was the Son of God. She watched him get crucified.

If I were him, and if someone were coming after me with nails and telling me I still had time to change my mind about being King of the Jews, then maybe I'd say 'Well, hang on a second, maybe I got it wrong.' He didn't do that. He believed he was the Son of God.

Mary watched her son die on a cross. For me, that means she has compassion. I see her as a woman who lost her son, her child. I see her as a woman who had a child who was ridiculed.

I don't believe there should be any hierarchy between me and Mary or Jesus. I don't need any hierarchy. We are told that when we pray our prayers go straight to God. So why would I need to speak to some man, who might be a paedophile, to communicate with Mary and Jesus? I don't. I've been abused by men in religious orders.

Until very recently I'd have called myself a Catholic, mainly because it was a convenient label. I don't do that any more. Now I call myself a Christian, and I'm a good Christian. I don't care whether people are Muslim or whatever. No matter what religion we are, we all know what's right and we all know what's wrong. Labels don't matter.

Why I had my sex-change operation

I had to do what I did to be true to me. I tried to put right the wrong. End of.

My greatest achievement

Having my operation was my greatest achievement because I had it against all odds. I didn't even have the money to pay for it. It cost seven thousand pounds back in 1989. But I got there in the end.

Priests and hell on earth

I went to see a priest in London. It was during one of my pretty dark days, a day of drinking, not long after I had my sex-change operation. I had been thinking about the whole Catholic thing, and I felt sure that, given all I'd done, I'd be doomed in the afterlife. When the priest heard my story, he said, 'You'll go straight to hell.' After that I went out and drank some more.

A few years later I went to another priest. He said: 'No. You won't go to hell. God loves you for you. He loves your soul. It's not about your body.' So I kind of went with his version. Looking back, I think that the second priest was a bit better than the first one. When the first priest said I'd go straight to hell, I wanted to say, 'I'm already there.' People like me who have been in the throes of addiction have already been to hell.

Women in business

It's tougher to be a success in business when you're a woman than when you're a man. When I was a 'bloke' – for the want of a better word – to the outside world, it didn't matter whether I was gay or straight or whatever. I was perceived as being male, and that's how I was treated in business.

The minute I became a woman I had a tougher job on my hands. The things I have to fight trebly hard for in business were handed to me on a plate twenty-five odd years ago when I was a man. When I go into a business meeting with a group of men I have a hard task, but I have difficulties with women too. Now that I'm a woman I find that if other women perceive me to be prettier, taller or blonder than they are – and I probably am most of the time – then I'm a threat to them. I feel that.

I've been 100 per cent female for twenty-five years, and I would stick by any woman and give her a chance. I love powerful women, but I don't understand the ones who, on becoming powerful, behave like men. Women are supposed to be different to men. Sometimes they get their power from that difference; from being sexy and female. I know about this, having gone from being a man to being a woman.

The jealousy of women

I thank God that one thing I've never been, as either a man or a woman, is jealous. I don't like people who look me up and down. If I see a beautiful woman or man, I will have huge admiration for them and I will be the first to say, 'You look amazing.'

But then someone will see me and they will look me up and down and resent me. And when that happens, I tell myself I'm fighting a losing battle.

My secret passion

The one thing that I've always wanted to do – my secret passion – is TV presenting. I've done a little of it, but my gender thing is holding me back. There still isn't a 100 per cent open door for me in TV presenting.

If my book became a movie

My book, *His Name is Rebecca*, is up for movie rights. If it becomes a movie, it will be amazing. Some say Madonna could play me, but I don't think so. I think that while Daryl Hannah could do it, Kim Cattrall would be perfect. She is exactly the same age as I am, and she would be wonderful in the fun parts. I'd like her to play me as I am now.

Euthanasia

If they start putting nappies on me, then let somebody shoot me, please. I couldn't live that way.

Home, pets and leaving the club scene behind

For years I couldn't stand silence and I couldn't stand my own company, but now it's the other way around. Now there are times when I want to kick myself for staying at home so much, and I ask myself: 'Why aren't you down in Lillie's Bordello every night? Why aren't you here? Why aren't you there?' And then I say to myself: 'It's because you've done all that, love. You're 55 years of age.'

When I'm out, I can't wait to go home in the evenings to my two little doggies. I've got a shih-tzu and a Tibetan spaniel cross. They're named Lulu Belle and Harvey. Harvey is Lulu Belle's son. They absolutely adore me and I adore them.

Acceptance

I used to have a chip on my shoulder, but I'm over it now. I had it because people put it there. I got it because people wouldn't accept me as me. It didn't matter what I did. They just wouldn't accept me, and most of my friends were no different.

In Ireland I spend a lot of my time with younger people who know me as 'Rebecca'; people who never knew me as 'Ross' or as 'Eamon'. They accept me for who I am now.

Very few Irish people stood by me through everything, but there are some. One is Mary McEvoy, the actress. Another is a Granard woman who knew me when I was growing up. She's probably only ten years older than I am, but she looked after me as a kid, and as the years passed I could go to her door as Eamon, Ross or whoever I was at the time, and she'd welcome me in. She is a humble countrywoman, yet she would be seen anywhere with me, no matter what was going on in my life.

Love

While I've been married three times, I never took husbands; I took prisoners. I've had near hits with love, or with what I've thought was love. I may have thought I loved or felt I loved in the past, but I don't think I ever really loved anyone. I fell in lust lots of times. I've had plenty of train crashes of relationships in my time, but I still hope there's light at the end of the tunnel, and that that light won't be a truck coming towards me. I think I will find love. I think it will happen for me.

Romance

There are more fingerprints on my arse than there are in Scotland Yard, but for all the subtle whoring and the rest of it, I haven't slept with anyone in over six years. Some will say: 'That's an awful bleeding waste of a lovely body like that,' and it's not good, I know. I don't think it's because I'm protecting myself, but it could be because I'm afraid. I don't know. Either way, it's really weird living this way, given all I've been through.

I've seen things that nobody should see. I've seen murder. I woke up with a dead man beside me in my bed. I've seen people die. One of my friends died in my lap. Through all of that, I found sex to be a form of love, and it got me through the tough times.

But when I got clean and sober, sex went out the window for me, and it hasn't come back. I'm not holding back. Once or twice I've seen a guy and I felt my heart flutter a bit, so there is still something there. But I don't think Irish men are ready for transgender women – not publicly, anyway – and I'm not going to have a relationship with someone who won't be seen out in public with me; someone who wants the whole thing hidden.

Why I should be the toughest bitch this side of Oklahoma

I can be defensive. Because of that people often say to me, 'Gosh you're very sensitive.' That really angers me, and I say to myself: Well, isn't sensitivity a great trait to have, given all I've been through? I could be as hard as nails.

That's just one of the things I love about my journey – whatever it has changed, it has changed for the better. It hasn't hardened me, and I find that remarkable because really at this stage I should be the toughest bitch this side of Oklahoma, and I'm not. Silly little things can still upset me.

My days at Terenure College

I never got bullied. Never. When I went to Terenure College, a Dublin rugby school, I was the ringleader in the classroom. I've friends on Facebook, old schoolmates of mine, who say to me: 'Just as well you didn't look back then the way you do right now, or I'd have ridden the ass off you.' And I think that's great. I'd like to go back there for a school reunion. Can you imagine what that would be like? I could say: 'Hi, boys. Look what you missed out on when you were behind the sheds smoking.'

A daft question I've been asked

I've been asked what it's like being a woman. To that I reply: 'I don't know. That's just what I am.'

Sure, when I was a man I got married; then did the gay thing. But I did all that because that was all that was available to me at that time. My identity isn't complicated to me: I'm Rebecca.

Why I'm quite homophobic

I hate obviously gay people. When I was going through my gender stuff, the people who gave me the hardest time were gay. Because of that, and because I don't really 'get' them, I have only a tiny tolerance for gay people. The ones I know are very fake, and they treat women like some kind of fashion accessory. I've lots of gay friends, but I wouldn't trust them as far as I'd throw them and I wouldn't depend on them either. They're very fickle. I've had first-hand experience of all levels of gay people. I'm actually quite homophobic really.

Prejudice

There were many times in my life when people had good reason for not wanting to know me. When I used to hit the bottle or take drugs they had an excuse for wanting to have nothing to do with me. In many ways, nothing much has changed. While I'm doing nothing wrong now, there are some who still want nothing to do with me. In their eyes I'm still doing wrong.

There are others who are prejudiced against me. But that's fine with me, as the same people will be prejudiced against lots of people. I've learned in recovery that that's their stuff, not mine.

Another daft question I've been asked

I've been asked: 'If a man fancies you, what does that make him?' I replied: 'It makes him a man who fancies a woman.' I'm no freak, I'm just a woman. Strip me naked and I'm like any other woman. You won't see any difference. Search inside and there is no womb, but that's the only thing missing. We're moving forward here in Ireland. We're on our way, but we've a long way to go.

Why I'm here

I feel we are all here for a reason. I think mine is to be a pioneer, an ambassador for my gender, the Coco Chanel of my gender.

Finally feeling comfortable in my skin

It's only in the last couple of years that I have felt really comfortable in my skin. I went through an anorexic stage in the early 'Rebecca years' when I was five-and-a-half stone. People would stare at me. Whether that was because of my gender or because I looked so terribly ill, I don't know. But people don't stare at me any more, and I don't miss the attention.

For a long time my life was on stage, but it's not any more. When I visit Granard, my hometown in County Longford, I'm one of the locals. I'd nearly have to walk up the town topless to get attention now.

I was always a bigmouth, but behind all that was this really insecure little person. That has changed too. I see my growth when I stand up in Trinity College and speak from the heart in front of 250 people.

I feel insecure sometimes in a superficial way. The beauty business is all about image, so there have been days as a model agency boss when I have felt a little insecure. As a woman, I'm not insecure.

My time as a junkie

What I remember most was that I had the most haunting highs on drugs. I also had dead-eye. My eyes are hazely brown, but they were black back then. I remember looking in the mirror and there was nothing looking back at me; just dead eyes staring.

Survival was paramount in those days. Life was a jungle. I could have a bad day or a weak day, but I still had to watch my back 24/7. That's how tough it was. Any sign of weakness and I was dead. The weak got preyed on. There were loads of times when I should have been dead, loads of times I shouldn't have survived, but I did.

I felt I was minded by Our Lady. I had rows with her. I fell out with her. I treated her like my mother, because my mother wasn't really like a mother to me. She really wasn't, God love her.

An incurable romantic

I am an incurable romantic. I cry at the soppiest movies. I'd love to fall in love and meet the man of my dreams – someone who will sweep me off my feet. But I'm a realist too, and if I was getting into a relationship now I'd want it to be with someone who is financially secure. At my age I've no interest in finding myself a toy boy. I'd want someone who leads a comfortable life; someone who owns his house.

What scares me

I don't own my house, and that scares me. I'm still renting because I was robbed of twenty-three years of my life in the most crucial years when I should have been earning enough money to buy property. Hopefully I will buy myself a house one day, and when I do that will be one of the big achievements in my life.

Why I'm no longer a chameleon

My first husband used to call me 'the chameleon', and I was a bit like that. There was a time when I'd constantly have to change my outfits, my looks and my hair. Those days are gone. Now

I'm happy with where I am in my life. I get Botox injections sometimes, but other than that I'm happy with who I am.

What life has taught me

Never take anything for granted, ever. Be thankful. You never know when anything might change. The phrase 'This too shall pass' applies to the good as well as the bad in life, so we need to savour what we have.

Another lesson is to learn from your mistakes. It's okay to make mistakes. We all do. But it's not okay to repeat them. I'm no angel. I've made mistakes, but I have learnt hugely from them.

If I had my time over again, I'd probably still put sleeping tablets in the coffee of one of my husbands. I used to do that so I could go out on the town without getting grief from him. To be honest, if I had to do it all over again, I'd probably put more in.

The voice in my head

All my life I've had this voice in my head that tells me I'm not good enough. I still have it. When I hear that voice, I fight harder to be better.

Power

People made decisions for me – decisions over which I had no power. I had no choice when I was put into boarding school. No choice when I was raped there. Later, I had no say when what I had to do to myself in order to change from Eamon to Rebecca became national news.

There was a very small part of my life when I did have a say, and look at how that turned out. If I didn't have surgery to change gender, I'd have killed myself. The fact that I've had a fair few misses tells me I'm meant to be here; that I'm here for a reason. So, if only one person gets something good out of learning about my life, that's good enough for me.

Reincarnation and how my past life came back and bit me on the arse

In my next life I'm coming back as Rebecca, bigger, stronger and better. I think I'm coming to the end of my journeys on earth. I imagine my next life will be my last. When you look at the people who seem so privileged, I think they are the ones who are being rewarded in their final life here.

Someone who read my cards told me that people are vessels, and that before we are born our spirits choose to live in us so it can grow through that experience. I think that might be true. I don't believe that every time a person dies another soul is released. If that were the case, there'd be a lot of souls out there on the day of judgement.

But I do believe there's something beyond us. I'd like to think it's a parallel life to the one we're living in now. I also believe in karma. I've no doubt at all that some things I did in my past have come back and bitten me on the arse.

I believe our souls are the same gender as our bodies. I think I did something pretty bad in my last life, but it wasn't bad enough, and that's why I was put into the wrong body, then managed to get out of it. In my view, that was karma.

Who I am at the core of me

At the core of me I'm an entrepreneurial, sensitive, complicated survivor. I don't see myself as brave. I don't see the brave because in making the choices I have, I only put right what was wrong.

What surprises me

What most surprises me is how insecure, two-faced and insincere people can be. Most haven't been through anything really tough in their lives, and yet they have the capacity to be these truly horrible, judgemental human beings. When I meet people like that, I feel both surprised and angry. And then I say to myself: how dare they be like that to me?

Deepest sources of solace

In times of trouble I go to Our Lady. I really do. I still don't trust any human being enough to go to them for help. So I talk to Our Lady and, out of respect for her, I pray to her every now and then, as I feel I should do that. Most of the time I'm probably more freaky about it than that, in so far as I usually speak to her as if she is my mother. If I feel she is not listening to me, I have rows with her and I don't talk to her for ages.

What is lovely for me is the knowledge that she is always there. When I tell friends about this they say: 'Ah, there is no such thing as that.' I disagree. We all have a spirit. Our Lady has one too, because she once lived on this earth. I definitely feel my spirit and hers connect.

Guardian angels

I've been told my grandmother is my guardian angel, but I don't believe that. If she is, then who was my guardian angel before my granny died? I believe in angels, but some of the stuff I hear about them is, to me, a little bit airy-fairy, so they're not something I think about often.

Best advice I ever got

My granny used to say: 'Keep your friends close and your enemies closer.' I wish I'd taken heed of that piece of advice more often.

'Always keep your cards close to your chest' sounds a little calculating, but it is probably good advice. Even so, I've never been one to do that – I continue to wear my heart on my sleeve.

As for 'good things happen to good people' – well, that's bollocks. You only have to take a look at what happened to me. But again, for me, that goes back to the reincarnation belief. Maybe we better ourselves in every life.

What some people don't realise is that we all need to go through shit to appreciate the good times. I'm aware that what I have experienced is nothing compared with what the people who were gassed in Auschwitz went through, and that I have it good compared with the mothers who, in places like Mombasa, wait with their kids for the dump truck to arrive so they can get something to eat.

Snippets from my bucket list

If I won the Lotto I'd live in Manhattan. I went there recently for the first time, and it was amazing. I am convinced that in another life I was a native New Yorker. I love it there. It's my favourite city in the world. If I get rich, I will move there. I will come back to Dublin for visits, and when I do I will stay in the Westbury, the Shelbourne and the Four Seasons.

I'd also love to stay around long enough to really get to know my granddaughter and to be there for her. I'd love to see her go through her schooling and getting married. I'd love to be someone in her life who she absolutely adores.

Obviously, it would be absolutely lovely to find love. But the New York thing is huge for me.

Some people believe I'm a bitch

I've been a people-pleaser down the years. I still can be, but I'm less that way now than I used to be. I'm beginning to see now that it's okay if some people believe I'm a bitch.

A prima donna and a perfectionist

I can be a prima donna. I think I always will be. I can take advice, but I can never be told what to do.

With that, I'm a perfectionist – that's the one thing about me I'd love to change. For me it means that when something is not right, it's horrible. I'm even a perfectionist about myself. Someone might say to me, 'You look amazing,' and I'll reply, 'What are you on about?' I'm too conscious of my imperfections.

Trust, and why it's not something I do

People often say to me: 'You obviously don't trust people, but one day you will.' I don't trust. Life has taught me that it's best not to have any real expectations.

Visualising

I have tried visualising in my mind the life I want, to see if that would help it to materialise for me. I don't know if that works for anyone, but it sure hasn't worked for me.

Shedding my Teflon casing and getting comfortable with pain

When I came back to live in Ireland I felt as though I were made of Teflon. Things were just bouncing off me. I'd come to a stage where I don't think anything else could have hurt me or caused me pain. Then I wrote my book and I thawed out, and the Teflon casing seemed to disappear. But then I became this really vulnerable person for a year or so. You couldn't say 'boo' to me or I'd nearly cry.

Looking back on the tough times when I used to hang around the streets of Soho, I think that that life somehow gave me an anaesthetic – something that protected me from feeling all the pain.

Sometimes you take on so much pain that it doesn't feel like pain any more. You kind of get comfortable with it. You're in that zone. So if somebody came and cut off your ear, you'd just go, 'Ah, well. I have another ear.'

When I think back, it's hard for me to believe that one person could have gone through all I did and survived.

Geminis, and why TV is my new dancing

Geminis are supposed to be two people in one. And I have been. I love being a Gemini because once you say that's your star sign, everyone replies, 'Oh no!' They think you're a schizoid. I love that reaction.

Geminis have dual personalities, and I definitely have dual personalities – but then again, I think most people do. When I want to chill out, I watch TV with my dogs. The minute I do, my worries are gone. Dancing used to do that for me, so did music, then it was television. That's the side of me that people see now. But there's a wild child in me. She was put away while I was preoccupied with running my model agency business and the goal of making enough money to be able to afford to have staff, sit back on my laurels, book hotels and do whatever I want.

In recent years my business began to threaten a lot of people, and the bitching was on. I liked that. It meant I was rattling cages, and that meant I had my mojo back. My wild child hasn't made an appearance for quite a while. The fact that I have been battling illness for the past year has been a factor in that.

Blame

I've done blame. I've blamed God. I've blamed my mother and father. I've blamed myself big time, and when I did, I've asked myself why I didn't just go on living as a male, why I didn't make the most of the body I'd been given. Then I'd remind myself that while I could have done all that for everyone else, I'd never have found me.

Fighting for my life

For a long time I was scared of going back to London for a visit. Life was so tough for me there that it wasn't until I had moved back home to Ireland that I began to feel like a human being again. I'm so glad I came home when I did, because if I didn't I honestly don't think I'd be alive today.

I had no way of knowing that what was on the horizon for me was a battle with blood cancer that could only be fought in London. Last year I had to conquer my fear of going back there, because the medical treatment I need is not available in Ireland.

Since I became ill I have often thought that, given the number of times I tried to kill myself, it's ironic that I am now fighting for my life. I now realise that I should never have feared returning to London, because what I found when I returned were some of the most amazing best friends I have ever had in the world; friends I left behind when I moved home to Ireland; friends who are still here for me.

Becoming so ill was another blow for me, but I feel strangely calm about it. Being so unwell has made me feel surreal, as if I'm on a parallel planet. There's a part of me that feels physically tired, emotionally worn out and fed up with fighting. But then something comes along, kicks me in the ass and tells me: hold on, you've a long way to go yet.

Acknowledgements

For their great support, heartfelt thanks to Marie Browne, Toni and Victor Chaltiel, Mary Walsh, Sarah Berkeley, Claire and Lar Bradshaw, Catriona and Jimmy Hughes, Catherine Neville, Agatha Clancy, Hannah and Johno Bowden, Clare Clarke, Liz Allen, Geraldine Timmons, Pat and Betty Browne, Antoinette and Glenn Monnelly, Sr Bridget Quinlivan, Sr Monica Sheehan, Fiona Kelly, Mary Clare Pigott, Brendan Kilty, Jean Murtagh, Sharon Plunkett, Eoin McHugh, Brian and Sophia Egan, Josephine, Fintan and Denis Shankey-Smith, and last but certainly not least, Mike O'Dea.

For giving me the time I needed to work on this book, sincere thanks to Esther McCarthy, Vickie Maye and Irene Feighan at the *Irish Examiner*, and to Siobhan Cronin for the fun we had while working on features during that time. For Trojan support through so much, thanks to James Fogarty and all the gang at the *Medical Independent*. You've all been so kind and such a pleasure to work with.

Thanks also to the *Daily Mail*'s Peter Carvosso, who so helpfully pointed out – many years ago when I first started writing *Irish Independent* features for him – that it was my job as a journalist to encourage the people I interviewed to tell me interesting things....

With special thanks too to *Irish Independent* editor and family friend Tom Coogan, for being the first to commission a piece of writing from me, and for doing so much to help get this project off the ground.

Finally, gracious thanks to Eoin Purcell for commissioning this book, and to all of the wonderful team at New Island, especially the exquisitely astute and enormously talented editor and dear friend that is Dr Justin Corfield.

Rita de Brún is an award-winning journalist. Her features have been published in the *Irish Independent*, *Irish Examiner*, *Ireland on Sunday*, *Irish Farmers Journal*, *Medical Independent* and several magazines. Her book and advice columns have been syndicated to a number of newspapers. Before working in journalism she worked as a headhunter. She also practised as a barrister for a very short while.